R

WorkBook

Criminal
Law

Second Edition

EDITOR: F. R. SAMPSON, LLB

HLT Publications

HLT PUBLICATIONS
200 Greyhound Road, London W14 9RY

First Edition 1991
Second Edition 1992
Reprinted 1992

ISBN 0 7510 0013-2

British Library Cataloguing-in-Publication.

A CIP Catalogue record for this book is available from the British Library.

Printed and bound in Great Britain.

CONTENTS

ACKNOWLEDGEMENT

Some questions used are taken or adapted from past University of London LLB (External) Degree examination papers and our thanks are extended to the University of London for their kind permission to use and publish the questions.

Caveat

The LLB answers given are not approved or sanctioned by the University of London and are entirely our responsibility.

They are not intended as 'Model Answers', but rather as Suggested Solutions.

The answers have two fundamental purposes, namely:

a) To provide a detailed example of a suggested solution to an examination question, and

b) To assist students with their research into the subject and to further their understanding and appreciation of the subject of Law.

INTRODUCTION

This WorkBook is based on examination papers set by the University of London over the last ten years. Unlike the *Criminal Law Suggested Solutions Pack* published by HLT Publications, this book has been divided into syllabus topics under broad headings eg 'automatism' appearing under 'Defences' (Chapter 10). Such classification has been done to assist students in their revision in a more structured way whilst, at the same time, providing students studying this subject with another Examination Board with ease of access to the topics they wish to revise.

As none of the topics exists in isolation there is necessarily some overlap between them, and so questions focussing on mens rea may include offences of murder or theft. Similarly, all the questions will involve some examination of mens rea and actus reus as there would be no crime without them.

The suggested solutions are just that - they are not intended to be model 'examination answers', indeed some of them could never be written in their entirety in the time allowed, nor are they endorsed by the University of London. They do, however, represent a very useful and effective revision medium, providing examples of previous examination questions, suggested answers and an up-to-date review of relevant cases and statutes. In order to maintain a certain amount of fidelity to past examination papers, where some questions are shorter than may be expected, they have been divided into two, eg, questions 2(a) and 2(b).

In this revised 1992 edition a new final chapter has been inserted which contains the complete June 1991 University of London LLB (External) Criminal Law question paper, followed by suggested solutions to each question. Thus the student will have the opportunity to review a recent examination paper in its entirety, and can, if desired, use this chapter as a mock examination - referring to the suggested solutions only after first having attempted the questions.

References for London University examination papers

Following each question is a reference to the University of London LLB Examination (for External Students) in which it was set for examination purposes. To focus more clearly on the chapter topic the Editor has generally amended or shortened the wording to some extent. To indicate this, the words 'Adapted from' are used in the reference. Some questions were specially written by the Editor.

Paper currency

Occasionally, in a question, a possible misdemeanour depends on confusion between a one-pound note and a note of higher value (eg five or ten pounds). These questions were prepared before Britain dispensed with the one-pound note in favour of a coin only for this amount. To make sense of the problem or issue involved the references to pound notes have not been changed.

HOW TO STUDY CRIMINAL LAW

Unlike many other 'compulsory' areas of law, Criminal Law is generally remembered by students as being one of the most interesting and therefore studying it becomes so much easier than some other disciplines. That is not to say, though, that it is an 'easy' subject, and there are certain crucial aspects of it which require a great deal of attention in order to understand them fully.

A considerable amount of Criminal Law appears in statutes and it is vital to be familiar with these enactments and their more important sections. Students must have a good working knowledge of which statutes create certain offences and which sections lay down criteria for determining questions arising from alleged offences (eg ss1-7 Theft Act 1968). You must know the ingredients of all the main offences covered by their respective syllabuses together with any defences.

Care should be taken not to confuse elements from one offence with those of another, such as 'reasonable excuse', 'lawful authority' and 'dishonesty'. One of the most difficult areas of Criminal law is that of mens rea. Which type of mens rea is applicable in a given case? The different types of mens rea must be clearly understood together with the various objective and subjective tests which have been developed by the courts.

Problems in this area are nowhere more apparent than in the area of murder - still governed by the Common law - and the epithet 'malice aforethought' which most laymen associate with 'pre-meditation' has had a turbulent and confusing passage through the courts over recent years.

When considering an accused's liability, one must not be blinkered; the facts will often reveal several (sometimes overlapping) offences. Some instances of criminal damage may also amount to theft. Separate offences of burglary and robbery may be disclosed on the same facts. Consider, too, how an offence has been committed; were any instruments, disguises, or 'props' used? If so, then other offences may have been made out. How many people were involved? Were they all acting voluntarily? Are they equally culpable? Were they acting in concert?

If you were able to defend the accused what possible defences, however remote, may be available? How restrictive are they and how have the courts interpreted them? Is there an essential element missing from the facts as presented thereby obviating the need for a defence?

In asking these questions one must establish the elements required in order to attract liability, and then consider each individual part in the light of statutory guidance and case law.

So, in an alleged burglary one should proceed logically through the facts to discover whether there has been an 'entry'; whether it was into a 'building'; whether it was made as a 'trespasser'; whether the accused had the requisite 'intent' and so on. One must then look at the attendant (possibly mitigating) circumstances, eg the accused had got drunk, he had been drugged, he was mistaken, he was acting under duress, he did it for a joke, etc. In other words, once the basic principles have been grasped from a thorough reading of the textbooks and cases, one should approach specific instances of alleged criminal conduct from the point of view of both prosecutor and defence counsel, finally weighing up the respective merits of each argument and coming to a conclusion.

As with any other legal topic, students should have a sufficient number of authorities in their 'armoury' to support the arguments they propose and by repeatedly practising the application of what they have learned to hypothetical cases, students can become competent and confident in answering problem questions favoured by examiners, and also in discussing broader concepts of Criminal Law such as impossibility and strict liability.

Finally it is suggested that students read the Criminal Law Review which, apart from containing the most recent cases on the subject also has regular articles of interest to academics and practitioners alike.

REVISION AND EXAMINATION TECHNIQUE

In tackling any examination one must first know the extent of the syllabus and although it seems a fairly obvious observation, a lot of valuable study time can be wasted on topics that are of little importance or oblique relevance in that syllabus. This pitfall is particularly hazardous to part-time external candidates who can labour for hours over points that will earn only a fraction of the marks for an examination question. Students must be aware primarily of the major areas of their subject such as those which are embraced by the topic headings in this WorkBook. With Criminal Law, it is fortunate that one is able to predict with some accuracy what areas are almost certain to be examined.

Revision

An inescapable part of learning the law is the committing of facts to memory and, despite the very large proportion of problem questions used in Criminal Law papers which test a candidate's ability to apply posited principles and opposing arguments, there is still a considerable amount of 'rote learning'.

Although everyone develops their own style of revision, there are certain universal features of learning that are worthy of note, particularly for those in their first year of degree-level study. The first is that repeatedly transcribing information from books and notes, and effective learning, are not by any means synonymous. In fact the converse can well be the case and mechanical duplication of written texts can be distracting, time-wasting and counter-productive in that it may give one the feeling of having done 'a lot of work'. Such time could be far better utilised by re-reading textbooks and concise annotations, which brings us to the second point. Legal tomes can seem extremely obscure and require sustained concentration which is best broken up into short but determined bouts. In this way the reader proceeds piece by piece until the whole area has been covered and, therefore, it is essential that students re-read their main textbooks (at least three times) in order to gain a sound overall view of the subject and, at the same time, to increase their retention of the salient points.

Unlike re-writing notes and texts, there is a direct correlation between the number of times one reads an article and the amount that is digested and retained.

Few of us have sufficient time to do all that we would like and when studying, especially part-time, it is essential that time is used to the best effect. What should be borne in mind when revising is that examination time limits are very restrictive and it is virtually impossible for the well-read student to rehearse all that he has learnt, which is relevant, in the examination room. Therefore the key points in each topic area should be grasped, together with the established current authorities. In reading cases and other textbooks it must be asked whether or not the expenditure of valuable time and effort is warranted by the potential improvement in understanding and learning. Even if students were allowed to take all their notes, textbooks, and law reports into the examination, it is unlikely that they would have time to refer to them - unless they were hopelessly unprepared.

A very important exercise in revision is to practise writing answers under examination conditions. It will quickly be seen that the forty or so minutes allowed for each question go very rapidly. More importantly, one can develop the knack of unravelling complex sets of facts and apportioning liability, and setting down arguments and opinions in a logical and persuasive manner while 'under pressure'.

A good way to test one's knowledge is to apply the principles learnt to everyday events - newspaper and television reports, films, occurrences at work, for example. If you read a story in the paper about an alleged 'robbery' or 'burglary', stop and consider the facts and call up the authorities you have learnt - it is surprising how often the nomenclature used in the press is misleading.

In more structured revision it is important to organise the time spent on each aspect of the subject, with 'goals' at the end. Concentrate primarily on what you do know and don't label one topic as 'easy' or 'done' and then ignore it until the examination. Learning the law is like juggling with, at first one, then many, different topics and keeping them 'in the air' until you sit the examination.

Examination technique

There are several crucial areas which students must bear in mind during examinations.

a) *Time*

After allowing time to review all the questions on the paper and selecting those that you intend to tackle, you will be left with just over half an hour - in a 3 hour examination of four questions - to do the actual writing of your answer. Given the amount of detail involved in most problem questions, this presents quite a hurdle in itself hence the need to practise writing specimen answers beforehand.

b) *Relevance*

If there is one thing that antagonises examiners it is the regurgitation by students of all they know on a topic. Unless the answer is directly relevant to the question, and addresses it in the manner required, you will be wasting your time and the examiner's.

c) *Structure*

Try to make your answers balanced and structured. In answering problem questions it is useful to follow the pattern:

i) Introduction - concise - maybe a few lines.

ii) Principles - look at the principles of law raised by the question - along the lines of the skeleton solutions used here.

iii) Application - apply those principles to the facts and consider any counter-arguments. Discuss any ways in which those facts differ from the decided cases.

iv) Conclusion - having applied the principles and weighed the arguments, arrive at some conclusion which is supported by your discussion.

Remember, it is the argument upon which you base your conclusion that is the most important part of the answer.

Also, if the examiner asks you to 'advise X' then do just that.

Finally, when studying for the London University LLB degree remember to follow their study guide and READ THE EXAMINER'S COMMENTS FROM THE PREVIOUS YEAR. These are obtainable from the University and will often indicate areas which were poorly covered in the examination. Quite often those areas are examined again the following year.

Remember too that Criminal Law papers carry few surprises and a good knowledge of the topics covered here will provide a very sound foundation for your revision.

Good luck!

TABLE OF CASES

TABLE OF STATUTES

1   CRIMINAL CONDUCT

1.1   Introduction

In most offences, certainly the more serious ones, there is a requirement that the accused has voluntarily brought about the proscribed consequences or/and circumstances and in doing so his 'actions' may be positive and deliberate, or they may take the form of an omission.

The acts/omission to act, together with the required consequences or/and circumstances make up the 'actus reus' or criminal conduct element of the offence.

In all cases there must be a causal link 'joining' the accused to the 'conduct' and the consequences/circumstances.

1.2   Key points

The following points must be understood.

a) *Acts and omissions*

The accused must voluntarily act or pursue a course of conduct which brings about the proscribed consequences/circumstances. If what he does fails to bring those consequences/circumstances about, there is no actus reus: *R v Hensler* (1870) 22 LT 691, *R v White* [1910] 2 KB 124.

If the accused's conduct initiates a sequence of events which are overtaken by a subsequent supervening event, then he has not caused the circumstances/consequences that follow that event and they cannot form part of the actus reus: *R v Smith* [1959] 2 QB 35; *R v Blaue* [1975] 3 All ER 446; *R v Malcherek and Steel* [1981] 2 All ER 422.

Although generally a failure by the accused to act will not be sufficient to establish the actus reus for an offence, there are occasions where an omission will suffice:

   i)   where the accused's relationship with another imposes a duty to act eg parent-child *R v Gibbins and Proctor* (1918) 13 Cr App R 134 or where an accused has taken it upon himself to look after another: *R v Stone and Dobinson* [1977] 1 QB 354;

  ii)   where the accused has a duty by virtue of his office to act (eg police officer): *R v Dytham* [1979] QB 722;

  iii) where a statute imposes such a duty eg the duty to stop after a road traffic accident (RTA 1988 s170) or where the accused is under a contractual duty (eg by virtue of his terms of employment: *R v Pittwood* (1902) 19 TLR 37) or other agreement: *R v Instan* [1893] 1 QB 450;

  iv) where a subsequent duty follows the accused's actions eg where he accidentally set fire to a room and, on realising what he had done went to sleep elsewhere and omitted to put the fire out: *R v Miller* [1983] 2 AC 161.

b) Cases of strict liability and involuntary conduct are dealt with in later chapters.

1.3   Recent cases and statutes

R v Shama [1990] Crim LR 411 - British Telecom operator omitted to complete required form when connecting calls - forms needed for accounting purposes - D's omission amounted to false accounting, s17 Theft Act 1968.

R v Stringer and Banks [1991] Crim LR 639 - theft committed by D signing cheque in the knowledge that it would be authorised by an innocent agent.

1.4   Analysis of questions

As the concept of actus reus is crucial to all criminal offences in assessing liability, almost every question will, to some degree, involve an examination of the required elements. The questions that follow enable students to concentrate primarily on the criminal liability of the actors.

1.5   Questions

Question 1

K was attacked in a street by a group of youths. L, who was the leader, caused K to be thrown to the ground where several of the gang kicked him until he became unconscious. They then left the scene. Whilst K was on the ground M passed by and removed K's wallet to see if there was anything worth stealing. M took five pounds from the wallet and kicked K twice before leaving causing severe bruising. N who was next to pass the scene saw that K was seriously ill but did nothing, deciding that he did not want to become involved. O, a doctor, also passed by without rendering assistance. P finally came over to K's aid but because of his inexperience in such matters, he moved K which in turn caused K's internal injuries to become severe.

Advise the parties of their criminal liability.

University of London LLB Examination
(for External Students) Criminal Law June 1987 Q4

General comment

Although primarily concerned with the offences of assault and theft, this question is a good illustration of some of the different types of mens rea in criminal law.

It is a complicated question involving a number of parties and students should take care not to get bogged down in generalities.

Skeleton solution

L   Meaning of cause - assault, incitement, accomplice

Youths Sections 47, 20, 18 OAP 1861 - causation

M   Section 1 TA, s8 TA and ss47, 20, 18

N   Causation, assault, omission

Suggested solution

Mens rea need be shown as to the consequences of actual bodily harm *R* v *Venna* (1975).

Section 20 Offences Against the Person Act 1861 provides that it is an offence unlawfully and maliciously to wound or inflict any grievous bodily harm upon any person. There is nothing to indicate that K has suffered a wound - which requires a break in the external skin: *JJC* v *Eisenhower* (1983). However it seems likely that there has been an 'infliction' of grievous bodily harm. 'Grievous bodily harm' means 'really serious bodily harm': *DPP* v *Smith* (1961). In order to inflict such harm there must be an assault of some kind, ie a use of force against the victim. In *R* v *Clarence* (1888) it was stated that the force had to be directly applied. However, in *R* v *Martin* (1881) an indirect assault was allowed.

The mens rea for s20 requires not only that the accused is intentional or reckless as to the act. In addition he must foresee the possibility of at least a little harm: *W* v *Dolbey* (1983).

Section 18 OAP 1861 contains the offence of wounding or causing any grievous bodily harm with intent to do grievous bodily harm. This is obviously the most serious of the assaults and it has a very high mens rea. Intention to do grievous bodily harm is required and recklessness will not suffice: *R* v *Belfon* (1976). On the facts in question there is nothing to indicate this high mens rea is satisfied.

The youths who performed the assaults would be the principal offenders as they are closest to the performance of the actus reus. Sections 47 and 20 are the most likely offences but it must be recalled that s20 requires a higher mens rea than s47. L would be an accomplice to these offences.

An aider and abettor is a person present assisting or encouraging at the scene of the offence: *R* v *Coney* (1882); *R* v *Clarkson* (1971). He must have full knowledge of the circumstances of the offence: *Johnson* v *Youden* (1950).

Section 8 of the Accessories and Abettors Act 1861 provides that for the purposes of trial and punishment accomplices are to be treated as principal offenders.

3

When M removes K's wallet to see if there is anything worth stealing he may commit an attempted theft. Section 1 Theft Act 1968 provides that theft is committed where an accused dishonestly appropriates property belonging to another with intention to permanently deprive the other of it.

In order to establish attempted theft the prosecution must show that M has done an act 'more than merely preparatory' (s1 Criminal Attempts Act 1981) with full mens rea. M takes the wallet to see if there is anything worth stealing. This is an example of 'conditional intention'. Provided the indictment is drafted broadly without reference to particular items, eg M attempted to steal from the contents of the wallet, the mens rea for attempted theft will be satisfied. In practice as M proceeds to the full offence it is unlikely the prosecution would pursue an attempted charge.

The full offence will be complete when M removes £5 from the wallet - at that time there is an assumption of the rights of an owner (s3 TA 1968) and this would amount to an appropriation. It is undoubtedly an act by way of adverse interference with or usurpation of an owner's rights: *R* v *Morris* (1983). There seems no doubt that the mens rea is satisfied. He has an intention to permanently deprive and he is clearly dishonest. Were there to be any difficulties in relation to dishonesty the jury should be directed in line with: *R* v *Ghosh* (1982). After he has stolen M kicks K twice causing severe bruising. At that point M commits an assault either under s47, s20 or possibly s18, depending on mens rea. The offences have already been outlined and on the assumption that the bruising amounts to grievous bodily harm M's criminal liability would depend on how high is mens rea.

It should be noted that he is not liable for robbery. Section 8 Theft Act 1968 provides that a person commits robbery if he steals and immediately before, or at the time and in order to do so he uses force on any person or puts any person in fear of being then and there subjected to force. M undoubtedly uses force. However this occurs after the theft is complete. Even allowing for the prosecution to argue that there is a continuing actus reus (*R* v *Hale* (1978)) it could still not amount to robbery as the force used is gratuitous force and not force in order to steal: *R* v *Shendley* (1970).

Omission:

N would appear to have no liability in this matter. Undoubtedly certain crimes may be committed by omission. But there can be no liability by this means unless there is a duty to act in law. In these circumstances N has no duty to act in law and therefore would have no liability. It should be noted in relation to matters already discussed that an assault cannot be performed by omission. It must invariably take place by means of a positive act: *Fagan* v *MPC* (1969).

N was under no legal liability to help K. Where English criminal law does impose a duty to act, there must be a close relationship ie family, a business or similar: *R* v *Marriott* (1838); *R* v *Nicholls* (1874); *R* v *Instan* (1893); *R* v *Stone and Dobinson* (1977) ; *R* v *Dalby* (1982)).

Similarly, O would not be liable unless he stood in such a special relationship to K (ie his family doctor). He has a moral duty to act but, in these circumstances that is not automatically translated into a duty under criminal law.

One could argue, on the lines of *R* v *Dytham* (1979) where a police officer was determined to be liable, virtute officii, to intervene and stop an assault, that O has a similar duty to act by virtue of his 'office' in which case his omission would be sufficient to attract liability.

Causation:

When P moves K causing his internal injuries to become severe, he would not become liable in criminal law. There are two main reasons for taking this view. Firstly as a matter of law he would not be regarded as the *legal* cause of the injuries. The chain of causation will not be broken in these circumstances - P would be regarded as an innocent or non-responsible intervener. Where such a person intervenes by an act instinctively done to assist someone he would not break the chain of causation and the harm resulting would not be in law attributable to him but rather to those who started the chain of causation. Furthermore the offences contained in s47, s20, and s18 are crimes of maliciousness and from the facts patently P is not acting in a malicious manner. It would not be sufficient mens rea to allege that P is reckless. Although recklessness may be sufficient mens rea for s47 it is *Cunningham* recklessness and not *Caldwell* recklessness that must be established. On the facts this is not shown.

Question 2

P, Q and R were climbing up a local church tower to raise money for a charity when P and Q fell. A crowd had gathered below to view the climb. R was having difficulty supporting P and Q on the rope to which they were all attached. Eventually after several attempts to secure a hold R said to Q: 'Cut the rope I cannot support you both for much longer. I shall be dragged off too!' Eventually, Q cut the rope and P was severely injured in the resultant fall. One of the spectators had a heart attack from seeing P fall.

Advise Q and R of their criminal liability. What difference if any would it make to your answer if the spectator had died?

University of London LLB Examination
(for External Students) Criminal Law June 1988 Q8

General comment

Again, another essay question more than a problem question, which deals with some of the fundamental issues in the criminal law, namely what constitutes an actus reus and what amounts to causation in law as well as in fact.

Skeleton solution

Actus reus - definition - causation - in fact - in law - criminal liability for injuries to P.

Criminal liability for injuries to spectator - non-fatal offence against the person - homicide - causation - mens rea.

Suggested solution

It is difficult to see on what basis R or Q have any criminal liability for P's injuries for, in order to be criminally liable, they must have caused P's injuries.

It is a general principle of criminal law that a person may not be convicted of a crime unless the prosecution has proved beyond reasonable doubt that the defendant has caused a certain event or that responsibility is to be attributed to him for a certain state of affairs which the criminal law has forbidden (the actus reus) and that the defendant had a defined state of mind in relation to the causing of the event or the existence of the state of affairs (the mens rea).

Mens rea may exist without an actus reus but if the actus reus of a specific crime does not exist or did not occur, then that crime cannot be committed (though there may be an attempt).

When the definition of an actus reus requires the occurrence of certain consequences it is necessary to prove that it was the conduct of the accused which caused those consequences to occur. If the consequences came about solely through some other cause then the crime has not been committed, even though all the elements of the actus reus and mens rea were present: *R* v *White* (1910); *R* v *Hensler* (1870). The general rule is that the defendant must have caused the actus reus: *R* v *Larsonneur* (1933); *Winzar* v *Chief Constable of Kent* (1983).

Therefore, the facts of this question raise the issue of causation. Did R and Q in any way 'cause' P's injuries?

For example, in the crime of homicide the defendant must 'kill' the victim, ie he must be the factual and legal cause of the death of his victim. A defendant's act cannot be held to be the cause of death if death would have occurred without his act. The defendant's act must be a sine qua non of the death and whether it is so is a question of fact.

However, even if an act is the sine qua non of homicide, it may not be the cause of the homicide in law. Whether a particular act which is a sine qua non of an alleged actus reus is also the cause of it is a question of law.

The first principle is that a defendant's act cannot be the cause of an event if the event would have occurred in precisely the same way had the act never been done. It must be proved that but for the defendant's act, the event would not have occurred. The act must be the sine qua non of the event, and, in law, also be the cause of the event.

On the facts, it appears that R and Q were neither the contributory cause of P's injuries nor a substantial cause of P's injuries.

Liability cannot be attributed to a defendant unless it can be shown that the culpability of his act contributed to the injury or death: *R* v *Dalloway* (1847).

On the facts, the issue was not whether P was going to be injured but whether Q and R were also going to fall, given that they were all roped together.

A defendant's contribution to the cause of injury or death need not be substantial but must not be so minute that the law will ignore it under the 'de minimis' principle. As killing is merely an acceleration of death, factors which produce a very trivial acceleration will be ignored: *R* v *Cato* (1976); *R* v *Malcherek and Steel* (1981).

Given that, P, Q and R were roped together and P and Q fell, dragging R with them, then the action of Q in cutting the rope and P falling a matter of seconds before all three would have fallen will not be the cause of P's injuries in law, even though factually it was the cause of P's injuries.

With respect to the spectator, again, it is hard to see how P, Q or R can be held criminally liable for the heart attack or death.

With respect to the heart attack none of the non-fatal offences against the person appear relevant. If death occurs, then on present case law it would not be possible to say that, P Q or R caused the death, leaving aside the issue of the apparent lack of mens rea.

2 STATE OF MIND

2.1   Introduction

2.2   Key points

2.3   Recent cases and statutes

2.4   Analysis of questions

2.5   Questions

2.1   Introduction

It is a fundamental rule of our criminal law that a man cannot be guilty by his actions unless he also has a guilty mind - '*actus non facit reum nisi mens sit rea*'.

The idea of a 'guilty' mind is not entirely accurate and the required 'state of mind' is a more appropriate way of regarding mens rea.

The requirement for mens rea is subject to some exceptions, notably negligence and strict liability. Furthermore, it is of paramount importance that the actus reus and the required mens rea be shown to have coincided.

2.2   Key points

a) Traditionally, offences are categorised by the extent of mens rea required for their commission, with those involving a very high degree of mens rea (and therefore being more difficult to prove) including crimes of ulterior or specific intent.

b) Crimes of general or basic intent require a lesser degree of mens rea, and those crimes which may be committed by negligence even less so.

Finally there are those crimes which may be committed with no 'guilty knowledge' or negligence at all ie crimes of absolute and strict liability.

i) Specific intent crimes require proof of a particular specific intention in the mind of the accused when he acted (eg an intention to kill or cause serious injury for murder).

Ulterior intent crimes require proof of an intention to do something in addition to the initial actus reus, eg burglary under s9(1)(a) Theft Act 1968 - entering a building as a trespasser with intent to go on to commit further offences therein (rape, steal, inflict gbh, cause damage). Similarly possessing a controlled drug with intent to supply, contrary to s5(3) Misuse of Drugs Act 1971 requires proof of this ulterior intent.

2 STATE OF MIND

ii) Crimes of basic or general intent require proof of mens rea but not a particular 'intention'. They cannot be committed by negligence but, in contrast to crimes of specific intent, recklessness may suffice to prove their commission.

iii) Crimes of negligence are almost all statutory in origin, except manslaughter (which may be committed by gross disregard for life), examples of which are driving without due care and attention: s4 RTA 1988, or failing to exercise proper control of a dog.

iv) Crimes of absolute and strict liability: absolute liability is a concept generally at variance with our legal system and is committed by a proscribed 'state of affairs': *R* v *Larsonneur* (1933) 24 Cr App R 74 and the offences it covers are rare. Strictly liability is less extreme and, unlike absolute liability, general recognised defences (eg automatism) are applicable.

Strict liability offences include - quasi-criminal offences: *Smedleys Ltd* v *Breed* [1974] AC 839; *Pharmaceutical Society of Great Britain* v *Logan* [1982] Crim LR 443 and offences aimed at regulating public nuisance: *Alphacell* v *Woodward* [1972] AC 824, *FJH Wrothwell* v *Yorkshire Water Authority* [1984] Crim LR 43.

There is also a trend towards strict liability in interpreting statutes which seek to penalize acts that pose a grave social danger: *Gammon (Hong Kong) Ltd* v *Attorney-General for Hong Kong* [1985] AC 1; *R* v *Bradish* [1990] Crim LR 723 - possesion of 'prohibited weapon' s5(1)(b) Firearms Act 1968 - no mens rea required.

Note however the presumption against such a construction: *Sweet* v *Parsley* [1970] AC 132, albeit a rebuttable one.

c) In addition to intention and negligence there is the complicated and very examinable area of 'recklessness', the third aspect of mens rea. Recklessness is insufficient mens rea for the specific and ulterior intent crimes. It is, however, sufficient to prove offences requiring basic intent and negligence.

The two leading cases in this area **must** be known: *R* v *Cunningham* [1957] 2 QB 396 and *MPC* v *Caldwell* [1982] AC 341.

R v *Cunningham* requires a conscious taking of risk, or a foresight of consequences with a subsequent act by the accused despite his having foreseen those consequences. It is therefore subjective in nature: *R* v *Stephenson* [1979] QB 695.

MPC v *Caldwell* requires a failure to consider whether any risk exists where, had it been considered, the risk would have been obvious. The question here is whether it would have been obvious to an ordinary, reasonable and prudent person. It is therefore objective in nature: *Elliot* v *C* [1983] 1 WLR 939.

If the accused, having recognised the risk, takes precautions against that risk but these precautions do not prevent the risk occurring, he is reckless under this head: *Chief Constable of Avon and Somerset* v *Shimmen* (1987) 84 Cr App R 7.

In relation to reckless driving the test in *R* v *Lawrence* [1982] AC 510 must be known, although that offence has been replaced by the new offence of dangerous driving by the Road Traffic Act 1991 (see 2.3 below).

d) One further aspect of mens rea and its operation is that of 'transferred malice' and the rule that the mens rea of one offence cannot suffice to support a conviction of another different offence: *R* v *Pembliton* (1874) 12 Cox CC 607

e) The need for 'intention' in murder cases is complex and again very examinable. It is dealt with later in the book, however, students must be aware of the interpretation of 'intention' embodied in *R* v *Moloney* [1985] AC 905; *R* v *Hancock and Shankland* [1986] AC 455 and *R* v *Nedrick* [1986] 1 WLR 1025.

2.3 Recent cases and statutes

The most recent cases in relation to mens rea concern recklessness and they are:

Large v *Mainprize* [1989] Crim LR 213 - recklessly furnishing information re fishing catch conscious indifference to truth/falsity of claim.

R v *Bradish* [1990] Crim LR 723 - possession of prohibited weapon under s5(1)(b) Firearms Act 1968 - no mens rea required.

R v *Gibson*; *R* v *Sylverie* (1990) Times 12 July - offence of outraging public decency - no need to show any such intent by D.

R v *Reid* [1991] Crim LR 269 - death by reckless driving - Court of Appeal accepted (obiter) existence of *lacuna* ie where person considers risk and decides that none exists he is not reckless in *Caldwell/Lawrence* sense.

Owing to the difficulties involved in proving recklessness in driving offences a new offence of causing death by dangerous driving has been created by the Road Traffic Act 1991. Thereunder the standard of D's driving will be judged against that of a competent and careful driver and whether it would have been obvious to such a driver that D's driving would be likely to cause a risk of injury to a person or serious damage to property.

2.4 Analysis of questions

As with actus reus, all questions will necessarily involve a consideration the relevant state of mind of the accused. There are frequently questions that specifically test the very important areas of intention in relation to murder, and recklessness in its recognised forms. Students are also required to show what category of mens rea will be required by different classes of offence eg recklessness and crimes of basic intent. Occasionally there will be essay questions on eg the rationale behind strict liability.

2.5 Questions

Question 1

U, who was 22 years but with a mental age of 10 years, was playing in the playground when a fellow pupil, V, shouted abuse at him. U lost his temper and pushed V to the ground. V, who had a thin skull, was concussed by the fall. X, who was U's best friend, tried to pull U away from V whom U was trying to kick. W, a schoolmaster, came on the scene and, misunderstanding what was going on, pulled X off U. Released, U ran and kicked V on the ground.

Advise the parties of their criminal liability on the basis that V had died as a result of concussion and internal injuries.

University of London LLB Examination
(for External Students) Criminal Law June 1987 Q7

General comment

A good question to tackle. Core elements of the syllabus were examined and all the main aspects were easily recognisable on the facts.

Skeleton solution

U   assault - s47, s20 OAP 1861 - causation - murder; diminished responsibility; constructive manslaughter

X   battery - lack of MR - accomplice role - s3 CLA 1967

W   assault - s3 CLA 1967 - mistake

Suggested solution

When U pushes V to the ground he may commit a number of assaults contrary to the Offences Against the Person Act 1861.

Section 47 OAP 1861 provides that it will be an offence to assault occasioning actual bodily harm. 'Actual bodily harm' includes 'any hurt and injury calculated to interfere with health or comfort': *R* v *Miller* (1954). The mens rea requirement for s47 was that, until recently, there must be intention or recklessness as to the act but no mens rea was required as to the consequence of actual bodily harm: *R* v *Venna* (1975). However, the Court of Appeal decision in *R* v *Spratt* (1990), which was approved by a differently constituted Court of Appeal in *R* v *Parmenter* (1991), held that it was also necessary as to the actual harm caused. In *Parmenter*, which directly conflicts with another decision of the Court of Appeal, *R* v *Savage* (1990), their Lordships expressed their dismay at the state of the law in this area which was beyond their resolution. It should be noted that recklessness in this context is subjective recklessness, ie the accused must know that he is taking the risk that he may assault.

Section 20 OAP 1861 provides that it is an offence to unlawfully wound or inflict grievous bodily harm. 'Grievous bodily harm' means really serious bodily harm. The term 'inflict' requires an assault either direct or possibly indirect: *R* v *Martin* (1881). Undoubtedly this is satisfied in the facts on question as U uses direct force on V. The mens rea for s20 is intention or recklessness as to circumstances (as for s47); *R* v *Parmenter* (1991). Furthermore the accused must foresee the possibility of at least a little harm: *W* v *Dolbey* (1983). Both s47 and s20 are 'result crimes', that is crimes where a consequence must be shown as part of the actus reus.

V who had a thin skull was concussed by the fall. In order to establish the actus reus of either s47 or s20 it must be shown that U is the legal cause of the injury sustained by V. However U must take his victim as he finds him, *R v Blaue* (1975), and therefore the chain of causation will not be broken because of the victim's special characteristic of a thin skull.

When U later returns to kicking V he will commit further assaults within s47 or s20 depending on his state of mind. If he has the necessary foresight he may be liable under s20. If he lacks this he will be liable under s47.

The victim dies as a result of concussion and internal injuries. V's possible liability for murder must be considered. In order to establish this as a very serious offence it must be shown that U is the legal cause of V's death. Furthermore it must be shown that U had the necessary mens rea for murder at the time of the actus reus. The mens rea for murder is very high. The prosecution would have to establish that U killed V intending to kill or intending to do grievous bodily harm. 'Intention' includes both desiring to kill or do grievous bodily harm (direct intent) or knowing that death or grievous bodily harm is certain or virtually certain to occur (oblique intent). Where the prosecution rely on oblique intent it is not sufficient to establish the accused foresaw the result as highly probable. While this may be useful as evidence it is no more than that. Foresight is not to be equated with intention. A jury should be directed that they are not entitled to infer the necessary intention unless they are satisfied that death or grievous bodily harm was virtually certain as a result of the defendant's actions *and* the defendant appreciated that this was the case *R v Moloney* (1985); *R v Hancock and Shankland* (1986); *R v Nedrick* (1986).

On the facts in question there seems little doubt that U is the legal cause of death. If he has intention to kill or intention to do grievous bodily harm at any time when the actus reus is continuing he may be liable for murder.

The statutory defence of diminished responsibility under s2 Homicide Act 1957 may be available. Section 2 provides that where a person kills he shall not be convicted of murder if he was suffering from such abnormality of mind (whether arising from arrested or retarded development or any inherent causes or induced by disease or injury) as substantially impaired his responsibility. Thus murder will be reduced to voluntary manslaughter. On the facts in question this may well be available.

If U lacked mens rea for murder he could be liable for constructive manslaughter. This is established where a person kills as a result of an unlawful act - in this case one of the assaults. Furthermore in addition to an intention to do the unlawful act it must be shown that a reasonable man would foresee the possibility of at least a little harm from the act. *DPP v Newbury* (1976).

X has no criminal responsibility on the facts as given. Undoubtedly he uses force against U when pulling him away and this could amount to a common law battery - a direct use of force, intentionally or recklessly committed. However, under s3 Criminal Law Act 1967, a person may use reasonable force in the prevention of a crime. It must be established that X was acting defensively and not aggressively: *R v Shannon* (1980). The question of whether the force used was reasonable must be considered by reference to the circumstances the accused found himself in: *Palmer* v *R* (1971); *R* v *Whyte* (1987). There seems little doubt on the facts that this would be available to X as a defence.

A similar approach should be adopted in considering any liability W may have. Undoubtedly he may commit a common law battery when he pulls X off U. However, W's position is complicated because of his mistake. He believed wrongly that X was the aggressor. He will still be able to claim s3 Criminal Law Act 1967 as a defence providing the mistake was honest. In *DPP* v *Morgan* (1975) the House of Lords confirmed that an honest mistake, whether or not it was reasonable, enabled an accused to be judged on the facts as he believed them to be. In *Albert* v *Lavin* (1981) the Divisional Court considered that a mistake in relation to a defence had to be both honest and reasonable before an accused could be judged on the facts as he believed them to be but in *R* v *Williams* (1984) that approach was disapproved of and *DPP* v *Morgan* was applied. Following the Privy Council decision in *Beckford* v *R* (1987), provided W's mistaken belief is honestly held, he will have a defence.

Question 2(a)

Jane, a young mother, noticed that her child was extremely white and covered in perspiration. Realising that the child was very ill, she picked up the baby and ran outside. She saw an unlocked car parked with its ignition key in it, placed her baby in the car and drove off to hospital. She drove through a red traffic signal. When she arrived at the hospital she discovered that her child was dead.

Discuss Jane's criminal liability.

University of London LLB Examination
(for External Students) Criminal Law June 1981 Q2

General comment

The question centres around the mens rea required for the offences of taking a conveyance and reckless or careless driving.

Skeleton solution

Section 12 TA 1968, 'belief' s12(6)

Sections 2 and 3 RTA 1988

Suggested solution

Jane may have committed an offence of taking a conveyance without the owner's consent or other lawful authority contrary to s12 of the Theft Act 1968.

There is no requirement for her to have an intention 'permanently to deprive' as there is in the offence of theft. All that is required is a 'taking' of the vehicle - completed when she moves it: *R* v *Bogacki* (1973) for her use as a conveyance: *R* v *Bow* (1976). She does not appear to have the consent of the owner, neither can she point any lawful authority for the taking of the car.

However, Jane may be able to avail herself of the provisions of s12(6) of the Act if she can show that she believed that the owner would have consented had he known of the taking and of the circumstances. Given the nature of her urgent need of the conveyance Jane would very likely be able to show that she had such subjective belief.

Jane may have committed a further offence contrary to s3 of the Road Traffic Act 1988 (as amended by the Road Traffic Act 1991) by driving without due care and attention. Alternatively, she may have committed an offence contrary to s2 of the Road Traffic Act 1988 of driving recklessly.

Section 3 contains the lesser offence and is an example of a crime where the mens rea required is that of negligence ie an objective standard. The court has to consider whether the accused was exercising that degree of care and attention that a reasonable and prudent driver would exercise in the circumstances: *Simpson* v *Peat* (1952).

The more serious offence of driving recklessly has been considered by the House of Lords in *R* v *Lawrence* (1981), where it was held that mens rea is required in the offence of driving recklessly and that the mental element required is that, before adopting a manner of driving that in fact involves an obvious and serious risk of causing physical injury to another person using the road, or of doing substantial damage to property, the driver has failed to give any thought to the possibility of there being such a risk, or, having recognised that there was some risk involved, has gone on nonetheless to take it. The House of Lords considered the case of *R* v *Murphy* (1980) was defective in certain respects in that it referred to 'due care and attention' which lowered the standard of care to that of the less serious offence contained in s3 of the Act. Once the 1991 Road Traffic Act comes into force, Jane's driving will be judged against that of a careful and competent motorist in order to determine whether such driving was dangerous.

Jane will not be able to claim a general defence to the offences shown on the basis of the necessity of her situation. The defence of necessity is not one recognised in English law. Lord Denning stated an opinion in *Buchoke* v *GLC* (1971) that the driver of a fire engine who crossed a red light to rescue someone in a blazing house would commit an offence although, in his view the man should be congratulated and not prosecuted. Similarly in *Brown* v *Dyerson* (1969) it was held that a medical emergency was not a defence to a charge of driving with excessive blood alcohol.

However, Jane may claim duress of circumstances caused by the threat of death/serious injury to her child: *R* v *Conway* (1988). (See chapter 10.)

Question 2(b)

Dan was driving one afternoon and felt increasingly drowsy. He fell asleep and his car mounted the pavement, crashed into a wall and trapped a young boy against the wall, seriously injuring him. The crash woke Dan, who, seeing the trapped boy, decided not to move his car. After some time he did decide to move, reversed and drove away. Jack, a passing pedestrian, witnessed the event and was very upset by the occurrence. In his efforts to erase the memory of the injured boy, Jack drank a large quantity of brandy and became extremely drunk. He stumbled into a hotel and did not realise that he had dropped his cigarette on the the the hall carpet. The hotel caught fire and two of the occupants died in the blaze. Jack escaped.

Discuss their criminal liability.

University of London LLB Examination
(for External Students) Criminal Law June 1981 Q3

General comment

The question centres mainly around the respective mens rea of both Dan and Jack, particularly with regard to their 'recklessness' and thereby tests knowledge of the types of recklessness relating to different offences.

Skeleton solution

Dan   Sections 2 and 3 RTA 1988 - recklessness - sections 47 and 20 OAP 1861

Jack   Sections 1 and 3 CDA 1971 - recklessness

Suggested solution

Dan may commit a number of offences contrary to the Road Traffic Act when his car mounts the pavement and injures a boy.

Section 3 of the Road Traffic Act 1988 (as amended by the RTA 1991), provides that if a person drives a motor vehicle (or mechanically propelled vehicle) on a road without due care and attention or without reasonable consideration for other persons using the road, he shall commit an offence.

Section 2 of the Road Traffic Act 1988, provides that a person who drives a motor vehicle on a road recklessly shall be guilty of an offence. This offence is, owing to probative difficulties in driving cases, to be replaced by one of dangerous driving, but the discussion of recklessness which follows is instructive. Section 2 creates the more serious offence and because of that it is generally considered that a higher standard of mens rea is required to satisfy the offence. A person could be driving 'without due care and attention' if he fails to exercise the degree of care and attention that a reasonable and prudent driver would exercise in the circumstances: *Simpson* v *Peat* (1952). This is an objective standard and it is an example of one of the few crimes of negligence in English criminal law.

It is not so easy to define the test which will indicate whether a person is driving recklessly. Certainly, recklessness denotes deliberate taking of an unjustifiable risk and mere inadvertence will not be sufficient without there being an essential element of the awareness of the risk involved. The test for deciding whether a person is driving recklessly has been considered by the House of Lords in the case of *R* v *Lawrence* (1981) where, following to the case of *MPC* v *Caldwell* (1982), the House of Lords held that mens rea was an essential element in the offence of driving recklessly, furthermore, the mental element necessary is that before adopting a manner of driving that in fact involves an obvious and serious risk of causing physical injury to another person using the road, or of doing substantial damage to property, the driver has failed to give any thought to the possibility of there being such a risk or having recognised that there was some risk involved, has gone on nonetheless to take it.

Lord Diplock's direction in *R* v *Lawrence* (1982) was approved as a model in *R* v *Madigan* (1983) and the need for the word 'obvious' to be included in such a direction was emphasised in *R* v *Khan* (1985).

In *R* v *Lawrence* the House of Lords considered that the earlier decision of *R* v *Murphy* (1980) was defective in that it referred to 'due care and attention' which in effect lowered the standard of care to that of the less serious offence contained in s3. This was an incorrect approach.

Obviously, it is necessary to consider what mens rea Dan had and whether the fact that he fell asleep may provide him with a defence. The fact that Dan fell asleep does not enable him to claim the defence of automatism. He would be convicted on the basis that at the time when he realised he was sleepy, he should have stopped and therefore, as he did not stop he committed an offence at that time. The defence of automatism could possibly have been claimed if Dan had started driving while concussed or sleep-walking and therefore, the act of driving itself was one which was involuntary in some way. The facts of the question can be distinguished from the situation where, for example, a swarm of bees stung a driver so that his driving became involuntary. In *Hill* v *Baxter* (1958) it was stated that in these circumstances there could be a defence of automatism. However, on the facts in the question, Dan had awareness of feeling drowsy and could have stopped the car and thus avoided the risk. The mental element required for driving recklessly is one which is for almost all purposes objective. It is immaterial that Dan has failed to give any thought to the possibility of there being a risk of causing physical injury to some other person or doing substantial damage to property.

There may be an assault against the injured boy when Dan reverses the car and drives away. It is not indicated whether any further injury results but there will at least be an assault and battery. In *R* v *Venna* (1975) it was stated the mens rea required is intention or recklessness. If some further injury results from the reversing of the car, then it may be s47 (assault occasioning actual bodily harm), or s20 (wounding or inflicting grievous bodily harm) Offences Against the Person Act 1861, but it must be shown that Dan intended to cause that further injury or was reckless as to that consequence: *R* v *Spratt* (1990); *R* v *Parmenter* (1991).

Jack may commit an act of criminal damage contrary to s1(1) of the Criminal Damage Act 1971, where intentionally or recklessly he destroys or damages property belonging to another with intent or being reckless as to whether such property is destroyed. Prima facie, there is the more serious offence within s1(2) of the Criminal Damage Act, in that he destroys or damages property intentionally or recklessly with intention to endanger life or being reckless as to whether life is endangered.

Because the offence is performed by fire, then it will come within s1(3) - arson. However, there may be difficulties in showing that Jack had the necessary mens rea in his drunken state. However, he will not be able to plead this as a defence unless it can be shown that the offences with which he could be charged are crimes of specific intent. In these circumstances, drunkenness may be a defence if it can be shown that

16

the drunkenness totally negatives the mens rea required: *DPP* v *Majewski* (1976). If it is a crime of basic intent, then drunkenness will be no defence even though the accused is incapable of forming mens rea. The House of Lords considered the defence of drunkenness in relation to the Criminal Damage Act in *MPC* v *Caldwell* (1982). The House of Lords considered that the term 'reckless' within s1 of the Act, held a meaning which it bore in in ordinary speech. That meaning included not only deciding to ignore the risk of harmful consequences resulting from one's acts that one recognises as existing but also, failing to give any thought to whether or not there was such risk in circumstances where if any thought were given to the matter, it would be obvious that there was. Therefore, the fact that the defendant was unaware of the risk of endangering lives owing to his voluntary intoxication would be no defence if the risk would have been obvious to him had he been sober. The result is that if Jack was charged under s1(2) of the Criminal Damage Act, with being reckless as to whether life was endangered, then he will not be able to claim drunkenness as a defence. However, if he were charged under s1(2) of the Criminal Damage Act, intending to endanger life, evidence of self-induced intoxication could be relevant as a defence. The result of the decision of *MPC* v *Caldwell* (1982) is, that within s1(2), there are two separate offences where one of which is a basic intent crime within the *DPP* v *Majewski* rule and the other is a specific intent crime. This goes against earlier case law where it has been held that s1(1) of the Act was a crime of basic intention where voluntary intoxication would offer no defence and s1(2) of the Act was a crime of specific intent where voluntary drunkenness could be raised as a defence: *R* v *Orpin* (1980).

The test of 'recklessness' outlined in *MPC* v *Caldwell* is open to quite severe criticism on the ground that it goes against the Law Commission recommendations and introduces a substantial objective element into the test.

Because of this objective element, it will not really be necessary to enquire into the state of mind of the accused even though, Lord Diplock states in *MPC* v *Caldwell* that 'mens rea is, by definition, a state of mind of the accused himself at the time he did the physical act that constitutes the actus reus of the offence; it cannot be the state of mind of some non-existent hypothetical person'.

Question 3

'Strict liability must be retained. It provides social benefits which would not be obtained through any of the supposed alternatives to it and the injustice caused by it is often exaggerated.'

Discuss.

University of London LLB Examination
(for External Students) Criminal Law June 1981 Q9

General comment

A very hard question which admits of detailed discussion. Therefore it is potentially hazardous in that answering essay questions such as this can quickly eat into one's time. Only students who are well-disciplined and well-organised in their examination technique should attempt such a question.

CRIMINAL LAW

Skeleton solution

Strict liability and absolute liability compared and contrasted - social benefits of 'no-fault' liability at criminal law - 'negligence' aspect - drawbacks of such liability and apparent inequity thereof.

Suggested solution

A crime of strict liability is one where mens rea (intention, recklessness or even negligence) is not required as to one or more elements in the actus reus. Such crimes are sometimes referred to as crimes of 'absolute liability'. However, this is a misnomer since apart from one or two exceptional situations, some mens rea must be shown the 'strict' element relating to only one or two elements of the actus reus.

Crimes of strict liability are generally the creation of statute. Under the common law it was, on the whole, accepted that every crime required mens rea of some kind. However, with the industrial revolution, Parliament began to legislate in such matters as safety in factories, selling impure food and the regulation of economic activities of all types. When it did so, it frequently laid down in detail what the prohibited act consisted of, but failed to specify any mental element. It therefore fell to the courts to decide whether this omission was intended to mean that strict liability was to be imposed or alternatively whether such statutes were to be interpreted in accordance with the general principles of criminal law where there is a presumption in favour of mens rea. On the whole, the courts have taken the first view and almost invariably have imposed strict liability when Parliament has omitted words like 'wilfully', 'knowingly'. Occasionally, the courts have even interpreted an offence as one of strict liability where such words have been present.

It is necessary to examine exactly what social benefits arise from imposition of criminal liability without fault before it can be considered whether or not strict liability must be retained. It has been argued particularly by Baroness Barbara Wootton, Social Scientist, that one of the main aims of criminal law must be to protect society from harmful acts. Such an act which must be prevented is one which would be harmful, whether done intentionally, recklessly, negligently or even inadvertently. However, this argument does not apply simply to crimes of strict liability and if it were a correct approach, it is one which could be applied to all crimes, so that simply performing the actus reus of any offence would amount to a crime.

Indeed, one of the very strong arguments against strict liability is that the influence of strict liability does tend to affect the court's attitude to all crimes and undermine greatly the strength of the presumption in favour of mens rea.

A further argument frequently put forward in support of strict liability is that it is generally applied only to offences of a minor nature, those that could be described as 'regulatory' or 'social' rather than 'real crimes'. Originally there may have been some truth in this argument. The first type of strict liability offences did relate to food and hygiene legislation and other social regulatory offences. However, it is not an argument which is supported when one looks at the present areas where strict liability is applied. Legislation relating to pollution is usually interpreted as giving rise to strict liability: *Alphacell* v *Woodward* (1972). However, the consequences of allowing rivers to become polluted can be extremely serious and it would certainly be wrong to say that such crimes have no moral content.

In *Atkinson* v *Sir Alfred McAlpine & Son Ltd* (1974), it was held that the company committed an offence contrary to the Asbestos Regulations 1969 by failing to give written notice that they were going to undertake work involving crocidolite. The company neither knew nor indeed had reason to know that the work did involve crocidolite. However, the court found that where a statute contained an absolute prohibition against the doing of some act, as a general rule, mens rea was not a constituent of that offence. Furthermore, it distinguished the situation from that where the law imposed a duty to act where mens rea was a necessary requirement, for example, failure to report an accident, where the defendant would not be guilty if he was unaware that the accident had occurred: *Harding* v *Price* (1948).

A further example of the application of strict liability in pure criminal law may be seen in the legislation concerning dangerous drugs. This has on occasions in recent years been defined as involving crimes of strict liability: *Yeandel* v *Fisher* (1966). Here the defendant was found guilty of 'being concerned with the management of premises for the purposes of smoking cannabis', even though he did not know and had no means of knowing that such smoking was taking place. However, this case was overruled by *Sweet* v *Parsley* (1969) where a conviction on similar facts to those in the *Yeandel* v *Fisher* case was quashed by the House of Lords. The Misuse of Drugs Act 1971 has to some extent moved away from imposing pure strict liability by allowing a statutory defence for an accused where charged with being in possession of prohibited drugs to show that he neither knew of or suspected nor had reasons to suspect the existence of some fact alleged by the prosecution which it is necessary for the prosecution to prove if he is to be convicted of the offence charged. Thus, if it can be shown that the accused did not know or believe that he has a controlled drug on him, he will have a defence. However, it will not be a defence for the accused to show that he did not know or believe the substance to be the particular controlled drug it in fact was, if he knew or suspected that it was a controlled drug which he was not entitled to have: *R* v *McNamara* (1988).

Neither will the fact that D 'forgets' he has such a drug absolve him: *R* v *Martindale* (1986).

A rather better argument in support of strict liability is one founded in practicality. If the courts were to accept that mens rea had to be proved in every case, the prosecutor's task would often be made impossible. Indeed, this aspect was one stressed by Lord Salmon in *Alphacell* v *Woodward* (1972) and by their Lordships in the Court of Appeal decision in *R* v *Bradish* (1990) where the appellant had been found in possession of a can of CS gas, a 'prohibited weapon' under s5(1)(b) of the Firearms Act 1968. The court held that a balance had to be struck between protecting the innocent possessor of such articles and the underlying policy behind legislation which sought to protect the public from such weapons.

19

In *Alphacell* v *Woodward* Lord Salmon said:

'If it were held to be the law that no conviction could be obtained of the 1951 Act unless the prosecution could discharge the often impossible onus of proving that the pollution was caused intentionally or negligently, a great deal of pollution would go unpunished, and undeterred to the relief of many riparian factory owners. As a result, many rivers which are now filthy, would become filthier still and many rivers which are now clean, would lose their cleanliness.'

This indeed is probably one of the most important historical explanations for the existence of such offences. However, the consequences of such a situation are very grave. If a prosecutor does not have to prove mens rea, it is unlikely that he will go to the bother of doing so. So, when it comes to sentencing, the court will often find it very difficult to distinguish between the worst cases of a deliberate breach of the law and instances of inadvertant failure to comply with the required standard. It is very difficult to impose a sentence in such a situation and generally the court will want to enquire into which category the convicted person falls. Treating the offence as a crime of strict liability simply removes the decision as to these very important facts, from the jury into the hands of the judge.

It has been argued in support of offences of strict liability that the guilty defendant will, in almost every case, at least have been negligent, otherwise the statute would not have been complied with. However, there are cases where the defendant is absolutely blameless - for example, *Alphacell* v *Woodward* (1972); *Atkinson* v *Sir Alfred McAlpine & Son Ltd* (1974) - so even in the absence of any fault, liability may still be imposed. This point is sometimes argued in a slightly different way by saying that there is a substantial amount of empirical evidence to show that prosecutions are frequently only brought where the prosecuting agency (eg the factory inspectorate) is sure that some degree of fault is present. If this is so, why does Parliament not specify in detail what degree of fault must be proved for the offence to be committed?

Certainly, therefore, there are some arguments that can be put forward in support of strict liability, although on the whole the arguments have rather shaky foundations. However, before it can be considered whether or not strict liability must be retained, it is necessary to look at the arguments against such offences. The two main arguments against strict liability, indeed arguments that have been touched on already in considering supporting arguments to strict liability, are firstly, that it is unnecessary. Strict liability results in the conviction of persons who have been found by the court to have behaved impeccably and who should not be required to alter their conduct in any way. Furthermore, and possibly more importantly, strict liability is unjust. It is no argument to say that strict liability offences are not 'real crimes'. Those convicted of strict liability offences are treated as criminals, they go through a criminal process and the stigma of a criminal conviction attaches to them. Strict liability offences may catch the large number of truly guilty defendants, but it also catches the small number of persons who are absolutely morally innocent.

A conviction in a criminal court in that situation will obviously make the defendant feel rightly aggrieved and have consequences far outside the courts as in *Sweet* v *Parsley* (1969). It is no answer to such an argument to say that where there is no moral guilt, then the penalty imposed by the court will be only nominal. The court's penalty is the least of many penalties which attach to an individual when convicted of an offence. The stigma attached to the conviction may be a much more severe penalty. Where such a sense of injustice arises from a conviction in an offence of strict liability, the aggrieved defendant's attitude to criminal law generally may be affected so that the public respect for the criminal law, which is necessary for its upkeep, is undermined.

A practical argument in favour of strict liability is the most persuasive of all the arguments in support and could possibly outweigh the arguments against strict liability if there were no alternative to such offences. The practical problems of showing mens rea, which is the basis of the argument for strict liability, could to some extent be mitigated by altering the burden of proof in such offences. Indeed, to some extent, this has been seen by the statutory defence contained in The Misuse of Drugs Act as outlined above. However, a simpler approach would be to provide for the imposition of liability for negligence. Thus, a person would be liable if it were shown that they had inadvertently taken an justified risk. However, they would be acquitted if it was found that their conduct was faultless. The imposition of liability for negligence does seem to meet the arguments of most of those who are in favour of strict liability. Roscoe Pound in 'The Spirit of the Common Law' writes that 'the good sense of the courts has introduced the doctrine of acting at one's peril with respect to statutory crimes which express the needs of society. Such crimes are not meant to punish the vicious will, but to put pressure upon the thoughtless and the inefficient to do their whole duty in the interest of public health or safety or morals'.

The 'thoughtless and inefficient' to which Roscoe Pound refers are obviously those who are negligent. They are certainly not those who have done everything they could possibly do and are in no way to blame for the act, omission or state of affairs which constitute the actus reus of the offence.

Furthermore, by providing for liability for negligence, the public will be encouraged to do their duty to the highest possible standard and thus, avoid a possible criminal conviction. The Law Commission Working Paper No 31 The Mental Element in Crime (1970), suggested various reforms in the law relating to the mental element in crime. The basis of the report was that mens rea in some form, be it intention, recklessness or negligence, should be a normal requirement of guilt. In relation to all future offences, the Law Commission considered that the presumption in favour of mens rea must operate unless expressedly excluded. Where intention, knowledge or recklessness is expressly excluded in the statute in respect of any element in an offence, negligence should be required unless the offence is specifically stated to be one of strict liability.

By this means, the burden would be on Parliament to state whether an offence is to be one of strict liability and not merely be a question for the courts. In relation to existing offences, negligence should be substituted for any offences which are at present strictly interpreted. Where negligence is the sufficient mens rea in any offence, it would be treated as being established in the absence of any evidence to the contrary.

Bearing in mind the alternatives available to strict liability in its present form, it is difficult to support a statement that it must be retained. It is certainly true to present a fairly strong argument that it provides social benefits. Furthermore, these social benefits might not be obtained where mens rea in the sense of intention or recklessness were a necessary requirement of every crime. However, in this social regulatory field, where the aim of the criminal law is to encourage the highest possible standards of care, this may be achieved by the imposition of liability for negligence without the very serious consequence of catching those who are blameless.

Question 4(a)

David hitched a lift home and was picked up by Gloria. They stopped at a pub for a few drinks and having resumed their journey, David persuaded Gloria to stop the car for sexual intercourse. Whilst participating, Gloria changed her mind asking David to withdraw. David gave Gloria venereal disease.

Advise David about what crimes have been committed.

University of London LLB Examination
(for External Students) Criminal Law June 1983 Q2

General comment

The question involves consideration of an area which is not specifically covered in the syllabus and it therefore appears to be quite difficult. However, the principles of consent and recklessness are the main feature of the question and students ought to be familiar with the basic elements of rape.

Skeleton solution

David - rape - recklessness - ss47 and 20 OAP 1861

Gloria - consent

Suggested solution

When David initially has sexual intercourse he commits no offence - assuming Gloria is at least 16 years old - as she consents to it. Such consent must be freely given and not obtained by duress, fear or fraud.

Without such consent he would be guilty of rape contrary to s1 of the Sexual Offences Act 1956 (as amended) if:

i)   he has sexual intercourse with a woman who, at the time, does not consent to it; and

ii) at that time he knows that she does not consent or is reckless as to whether she consents or not.

Does the consent end when Gloria changes her mind? The Privy Council in *Kaitamaki* v *R* (1985) held that if a man continues intercourse under these circumstances it would amount to rape if he knows or is reckless as to whether the consent has been withdrawn. Here Gloria asks him to withdraw so David may thereafter be guilty of rape.

David's recklessness as to whether Gloria consents or not will be judged on the subjective *R* v *Cunningham* (1957) principles (ie consciously taking the risk) *R* v *Pigg* (1982) and it was held in *R* v *Bashir* (1982) by the Court of Appeal that the test was whether D had acted recklessly and not whether a reasonable man would have so acted. If David is indifferent to Gloria's consent in that he 'could not care less either way' then he is 'reckless' for this purpose: *R* v *Kimber* (1983); *R* v *Breckenridge* (1984).

The question of consent and/or withdrawal of consent is also relevant in deciding whether David bears any criminal responsibility for infecting Gloria with venereal disease. It seems almost certain that venereal disease would be regarded as grievous bodily harm and therefore the offences of s20 and s18 of the Offences Against the Person Act 1861 should be considered.

Section 20 of the Offences Against the Person Act 1861 provides that it would be an offence if the accused unlawfully and maliciously 'inflicts grievous bodily harm'. The term 'inflicts' includes a direct assault or an indirect assault, *R* v *Wilson* (1983). However, if consent has been given to the act there would be no assault at all. In *R* v *Clarence* (1888) a husband was acquitted of a charge under s20 of the 1861 Act when he had infected his wife with venereal disease. Because the wife consented to intercourse there was no assault, even though had she been aware of the disease which her husband knew he was suffering from, she would not have consented. In *R* v *Clarence* an important factor was the implied consent given by a wife to have sexual intercourse with her husband. For this reason a husband cannot generally be liable for rape of his wife. However, on the facts of the question there is no marital tie. Therefore it could possibly be argued that when Gloria withdrew her consent to intercourse and David refused to desist he may have committed an assault. Applying *Fagan* v *MPC* (1969) the actus reus was a continuing act which at that time combined with the necessary mens rea to complete the offence.

Under s20 it is not sufficient simply to show an assault which results in grievous bodily harm. It is also necessary to show that the assault was 'malicious' ie that the accused foresaw the possibility of some harm, *R* v *Mowatt* (1967). If David has no knowledge that he was suffering from venereal disease then it is possible to argue that even though he committed the actus reus of a s20 offence he lacked the necessary foresight of harm. In these circumstances an alternative charge could be made out under s47 of the Offences Against the Person Act 1861 which renders an offence to assault occasioning actual bodily harm. However, since the Court of Appeal's decision in *R* v *Parmenter* (1991), where their Lordships approved the earlier decision in *R* v *Spratt* (1990), the requirement for an intention to cause the actual harm specified in the charge or a recklessness to that consequence also applies in cases of s47. Therefore on the given facts it seems unlikely that David has sufficient mens rea to support either charge, despite the conflicting Court of Appeal decision in *R* v *Savage* (1990).

In either case, there must in any event be an assault and if there is consent there is no assault.

It should be noted that undoubtedly David has 'caused grievous bodily harm', that being the actus reus of the offence contained in s18 of the Offences Against the Person Act 1861. However, it is necessary to show in order to complete the offence, not only that the accused intended to do the act, but also that he intended to cause grievous bodily harm, ie that he desired it or knew that it was certain to occur. Recklessness as to whether or not he caused the injury is not sufficient *R* v *Belfon* (1976). In *R* v *Clarence* (1888) Hawkins J was of the opinion that although the charge under s20 failed because there was no assault, had the charge been under s18 in his view the accused would have fallen within the precise language of the section. Certainly, the criteria for actus reus under s18 are much more easily satisfied and, applying that to the facts in question, a charge under s18 would avoid any problems of causation which would necessarily have to be hurdled if a charge were made under s20 or s47. It should be remembered that the assault must cause grievous bodily harm, and if the harm was caused while the consent was still operating then there will be no causal link between the assault and the injury sustained.

The question refers to David and Gloria having had a few drinks. However, there is nothing in particular to indicate an offence of driving with excess alcohol in the blood. As to the defence of voluntary intoxication David does not appear to be sufficiently affected by drink to be able to claim he lacks mens rea. In *DPP* v *Majewski* (1976) it was stated that voluntary intoxication would afford a defence to a crime of specific intent but only if the intoxication resulted in the accused being unable to form mens rea. However, it would afford no defence to a crime of specific intent. Rape has been categorized as crime of specific intent (*DPP* v *Majewski*) but in *MPC* v *Caldwell* (1982) the House of Lords considered that any crime that included recklessness within its mens rea was a crime of basic intent.

Question 4(b)

Fitzgerald, aged 13 years, was playing on an embankment near a highway. He threw stones at passing cars. Gordon, who was driving his car very fast hit a stone. The car crashed into the control barrier and Gordon was severely injured.

Fitzgerald who was not very bright had not realized the danger his stone-throwing constituted. He also threw a stone at Dan but it missed him, hitting John.

Advise Fitzgerald.

University of London LLB Examination
(for External Students) Criminal Law June 1983 Q3

General comment

This question again examines the elements of recklessness, in relation here to criminal damage and offences against the person. Also considered is the doctrine of transferred malice.

Skeleton solution

Fitzgerald - Sections 1(1) and 1(2) CDA 1971; recklessness

Sections 20 and 18 OAP 1861; recklessness; doli incapax

Suggested solution

Fitzgerald should be advised that he may have committed an offence contrary to s1(1) of the Criminal Damage Act 1971 which provides that it is an offence to destroy or damage any property belonging to another, intending to destroy or damage any such property or being reckless as to whether any such property would be destroyed or damaged, without lawful excuse. The mens rea for s1(1) is intention or recklessness as to all the circumstances and consequences that constitute the actus reus of criminal damage under s1(1)(b).

Furthermore, Fitzgerald may have committed the more serious offence contained in s1(2) of the Criminal Damage Act which provides that it will be an offence for a person without lawful excuse to destroy or damage any property, whether belonging to himself or another:

a) intending to destroy or damage any property or being reckless as to whether any property would be destroyed or damaged; and

b) intending by the destruction or damage to endanger the life of another, or being reckless as to whether the life of another would be thereby endangered.

In relation to both of these offences certain aspects need further consideration. Firstly, the question of causation could be a problem. We are told that Gordon was driving very fast when he hit the stone on the road, and it could be argued that he was the cause of the damage to the property and the consequent injuries because of his excessive driving speeds. Only if the jury are satisfied that Fitzgerald was in law a substantial and operating cause of the consequences that occurred will he be held to be liable. It should be noted that it is unnecessary to show that Fitzgerald is the only cause in law. There may be other causes contributing to the consequence which actually flows. The second point requiring consideration is whether Fitzgerald would be viewed as reckless in relation to the circumstances and consequences contained in the actus reus of s1(1) and (2). In *MPC* v *Caldwell* (1982) Lord Diplock considered the meaning of the word in the context of the Criminal Damage Act.

'In my opinion, a person charged with an offence under s1(1) of the Criminal Damage Act 1971 is "reckless as to whether or not any property would be destroyed or damaged" if:

a) he does an act which in fact creates an obvious risk that property will be destroyed or damaged;

b) when he does the act he either has not given any thought to the possibility of

25

there being any such risk or has recognised that there was some risk involved and has nonetheless gone on to do it.'

This definition of recklessness is a departure from the earlier definitions contained in cases like *R* v *Stephenson* (1979) where emphasis was placed on the accused subjectively having appreciated the risk. In Lord Diplock's definition of recklessness many more states of mind would be in decided, ranging from failure to give any thought at all to whether or not there is any risk of those harmful consequences to recognising the existence of the risk and nevertheless deciding to ignore it.

The result of this much wider definition of recklessness is that thoughtless people or people of low intelligence who may not have appreciated a risk that would be obvious to the ordinary person may now be caught within the definition of recklessness and therefore be liable in criminal law.

This 'objective' type of recklessness was confirmed in *R* v *Sangha* (1988) where the Court of Appeal held that in criminal damage cases - here arson of a flat - the test was whether an ordinary and prudent bystander would have perceived an obvious risk that property would be damaged and life endangered thereby.

It could be argued that Fitzgerald has committed an offence contrary to s18 or s20 in the Offences Against the Person Act 1861. Section 18 is the more serious offence and it provides that a person who unlawfully and maliciously wounds or causes any grievous bodily harm to any person with intent to do any grievous bodily harm shall commit an offence.

The actus reus of this offence may well be satisfied providing the jury are satisfied that in law Fitzgerald was the legal 'cause' of the injuries sustained by Gordon. However, the mens rea element of s18 would not be satisfied. There is no 'intention' to cause the grievous bodily harm as Fitzgerald does not desire it nor does he know it is certain to occur.

Under s20 it is an offence for a person unlawfully and maliciously to wound or inflict any grievous bodily harm upon another. The problem on the facts would be whether or not there has been an infliction of grievous bodily harm. In the case of *R* v *Clarence* (1888) it was held that the term 'inflict' implied an assault in the sense of a battery, although this has been interpreted to mean both a direct assault and a more indirectly inflicted injury, *R* v *Martin* (1881) and *R* v *Wilson* (1983). However, even if it were held that there was an 'infliction of grievous bodily harm' it would have to be shown that Fitzgerald acted 'maliciously'. In the case of *R* v *Mowatt* (1968) it was stated that the term 'maliciously' imported upon the part of the person who unlawfully inflicts the wound or other grievous bodily harm an awareness that his act may have the consequence of causing some physical harm to some other person.

Moreover, it must be shown that Fitzgerald intended to cause the injury received by Gordon or was reckless as to that consequence: *R* v *Spratt* (1990); *R* v *Parmenter* (1991). Such recklessness will be judged subjectively ie *Cunningham* recklessness; *R* v *Parmenter* and the fact that serious injury was a probable consequence of Fitzgerald's action will not allow a jury to infer that he himself foresaw it (s8

Criminal Justice Act 1967). It must be shown that Fitzgerald actually foresaw the possibility of some harm. In *R v Sullivan* (1981) the Court of Appeal viewed s8 as applicable in deciding whether an accused acted maliciously or not.

Fitzgerald would be able to claim the defence of infancy to any of these offences charged as he is 13 years old. A child under ten is presumed to be incapable of committing a crime and this presumption is irrebuttable. If a child is over ten but under 14 the same presumption arises but can be rebutted. This presumption may be rebutted by showing that he has 'mischievous discretion'. It must be shown that he knew what he was doing was seriously wrong: *R v Gorrie* (1918), *McC v Runneckles* (1984).

When Fitzgerald throws the stone at Dan but hits John the mens rea he has toward Dan is, under the doctrine of transferred malice, transferred to John, provided the actus reus and mens rea are the same: *R v Latimer* (1886). Had he intended to hit a car when he threw the stone, his hitting John could not be subject to the doctrine as the actus reus and mens rea would not be the same: *R v Pembliton* (1874). Likewise if he had intended to hit Dan but had missed and damaged John's property.

One could have argued that Fitzgerald was reckless in throwing the stone.

Additionally, once the Road Traffic Act 1991 is in force Fitzgerald would commit an offence (under s22A RTA 1988) of causing danger to a road user.

3 PARTICIPATION

3.1   Introduction

3.2   Key points

3.3   Recent cases and statutes

3.4   Analysis of questions

3.5   Questions

3.1   Introduction

The commission of an offence naturally implies the existence of an offender and that will usually be the person who, with the requisite mens rea brings about the actus reus of the offence.

However, there may be more than one such 'principal' offender and they in turn may be assisted by others who aid, abet, counsel or procure the offence, or who incite it. They may also conspire to commit the offence.

It is also possible for a person to be used as an 'innocent agent' in an offence.

3.2   Key points

a) A person may commit an offence as a principal offender even where he does not carry out the actus reus himself, if he uses an 'innocent agent' eg a child or someone who lacks the mens rea to be guilty of the offence. In such cases it is the person using the 'agent' as a conduit through which to carry out his own criminal purpose who will be the principal and not the agent himself who is merely used as an instrument.

b)   i)   Although a person may not directly take part in a crime he can still be liable to be tried as a principal if he aids, abets, counsels or procures an offence s8 Accessories and Abettors Act 1861 and s44 Magistrates' Courts Act 1980. Examples of each of these aspects of complicity should be known eg driving the accused to the locus of the crime will be 'aiding': *DPP for Northern Ireland* v *Lynch* [1975] AC 653; *Attorney-General's Reference (No 1 of 1975)*. Abetting may be any conduct which instigates or even incites the offender at the time of commission, whereas counselling will generally occur prior to the offence being committed, and both aspects requires some consensus between the parties.

Procuring does not require such consensus but there must be a causal link between that which is finally carried out and the procuring. This causal link is not required in abetting or counselling.

ii) To be liable, the secondary party must intend to aid, abet, counsel or procure the offence charged. It is, however, sufficient that he knows of the type of offence which it is intended will be carried out *R* v *Bainbridge* [1959] 3 All ER 200 or indeed that he is aware ie that the principal may commit are of a given number of offences within a 'type': *DPP for Northern Ireland* v *Maxwell* [1978] 3 All ER 1140.

iii) Mere presence of another at the scene does not make him a secondary party to any crime committed *R* v *Clarkson* [1971] 3 All ER 344, but if his presence encourages the commission of the crime he may be liable: *R* v *Coney* (1882) 8 QBD 534.

c) Note the difficulties associated with the principal causing other consequences which were unforeseen or unintended by the secondary party. He will generally be liable for all such consequences: *R* v *Anderson and Morris* (1966) 50 Cr App R 216; *Chan Wing-Siu* v *R* [1985] AC 168; *R* v *Slack* [1989] 3 WLR 513; *R* v *Wakely and Others* [1990] Crim LR 119; *R* v *Hyde and Others* [1991] Crim LR 133.

If the principal carries out an unauthorised act outside the terms of their agreement, the secondary party will not be liable therefor: *R* v *Creamer* [1966] 1 QB 72.

d) Although the criminal law does not have a general rule of vicarious liability there are occasions where such liability may be imputed to another provision, eg 'using' offences under the Road Traffic Act of 1988, or where the person held vicariously liable is the employer of the actor, eg as a licensee or where the employer delegates his authority to act.

e) Conspiracy, although sometimes dealt with under 'inchoate offences', is included here. It must be remembered that conspiracy is covered partly (and mainly) by statute - the Criminal Law Act 1977 and partly by the common law. Conspiracy to defraud, to corrupt public morals and to outrage public decency still exist at common law and, after some confusion as to which charge should be used in each case, the Criminal Justice Act 1987 s12 now permits the prosecution in cases involving fraud to use either.

For a conspiracy to be made out there must be an agreement with another (others) to pursue a course of conduct which will result in an offence if the agreement is carried out as intended. Impossibility will not negate their liability (s1(1)(b)), but an accused cannot conspire if the only other party is:

i) the spouse;

ii) under ten years old or suffering from mental illness;

iii) the intended victim;

iv) a registered company where D is a director.

f) Allied to conspiracy is incitement which remains a common law offence and students should note the difficulties regarding inciting 'impossible' offences at common law: *R v Fitzmaurice* [1983] QB 1083.

Incitement involves persuading or inducing another to commit or participate in an offence.

g) Finally thought should be given to corporate liability which is a very topical development in English law today. As a registered company is a legal 'person' it attracts duties and liabilities in the same way as an individual and as such may be criminally liable either under statute or the 'doctrine of identification': *Tesco Supermarkets v Natrass* [1972] AC 153. Note also the DPP's decision that the owners of the Herald of Free Enterprise could be charged with corporate manslaughter following the Zeebrugge disaster.

3.3   Recent cases and statutes

R v Howe [1987] AC 417 - mens rea of secondary party - defence open to principal irrelevant.

R v Ward (1987) 85 Cr App R 71

R v Phillips (1987) 86 Cr App R 18 - no need to identify other parties to conspiracy.

R v Grundy (1989) The Times 9 February - joint assault on police officer - D joined in after main injuries inflicted.

R v Wakely; *R v Symonds*; *R v Holly* [1990] Crim LR 119 - joint enterprise - foreseeability that one member might use violence not enough to impute liability to others - held here that such foreseeability was indistinguishable from express tacit agreement required by *R v Slack* (1989).

R v Hyde and Others [1991] Crim LR 133 - for secondary party to be guilty of murder it must be shown that he foresaw the consequence of killing/gbh which might follow from the actions of the primary party.

3.4   Analysis of questions

Questions concerning participation are usually incorporated into problem questions based on specific offences such as burglary, theft, robbery etc and it is rare for a problem question to include only one actor.

3.5   Questions

Question 1(a)

Arnold and Benjamin agree to pick the pockets of the person they saw in the distance, standing alone at a 'bus-stop'. Arnold attracted the person's attention whilst Benjamin put his hand in the man's coat pockets. They were empty. In his anger and frustration, Benjamin took out a knife (the existence of which had been unknown to Arnold) and threw it away in the direction of a crowd standing outside a club.

Benjamin realised there was a grave risk that the knife would seriously injure one of the crowd but Benjamin was indifferent as to that risk. In fact the knife hit a boy and injured him. Arnold and Benjamin ran off.

Discuss their criminal liability.

Adapted from University of London LLB Examination
(for External Students) Criminal Law June 1981 Q3

General comment

The question involves the apportionment of liability between the two actors and their participation in the various offences:

Skeleton solution

Arnold and)   conspiracy s1 CLA 1977 and common law - ss1 and 1(2) CAA 1981
Benjamin)   - ss20 and 18 OAP 1861 - s8 A and AA 1861

Suggested solution

When Arnold and Benjamin agree to pick-pocket, they may commit an offence contrary to s1(1) of the Criminal Law Act 1977, which provides that 'if a person agrees with any other person or persons that a course of conduct shall be pursued which will necessarily amount to or involve the commission of any offence or offences by one or more of the parties to the agreement, if the agreement is carried out in accordance with their intentions, he is guilty of conspiracy to commit the offence'. From the facts of the question, the most obvious charge would be a conspiracy to steal.

There would still be a possibility of a charge under the old common law. The common law offence of conspiracy has been abolished by the Criminal Law Act 1977 with the exception of conspiracy to defraud and conspiracy to corrupt public morals and outrage public decency. A conspiracy to defraud is an agreement by two or more persons to deprive a person of something which is his: *Scott* v *Metropolitan Police Commissioner* (1975). This would obviously cover the conduct envisaged by Arnold and Benjamin. However in *R* v *Duncalf* (1979), it was stated that if a course of conduct is capable of coming within the s1 of the Criminal Law Act 1977, a charge should be brought under that section in preference to the common law even where retained.

Benjamin is guilty of attempted theft under s1(1) of the Criminal Attempts Act 1981 in that he, with intent to commit an offence - theft - does an act - putting his hands in pockets - which is more than merely preparatory to the commission of the offence whereas prior to the 1981 Act Benjamin might have argued that the pocket being empty made any such attempt impossible and therefore not an offence: *Haughton* v *Smith* (1975). Section 1(2) of the Act states that a person may be guilty of attempting to commit an offence even though the facts are such that the commission of the offence is impossible.

Following *R* v *Shivpuri* (1987) any argument based upon impossibility will not succeed.

Arnold may be liable as aiding and abetting Benjamin and under s8 of the Accessories and Abettors Act 1861 he will be liable to be tried, indicted and punished as a principal offender. By distracting the victim's attention to facilitate the attempted theft, Arnold would seen to be 'aiding' Benjamin in the same way as eg a 'look out' *R* v *Betts and Ridley* (1930) or one who holds another while he is assaulted *R* v *Clarkson* (1971).

Benjamin may be guilty of wounding the boy under s18 or s20 of the Offences Against the Person Act 1861 although he lacks the mens rea ie an intention to wound - for the s18 charge: *R* v *Mowatt* (1968).

He may commit the s20 offences (one of basic intent) of wounding if he is shown to be 'reckless' in the *R* v *Cunningham* (1957) sense (ie consciously takes the risk): *R* v *Morrison* (1988). Here we are told that he realises the grave risk of injury and so he would appear to be reckless in this required sense.

Arnold's liability for the injury is less clear. Generally, one who assists a principal offender in his criminal conduct will be liable for the consequences arising therefrom, whether or not those consequences were intended or foreseen, provided the relevant mens rea is present: *R* v *Chan Wing-Siu* (1985); *R* v *Ward* (1987). In order for him to be liable for the violence used by Benjamin, though, there must have been some express or tacit agreement between them that such violence would be used if necessary: *R* v *Slack* (1989). Mere foreseeability that Benjamin might resort to violence is insufficient: *R* v *Wakely and Others* (1990).

However, if the principal goes beyond that which is agreed or contemplated, the other party cannot be held liable for the unauthorised act or its consequences: *R* v *Creamer* (1966).

As the original plan here was simply to steal, it is unlikely that Arnold, who knows nothing of the knife, would be liable for Benjamin's use of it: *Davies* v *DPP* (1954).

Question 1(b)

Quinn agreed with Robert to sneak into a nearby stadium to watch a wrestling match. Quinn kept a gatekeeper talking whilst Robert entered without paying. Robert then threw down a rope by which Quinn climbed in. Inside, Quinn was challenged by a security officer. Quinn pushed him aside and ran away.

Robert ordered food for himself and Quinn. They both ate the food and ran away without paying though this was not noticed by the waitress. During the meal Quinn had assumed that Robert was going to pay for both meals and was surprised when told to run by Robert.

What crimes have been committed?

University of London LLB Examination
for (External Students) Criminal Law June 1982 Q4

General comment

The question here again examines the degree of involvement of each party in the crimes revealed.

Skeleton solution

Quinn and Robert - conspiracy s1 CLA 1977 - common law - conspiracy to defraud - obtaining service by deception s1 TA 1978 - obtaining property by deception s15 TA 1968 - making off s3 TA 1978 - causing gbh s20 OAP 1861 - common assault

Suggested solution

When Quinn and Robert agreed together to sneak into a stadium to watch a wrestling match, that agreement may constitute a conspiracy to defraud under the common law. In *R* v *Landy* (1981) the Court of Appeal stated that a conspiracy to defraud was an agreement to dishonestly do something which will or may cause loss or prejudice to another.

It would be appropriate to charge under a common law conspiracy to defraud so long as the agreement between the parties had not reached such a stage that the agreement amounted to a particular offence. Once a particular offence can be shown it is more appropriate to charge under s1 of the Criminal Law Act 1977 which states that a statutory conspiracy is committed if a person agrees with any other person that a course of conduct shall be pursued which if the agreement is carried out in accordance with their intentions will amount to an offence or would do but for facts which render it impossible: *R* v *Ayres* (1984).

At the time when Quinn and Robert's agreement is not sufficiently formulated to amount to a crime, a conspiracy to defraud would be the appropriate charge, but once the agreement is sufficiently detailed to amount to a conspiracy under s1 of the Criminal Law Act 1977 then applying the principle laid out by the Court of Appeal in *R* v *Duncalf* (1979) the appropriate charge should be under the Criminal Law Act. However, the prosecution may bring a charge under either heading s12 CJA 1987.

When Quinn diverts the gatekeeper thus allowing Robert to enter without paying he may commit an offence contrary to s1 of the Theft Act 1978 which states that a person who by any deception dishonestly obtains services from another shall be guilty of an offence.

'Deception' under the 1978 Act has the same meaning as in s15 of the Theft Act 1968. It means 'any deception (whether deliberate or reckless) by words or conduct as to fact or as to law including a deception as to the present intentions of the person using the deception or any other person.

As with s15 of the Theft Act 1968 the deception must be operative, ie it must be the factor which enables the accused to obtain service and the conduct must be 'dishonest'. This is a question for the jury to decide: *R* v *Feely* (1973). In *R* v *Ghosh* (1982) it was stated that the jury had to apply a subjective test in ascertaining whether the accused was dishonest. However an accused would be dishonest if he appreciated that the average person would have viewed his conduct as such, whether or not he did.

It is necessary to consider the effect of s1(2) which states that it is in obtaining the services 'where the other is induced to confer benefit by doing some act, or causing or permitting some act to be done, on the understanding that the benefit has been or will be paid for'. Certainly, admission to a stadium would be 'a benefit' within s1(2), but there may be problems in showing that the gatekeeper was 'induced to confer a benefit' when he did not know that the parties had entered without paying. Had Quinn and Robert persuaded the gatekeeper to allow them by pretending that they had lost their entrance tickets which they had already purchased, then that element of the offence would have been satisfied. However, on the facts as shown there may be a problem on this point.

The trespassary entry into the stadium is not an offence on its own. There may be an offence contrary to s9 of the Theft Act 1968 but only if the stadium amounted to 'a building'. Furthermore, it would be necessary to show for an offence under s9(1)(a) that they intended to steal, inflict grievous bodily harm, rape or do unlawful damage to property or, under s9(1)(b), having entered any building or part of the building as a trespasser they stole or attempted to steal anything in the building, or inflicted or attempted to inflict on any person therein any grievous bodily harm.

The term 'building' is not defined in the Theft Acts and therefore its meaning must be judged from its ordinary usage. Certainly a stadium is capable of being a building providing it is a structure with a certain degree of permanence. However, if the stadium is simply a walled pitch, it seems unlikely that it would amount to a building. Furthermore, there is no evidence that either of the accused had the intention of committing an offence within s9(1)(a) at the time of entry. If the stadium were sufficient to amount to a building then Quinn may commit an offence under s9(1)(b) when he pushes the security officer aside and runs away.

However, it would be necessary to show that as a result of being pushed the security guard was sufficiently seriously injured for those injuries to amount to grievous bodily harm within s20 of the Offences Against the Person Act 1861. On the facts of the question there is nothing to indicate that there were any injuries at all and, indeed, if this were the case then the only offence committed in pushing the security officer would be a common law battery which is committed when there is a direct infliction of force against someone intentionally or recklessly performed: *R* v *Venna* (1976).

When Robert and Quinn leave the restaurant without paying they may commit an offence contrary to s3 of the Theft Act 1978, which states that a person who 'knowing that payment on the spot for any goods supplied or services done is required or expected of him dishonestly makes off without having paid as required or expected of him and with intent to avoid payment, shall be guilty of an offence'.

Under s3 it is not necessary to show any deception at all. Furthermore, dishonesty does not have to be present at the outset of the transaction but only when the accused makes off without having paid the bill.

Robert ordered the food and on this basis there was no problem in showing that payment was required or expected from him. However, in order for Quinn to be liable as a principal, it must be shown that Quinn knew that payment for the service was required or expected from him, even though he himself may not have expected to pay for it. If this element cannot be shown then Quinn may not be liable as a principal but may be liable as an aider and abettor to the offence committed by Robert, in which case he may be tried as a principle s8 Accessories and Abettors Act 1861.

A person who 'aids and abets' is present at the time of the committing of the offence, and assists or encourages the principal offender. Mere presence alone is not sufficient: *R* v *Coney* (1882). Furthermore, it must be shown that the aider and abettor has knowledge of all the circumstances which constitute the offence: *Johnson* v *Youden* (1950).

Furthermore, Robert may have committed an offence contrary to s15 of the Theft Act 1968 when by deception he dishonestly obtained property belonging to another with the intention of permanently depriving the other of it. A deception within s15(4) would be shown if Robert had the intention of not paying before he ordered the meal. If that were the case then there would be a deliberate implied deception by conduct which would operate to enable him to obtain the property.

Question 2

A agreed with B that they would sneak into a nearby amusement park in order to enjoy the various rides. A climbed over the perimeter fence in order to avoid paying the £15 entrance fee. A then kept the attendant talking, and while the attendant's attention was elsewhere, B was able to sneak past without paying.

B took several rides on the ghost train and on each occasion he examined handbags belonging to other passengers because he was looking for a special type of perfume which his mother used. None of his fellow passengers had that brand of perfume so he left disappointed.

Advise A and B of their criminal liability if any.

Adapted from University of London LLB Examination
(for External Students) Criminal Law June 1987 Q1

General comment

Although the question at first sight appears relatively straightforward there are many pitfalls that an unwary student could fall into, particularly in relation to the property offences.

Skeleton solution

A   Conspiracy - entry to the park as a trespasser but no burglary - s2 Theft Act 1978 Self defence - s3 CLA 1967 - mistake

B   Conspiracy - s1 TA 1978, attempted theft - impossibility or conditional intent - s1 CAA 1981

CRIMINAL LAW

Suggested solution

When A and B agree to sneak into the amusement park there may be a conspiracy within the common law or under s1 Criminal Law Act 1977. However a conspiracy under s1 CLA 1977 requires the carrying out of the agreement to necessarily amount to or involve the commission of a substantive offence and therefore it is convenient to consider the conspiracy aspect after the substantive offences have been considered.

When A climbs over the perimeter wall in order to avoid paying the entrance fee he undoubtedly enters the park as a trespasser. This would give rise to possible civil liability but there is nothing in the question to suggest that a crime has been committed at this stage. Section 9 Theft Act 1968 (burglary) does not need consideration as this is only satisfied where there is entry into a building as a trespasser. An amusement park would obviously not amount to a building.

When A keeps the attendant talking thus allowing B to sneak past without paying, he may commit an offence contrary to s2(1)(c) Theft Act 1978. Section 2(1)(c) provides that it will be an offence where a person by a deception dishonestly obtains any exemption from or an abatement of liability to make a payment. 'Obtains' within s2(1)(c) includes obtaining for another or enabling another to obtain.

Undoubtedly there is a deception practised on the attendant by A when he kept the attendant talking. Section 15(4) Theft Act 1968 provides that 'deception' means any deception (whether deliberate or reckless) by words or conduct as to fact or as to law, including deception as to the present intentions of the person using the deception or any other person. However it may be that a prosecution under s2(1)(c) could encounter difficulties on the ground that the term 'exemption' covers more appropriately the type of situation where, for example, an accused by deception dishonestly secures a rate rebate to which he is not entitled.

The only other offence within s2 that might be appropriate is s2(1)(b) which provides that an offence is committed where a person by deception with intent to make permanent default in whole or in part of any existing liability to make a payment, or with intent to let another do so, dishonestly induces the creditor or any person claiming on behalf of a creditor to wait for payment or forgo payment.

This offence, unlike s2(1)(a) may be committed by a unilateral act. Consensus between the creditor or debtor is not required. However it could be argued that at the time of the deception there is no existing liability - this only being created once B has gained entry.

More than one offence under s2 TA 1978 may be satisfied at the same time on the same facts. It is therefore possible that both s2(1)(b) and s2(1)(c) could be established: *R* v *Sibartie* (1983).

If A does commit an offence contrary to s2, B could be liable as an accomplice. An aider and abettor is a person; who is present assisting or encouraging the offence: *R* v *Coney* (1882); *R* v *Clarkson* (1971).

Under s8 Accessories and Abettors Act 1861 persons who are accomplices are to be treated as principal offenders for the purposes of trial and punishment.

When B rides on the ghost train he may commit an offence contrary to s1 Theft Act 1978. Section 1 provides that a person who by any deception dishonestly obtains services from another shall be guilty of an offence.

Section 1(2) provides that it is an obtaining of a service where the other is induced to confer a benefit by doing some act, or causing or permitting some act to be done, on the understanding that the benefit has been or will be paid for.

Certainly it could be that B is representing himself as having paid the entrance fee and this could amount to a deception within s15(4) TA 1968. However it must be shown that the deception operates on a human mind and if there is no one who allows B to ride the ghost train on the basis that he has paid there will not be an operative deception. It has also been argued that B commits the offence of travelling upon a railway without having paid his fare and with intent to avoid payment thereof (s5(3)(a) Regulation of Railways Act 1889), although this scarcely seems to fall within the spirit of that piece of legislation!

When B examines the contents of the handbag looking for a particular perfume he may become liable for attempted theft. Section 1 Theft Act 1968 provides that the offence of theft is established if he dishonestly appropriates property belonging to another with intent to permanently deprive the other of it. An attempted theft would be established if it was shown that there was an act more than merely preparatory towards the full offence with mens rea, s1 Criminal Attempts Act 1981.

There seems little doubt that the actus reus would be satisfied. However there could be difficulties in establishing an intention to permanently deprive. The facts of the question are similar to the facts in *R v Easom* (1971) where the accused was found rummaging through the contents of the handbag. The Court of Appeal quashed a conviction for theft of certain items because there was no intention to permanently deprive but merely a conditional intention, ie an intention to take any items that were worth taking. Their Lordships were of the opinion that an attempt charge would similarly fail if the charge made reference to particular items because unless it could be shown that an accused had mens rea towards those items the elements of theft are not established. This problem would be avoided if a charge of attempted theft were drafted in broad terms alleging that B intended to steal some or all of the contents of the handbag: *Attorney-General's References (Nos 1 and 2 of 1979)* (1979).

The facts in question differ in that B has in mind a particular perfume. It would therefore be necessary to establish that B had mens rea sufficient for theft of the perfume if the indictment alleges that he attempted to steal the particular item of perfume. The perfume is not there and therefore this could be regarded as an example of impossibility where there is no object. Under the CAA 1981 impossibility is no longer to be regarded as defence: s1(2). Under s1(3) in deciding where a person has the necessary intention he must be judged on the facts as he believed them to be. This could be a difficult point on the facts in question. B merely hoped that the handbag would contain the perfume - that is not the same as a belief.

Any difficulties that might arise from this would be avoided if the approach indicated in the *Attorney-General's References* were adopted and an indictment for attempted theft was broadly drafted without reference to the perfume.

B could possibly be liable under s9 Theft Act 1968. Burglary is established where a person enters a building as a trespasser with intent to steal (s9(1)(a)) or where a person having entered a building as a trespasser steals or attempts to steal. Usually a ghost train ride will pass through a tunnel or structure. If this were sufficient to amount to 'a building' s9(1)(a) and s9(1)(b) could be satisfied. B would be a trespasser as he has not paid for his entrance as required. To be a building the structure must have some degree of permanence but beyond that the term may vary considerably in its meaning. On the facts it is impossible to conclude whether s9 is satisfied.

Returning now to the question of liability for conspiracy. A conspiracy contrary to s1(1) Criminal Law Act 1977 would be established if a person agrees with any other person that a course shall be pursued which, if the agreement is carried out in accordance with their intentions:

a) will *necessarily* amount to or involve the commission of any offence by one or more of the parties to the agreement; or

b) would do but for the existence of facts which render the commission of the offence impossible.

The agreement between A and B appears only to extend to the entry and enjoyment of the amusement park. None of the charges that could arise from that are without difficulty. This means that it may not be possible for the prosecution to establish that their plan will necessarily involve the commission of an offence.

An alternative charge would be a common law conspiracy to defraud which would be established where there is a dishonest agreement which would result in a person suffering economic disadvantage: *Scott* v *Metropolitan Police Commissioner* (1975).

Undoubtedly s1 and the common law do on occasions overlap. Where this occurs s1 must be charged: *R* v *Ayres* (1984). Conspiracy to defraud should only be charged where either there is no substantive offence *necessarily* resulting from agreement or where beyond any agreement to commit a substantive offence there is a separate common law conspiracy: *R* v *Cooke* (1986). However, a prosecution may be brought under either head: s12 CJA 1987.

B may be liable as a co-conspirator providing he has, in addition to the normal mens rea requirement, mischievous discretion.

Question 3

A telephoned B inviting B to join him to take a Picasso painting from nearby Ascot Manor. B said that he would help A, but he did so only because he wished to entrap A and report him to the police. B informed the police and they advised B to participate so that A could be caught red-handed. A and B drove in A's car to Ascot Manor. A tricked his way past the custodian by representing that he was from the electricity board. B kept watch outside. A removed the painting and was in the process of leaving when he was apprehended by a security guard.

Discuss the criminal liability of A and B.

Adapted from University of London LLB Examination
(for External Students) Criminal Law June 1984 Q1

General comment

This question requires quite detailed consideration of a range of offences including incitement, conspiracy and burglary. However, the most difficult aspect of the question for any student would probably be to decide to what extent B will be liable as an accomplice for the offences committed by A and whether there is a defence of entrapment open to A. Careful planning of any answer will be required if the answer is not to appear confused.

Skeleton solution

Incitement - conspiracy s1 CLA 1977/Common Law - Burglary s9(1)(a) TA 1968 - Theft s1 TA 1968 - 'Dishonest' - obtaining property by deception s15 TA 1968.

Suggested solution

When A telephoned B inviting him to join him in taking the painting A will commit the offence of incitement at common law as he is endeavouring to induce or pursuade B to participate in a crime or in an act which would have been a crime had B done it of his own volition.

When B agrees to help A the incitement may have developed into a conspiracy. The conspiracy would be a statutory conspiracy within s1 of the Criminal Law Act 1977 which provides that the offence of statutory conspiracy is committed if a person agrees with any other person or persons that a course of conduct shall be pursued which, if the agreement is carried out in accordance with their intentions, either:

a) will necessarily amount to or involve the commission of any offence; or

b) would do but for the existence of facts which render the commission of the offence or any of the offences impossible.

In order to satisfy s1 of the Criminal Law Act 1977 it is necessary to show that a particular crime would have taken place with all aspects of its mens rea and actus reus being satisfied. On the facts there would seem to be a conspiracy to steal or to commit burglary contrary to s9 Theft Act 1968.

An alternative charge of conspiracy to defraud under the common law may be available. In *Scott* v *Metropolitan Police Commissioner* (1975) it was stated by the House of Lords that 'defraud' in this context meant depriving a person dishonestly of something to which he is, would, or might (but for the fraud) be entitled. Obviously there is a certain amount of overlap between s1 of the Criminal Law Act 1977 and the common law conspiracy to defraud. In *R* v *Ayres* (1984) the House of Lords stated that only in exceptional cases should fraudulent agreements be charged as common law conspiracies. In the majority of cases it would be clear that the performance of the agreement would necessarily involve commission of a particular substantive offence and in such a case the conspiracy should be charged under s1 of the Criminal Law Act 1977.

It could be argued that on the facts in question there was no conspiracy on the basis that B lacked an intention to enter into a true agreement and if this were the case or if, for example, it was held that B was not acting dishonestly, there would be no offence of conspiracy as no other parties are involved.

Note that there could be no offence of attempting to conspire (Criminal Attempts Act 1981 s1(4)). It could also be argued that B is not actually incited to commit the offence - his motivation being to help the police catch A - in which case the offence of attempting to incite may be committed: *R* v *Banks* (1873).

When A gains entry into Ascot Manor by pretending he is from the Electricity Board he may commit the offence of burglary contrary to s9(1)(a) of the Theft Act 1968. Under s9(1)(a) a person is guilty of burglary if he enters a building or part of a building as a trespasser with intent to steal anything in the building. A possible point of difficulty is whether or not A enters as a trespasser or whether he is an invitee. The meaning of the phrase 'enters as a trespasser' was considered in *R* v *Collins* (1973). The Court of Appeal implied that the entry had to be 'effective and substantial'. Furthermore it was not sufficient that the accused was a trespasser in civil law; he had to enter knowingly as a trespasser or be reckless as to whether or not he entered as a trespasser. It is submitted that in this context recklessness requires a subjective appreciation of the risk involved. On the facts in question where consent to entry is obtained by fraud undoubtedly there would be entry as a trespasser. A's license to be in the building extends to a particular purpose only and as he enters for some other purpose there would be a trespassary entry.

At the time of the entry into the building as a trespasser A intends to steal. Under s1 of the Theft Act 1968 a person is guilty of theft if he dishonestly appropriates property belonging to another with the intention of permanently depriving the other of it. A would appear to have satisfied the necessary mens rea of theft. However, it should be remembered that the question of dishonesty is always for the jury to decide in the absence of s2 of the Theft Act 1968 being applicable: *R* v *Feely* (1973). The test to be applied was outlined in *R* v *Ghosh* (1982). In that case the Court of Appeal stated that the test of dishonesty was subjective although in determining whether the prosecution had proved that the person charged was acting dishonestly a jury had first of all to decide whether, according to the ordinary standards of reasonable, honest people, what was done was dishonest. If it was not dishonest by those standards, that was the end of the matter and the prosecution failed. If it was dishonest by those standards then the jury had to consider whether the person charged *himself* must have realised that what he was doing was by those standards dishonest. Furthermore, it is dishonest for a person charged to act in a way which he knows ordinary people consider to be dishonest, even if he asserts or genuinely believes that he is morally justified in acting as he has. However, what has become known as a *Ghosh* direction should not be given to juries automatically in every case involving dishonesty: *R* v *Spencer and Turner* (1989), and as A is unlikely to raise his own subjective belief in the honesty of what he was doing as a defence, such a direction will not be needed: *R* v *Price* (1990).

When A removed the painting he commits the offence of theft contrary to s1 of the Theft Act 1968. At the point of removal he will have satisfied the actus reus of theft. Section 3 of the Theft Act 1968 provides a partial definition of 'appropriation'. Any assumption by a person of the rights of an owner amounts to an appropriation within s3. In *R* v *Morris* (1983) the House of Lords considered that the concept of appropriation involved an element of 'adverse interference with or usurpation of some right of the owner'. At the time when the theft is complete there will be a further offence under s9(1)(b) of the Theft Act 1968 which provides that a person is guilty of burglary if having entered any building or part of a building as a trespasser he steals.

Two further offences require very brief consideration. Firstly, when A tricks his way into the building and then steals it could be argued that an offence of s15 of the Theft Act 1968 has taken place. Under s15 it is an offence dishonestly by deception to obtain property belonging to another with an intention permanently to deprive. However, on the facts in question it would appear that the deception is too remote from the obtaining of the property and therefore could not be said that the deception was the operative reason for the obtaining of the picture.

B's liability as an accomplice to the offences committed by A would depend on whether or not he could be regarded as an aider or abettor. A person who 'aids and abets' is present at the time of the committing of an offence (or constructively present, as here, keeping watch) assisting, or encouraging the principal offender: *R* v *Coney* (1882). A person cannot be an aider or abettor unless he knows the facts which constitute the offence: *Johnson* v *Youden* (1950). B would argue that he had no intention to assist or encourage A but rather his only intention was to entrap him. However what he did was done voluntarily, knowing it would assist A in his offence. Therefore it would seem likely B would have mens rea. In *R* v *Sang* (1979) the House of Lords by a majority considered that such a person as B could commit an offence as an accomplice.

B's driving the car to the Manor will be sufficient for the actus reus of 'aiding' A - *DPP for Northern Ireland* v *Lynch* (1975) and, as he provides this aid with intention that A should commit the later offences - for whatever reason - such an intention would appear to make him guilty of aiding and abetting: *NCB* v *Gamble* (1959).

It should be noted that A will not be able to claim a defence of 'entrapment' although in the United States such a defence has been allowed where the accused who was not otherwise intending to commit an offence has been enticed into it by the police or an undercover agent. However, this defence has never been accepted in English law. Furthermore, even if it was available, it would seem that it would be inappropriate from the facts in question as A has not been enticed into committing any offence which he was not already disposed to commit.

Question 4

A telephoned B and suggested that together they should steal a rare diamond from a local jewellery exhibition. B replied that he would not help. B thought the matter over and decided to steal the diamond for himself. In order to 'case' the exhibition B bought an entry ticket. After inspection B decided it would be too difficult to steal the jewel. On the way out from the exhibition he took a coat from a cloakroom.

On discovering what B had done, A challenged him to a wrestling match. B agreed to the fight but, because he was afraid of A, he later changed his mind and failed to keep his 'appointment'.

Discuss A and B's criminal liability if any.

Adapted from University of London LLB Examination
(for External Students) Criminal Law June 1985 Q1

General comment

A relatively straightforward question although careful thought and discussion is required on the overlap between counselling and incitement. Another area that would need a very careful approach is the question of whether or not the necessary elements of burglary are satisfied, in particular whether or not there is 'entry as a trespasser'.

Skeleton solution

Incitement - counselling a crime - attempted theft - burglary under s9(1)(a) Theft Act 1968 - burglary under s9(1)(b) Theft Act 1968 - theft

Suggested solution

When A telephones B and suggests that they should steal a rare diamond A commits the common law offence of inciting another to commit an offence. The inciter must spur on or urge on by advice, encouragement, persuasion, threats or pressure: *Race Relations Board* v *Applin* (1973). It is immaterial that the encouragement is unsuccessful provided it has been communicated to the incitee. It could not be argued that A has incited B to conspire because there is no such offence. Section 5(7) Criminal Law Act 1977. A and B do not enter into any agreement, therefore there is no conspiracy either under the common law or under the Criminal Law Act 1977. B proceeds on his own although it may be possible to argue still that A is an accomplice.

When B buys the ticket in order to 'case' the exhibition he may commit an offence contrary to s9(1)(a) of the Theft Act 1968. Under s9(1)(a) the offence of burglary is committed where there is entry by an accused into a building as a trespasser with intent to steal. The entry must be 'effective and substantial' and the accused must have intention or at least recklessness as to the facts which make him a trespasser: *R* v *Collins* (1972). Considering the facts in question there are two main difficulties.

Firstly, B has bought himself a ticket and therefore it could be argued that he has not entered the building as a trespasser. However, B's permission to enter was not given to help plan a theft. B has entered the building for a purpose other than the purpose for which he was given permission and therefore he may have entered 'as a trespasser': *R* v *Jones and Smith* (1976).

Secondly, it seems doubtful that B entered with intent to steal. B's entry was done with the purposes of assisting him in planning the burglary and therefore the requirement of an intention to steal would not appear to be satisfied unless B had a more general intention to steal anything that took his fancy while in the building: *Attorney-General's References (No 1 and 2 of 1979)* (1979).

B could not be liable for an attempt to steal the diamond because he must have done an act which is more than merely preparatory to the full offence with full mens rea, s1 Criminal Attempts Act 1981. This would seem unlikely on the facts here although it is for the jury to decide. If there was an attempt to steal the diamond there may be a further offence under s9(1)(b).

When B removes a coat from the cloakroom he commits the offence of theft contrary to s1 Theft Act 1968. Under s1 a person is guilty of theft if he dishonestly appropriates property belonging to another with the intention of permanently depriving the other of it.

Section 3 provides that an assumption by a person of the rights of an owner will amount to an appropriation. In *R* v *Morris* (1983) the House of Lords held that it was not necessary for the prosecution to prove that an accused assumed all the rights. It is sufficient to prove that he assumed any of the rights.

Furthermore, the concept of appropriation involved an act by way of 'adverse interference with or usurpation of those rights'. The question of dishonesty must be left to the jury: *R* v *Feely* (1973). On the facts given it is unlikely that the jury will require a *Ghosh* direction.

B may also be liable for the offence of burglary under s9(1)(b) of the Theft Act 1968. Under s9(1)(b) a person will be guilty of burglary if he enters a building as a trespasser and steals or attempts to steal. The question of whether or not the entry was a trespassary entry has already been considered.

Returning now to A's possible liability as an accomplice for the offences committed by B. A person who aids, abets, counsels or procures an offence is treated the same as a principal offender. A is not present or constructively present and therefore could not be an aider or abettor.

Possibly he could be said to be a counsellor. However, to establish this it must be shown that the offence he counselled actually took place, and it is fairly doubtful that there was even an attempt to steal the diamond. It could not be argued that he counselled any other of the offences, as they were not within the scope of what he contemplated. A further difficulty with regard to any counselling charge is that while there need not be any causal link there has got to be consensus between the counsellor and the principal offender. Undoubtedly A would contend that this was not present and he had never had in mind that B should proceed as he did.

With regard to the wrestling match, when A challenges B he may again be 'inciting' an offence at common law. He has communicated the encouragement to B and he intends the offence to be committed by B.

The 'offence' to be committed - ie the wrestling match - presents some difficulty. If the match is to take place in public or private it could be an offence under the Public Order Act 1986 or a breach of the peace.

A and B may, in agreeing to fight, be guilty of conspiracy under s1 Criminal Law Act 1977 However, their agreement must be to do an act which would necessarily amount to an offence *R* v *Walker* (1962). Moreover, it will not be a conspiracy here if the only person with whom A agrees in the intended victim of the offence (s2(2)(c)). If it is argued that the match itself is an offence and that B is not the 'intended victim', it would seem that the conspiracy is made out.

4 NON-FATAL OFFENCES AGAINST THE PERSON

4.1   Introduction

It is traditional to separate the various offences against the person into those of a non-fatal type, a sexual type and murder/manslaughter although the former may often lead to the latter.

The offences ranging from threats to injure, through to grievous bodily harm, form the basis of many examination questions and it is vital that students are familiar with the requirements for each type of 'assault'.

4.2   Key points

a) Note the distinction between 'battery' and 'assault' although the two invariably coincide.

There are peculiar defences available in relation to assaults and these should be known.

   i)   Consent - *R* v *Coney* (1882) 8 QBD 534; *R* v *Donovan* (1934) 25 Cr App R 1 and the importance of public interest: *Attorney-General's Reference (No 6 of 1980).*

   ii) Chastisement of child by parent. Guardian or teachers: *Campbell* v *Cosans* (1982) unreported (European Court of Human Rights).

   iii) Accident and the *de minimis* rule.

b) The statutory provisions under the Offences Against the Person Act 1861 **must** be known and in particular the distinction between s18 and s20 mens rea, and the applicability of recklessness. The judicial interpretation of various words eg 'maliciously', 'grievous bodily harm' - *DPP* v *Smith* [1961] AC 290; *R* v *Saunders* [1985] Crim LR 230, 'bodily harm' - *R* v *Miller* [1954] 2 QB 282; *R* v *Dawson* (1985) 81 Cr App R 150, 'inflict' - *R* v *Clarence* (1888) 22 QBD 23; *R* v *Wilson* [1984] AC 242; *R* v *Martin* (1881) 8 QBD 54. One area that is commonly overlooked is the second arm of s18 where teaching generally concentrates on the 'intent' to cause grievous bodily harm. The offence will also be made out if the wounding/gbh is done to prevent 'the lawful arrest or detainer of any person'.

c) The provisions of s51 of the Police Act 1964 should be known, together with the question of 'in the execution of his duty'. Also, the defence under s3 of the Criminal Law Act 1967.

d) Students should be aware of the offences of kidnapping and false imprisonment which occasionally feature in OAP questions.

Child destruction under the Infant Life (Preservation) Act 1929 should be known, together with the corresponding provisions of the Abortion Act 1967 and s58 of the Offences Against the Person Act 1861. See *Rance* v *Mid-Downs Health Authority* below.

4.3   Recent cases and statutes

R v *Spratt* (1990) 91 Cr App R 362.

R v *Parmenter* (1991) 92 Cr App R 68.

The unsatisfactory position of s47 and s20 assaults, as lamented by the Court of Appeal in *R* v *Parmenter* (1991) must be noted.

In *R* v *Spratt* the Court of Appeal held that the requisite mens rea in either case was either an intention to cause the harm specified in the charge or a recklessness as to that consequence. It was not sufficient to show such intention/recklessness toward the act which resulted in the harm.

The decision directly conflicts with the court's decision in *R* v *Savage* [1990] Crim LR 709 and creates a situation where the appropriate charge will now depend upon the degree of harm caused - with the appropriate state of mind. As the court point out in *R* v *Parmenter* this is often merely a product of chance.

The situation, however, will require guidance from the House of Lords in the absence of the implementation of the Draft Criminal Code (Law Com No 177 1989). In the meantime the Court of Appeal has stated that trial judges must use 'subjective intent' and 'subjective appreciation of risk' as touchstones for which the jury should look and, as long as *Mowatt* remained the law, the possibility of any harm was what they should consider when assessing the subjective element.

R v *Morrison* (1988) The Times 12 November - recklessness and wounding - non-applicability to s18.

R v *Gillard* (1988) 87 Cr App R 189 - spraying CS gas into face - s24 OAP?

Rance v *Mid-Downs Health Authority* (1990) 140 NLJ 325 - if a foetus has developed to the stage where it is capable, if born, of breathing through its own lungs and of living without any connection to its mother, it is a child 'capable of being born alive' within meaning of s1 Infant Life (Preservation) Act 1929. Aborting such a foetus will be unlawful even if done within the 28 week period provided for in s2 of the Act.

NB   This is first time the interpretation of the statutory wording has arisen in an English court.

R v *Tait* [1989] 3 WLR 891 - Youths threatened pregnant mother that they would return and kill child - held that foetus *in utero* was not a person for purposes of threatening to kill another contrary to s16 OAP Act 1861.

Riley v *DPP* (1989) Times 13 December - Assault on police officer in execution of duty - essential element of offence that the officer's actions prior to being assaulted be lawful.

R v *Lamb* [1990] Crim LR 58 - Assault on police officer after officer had been told to leave D's house - officer reasonably apprehended a breach of the peace and therefore entitled to remain on D's property after order to leave, therefore still 'in execution of duty'.

Criminal Justice Act 1988 s39 - makes common assault triable summarily only.

4.4   Analysis of questions

Students can almost guarantee that they will have at least one question which deals with assaults. The usual format is a problem question with several potential offenders committing various assaults with different mens rea and possible defences. Students will be required to pick their way clearly through quite complex sets of circumstances and to do so they must be able to distinguish the different types of assaults and woundings and to identify the required mens rea for, and defences to each.

4.5   Questions

Question 1

Andy was of a nervous disposition. He saw three youths walking towards him down a dark street. One of the youths, Basil, was carrying and swinging a bicycle chain. Andy was apprehensive that they were going to attack him. Andy crossed the road. The youths followed. Andy said, 'Not one step further or I'll have to defend myself.' The youths believed that they were being threatened. One ran away. Basil was unable to run because he had a heart illness. His brother Charles stayed with him. Basil, who then began to feel very unwell, stumbled forward and fell on Andy who believed he was being attacked and kicked Basil, inducing a severe heart attack. Charles entered the melee to protect his brother and kicked Andy before a passer-by stopped the fight. The youths had not intended to attack Andy but had been going to retrieve Basil's broken bicycle.

What crimes, if any, have been committed?

University of London LLB Examination
(for External Students) Criminal Law June 1983 Q1

General comment

This question requires detailed consideration of a range of assaults together with two difficult defences, that of mistake and self-defence. A student should be careful not to confuse all the elements together but should clearly state what type of possible charges the parties may face and then go on to explain how the various defences working in conjunction with each other may operate to relieve any party of responsibility. Unless care is taken to plan the answer to this question it will appear confused.

Skeleton solution

Andy   - Assault; ss47 and 20 OAP Act 1861; possibly s18 OAP Act; self-defence; s3 CLA 1967 - mistake

Basil   - Assault; involuntary battery; recklessness

Charles   - Battery; s47 OAP Act

Suggested solution

The offences which may have been committed by Andy will be considered first. When Andy, fearing attack informs the youths that if they come any further he will have to defend himself he may commit a common law assault. This is committed where an accused intentionally or recklessly puts a victim in fear of being then and there subjected to harm. There is authority for the proposition that words alone cannot constitute an assault (eg *R* v *Meade* (1823)). However, this was not supported by Lord Goddard in *R* v *Wilson* (1955) who was of the opinion that when a thief shouted 'Get out the knives' that would amount to assault.

In *Tuberville* v *Savage* (1669) a declaration by the accused that he would not attack P as it was Assize time was held not to be an assault. Clearly, therefore, words can negative an assault. However, the principle of this case should not be taken too far. Indeed, in *Read* v *Coker* (1853) a threat by D to break P's neck if he did not leave the premises was held to be an assault.

When Andy kicked Basil, inducing a severe heart attack, he may have committed an offence contrary to s47 or s20 or possibly s18 of the Offences Against the Person Act 1861.

The most likely of those offences is s20 of the 1861 Act which provides that any person who unlawfully and maliciously wounds or inflicts any grievous bodily harm upon any person shall commit an offence. Certainly on the facts in question, there is an 'infliction' of grievous bodily harm. There is a direct assault on the victim which is in keeping with the House of Lords' decision in *R* v *Wilson* (1984) - a decision in conflict with other authorities like *R* v *Martin* (1881). Furthermore, undoubtedly the heart attack would be regarded as grievous bodily harm, ie really serious bodily harm *DPP* v *Smith* (1961). However, it will still be necessary to show that Andy acted 'maliciously'. According to *R* v *Mowatt* (1968) the term 'maliciously' imports upon the part of the person who inflicts the injury an awareness that his act may have the consequences of causing at least some physical harm if not the serious injury actually resulting. In *R* v *Sullivan* (1981) the Court of Appeal considered that s8 of the Criminal Justice Act 1967 required the *R* v *Mowatt* test to be proved subjectively.

An alternative would be to charge under s47 of the Offences Against the Person Act 1861 which provides that it is an offence to assault occasioning actual bodily harm.

This covers 'any harm or injury calculated to interfere with health or comfort'. *R v Miller* (1954) would be included in grievous bodily harm. However, since the Court of Appeal's decision in *R v Parmenter* (1991), approving its earlier decision in *R v Spratt* (1990), it is necessary to establish for both s47 and s20 offences that the accused intended to cause the particular kind of harm specified in the section or was reckless as to that consequence.

It seems unlikely that an offence under s18 has been committed, as it would be necessary to show that Andy 'intended to do grievous bodily harm'. Intention requires a desire to bring those consequences about or knowledge of the certainty of them occurring. Recklessness is not sufficient. *R v Belfon* (1976).

Andy would undoubtedly wish to claim that he committed no offence at all because he was acting in self-defence. At common law a person may use such force as is necessary to protect himself or his family. In *R v Shannon* (1980) the Court of Appeal held that it was necessary for the jury to consider the accused's state of mind and that a defence of self defence would not be available where he was acting in retaliation or aggressively. Furthermore, Andy would also wish to claim that he had a defence under s3 of the Criminal Law Act 1967 in that he was using reasonable force to prevent a crime. In deciding whether Andy's use of force was reasonable, a jury would have to take account of the honesty of his belief at the time. The question of whether his belief was reasonable or unreasonable would be irrelevant, save in so far as it might assist the jury to decide whether he did actually hold that belief (*R v Kimber* (1983)). Furthermore, the prosecution must eliminate the possibility that the defendant was acting under a genuine mistake of fact: *R v Williams (Gladstone)* (1987).

In *Beckford* v *R* (1987) the Privy Council approved *R v Williams* and held that, in relation to assaults, 'the mental element necessary ... is the intent to apply unlawful force' and that, if the accused believed, reasonably or not, in the existence of facts which would justify his using that force in self-defence, then he would not have the required mens rea (see chapter 10: *Defences*).

Applying these principles to the facts in question, Andy's belief that he was about to be attacked would seem to be honestly held and it is submitted that he would be able to claim the statutory self-defence.

In so deciding the jury would look at evidence eg of the amount of force used, the numbers of persons involved and any reluctance to use violence: *R v Bird* (1985) (such as Andy's crossing the road).

Basil may have committed the offence of common law assault ie putting a person in fear of being then and there subjected to harm by carrying and swinging a bicycle chain. The difficulty in proving that offence on the facts in question would be that he does not appear to have mens rea. The offence may be done intentionally or recklessly. While Basil may not have had any subjective intention to frighten or indeed may not have subjectively seen the risk that he might frighten somebody by swinging the bicycle chain it could be argued that he is still reckless, although it would seem that Cunningham recklessness is to be applied to statutory basic-intent assaults - *R* v *Morrison* (1988) - and such conscious risk-taking is not evident here. Within the *MPC* v *Caldwell* (1982) definition if he did the act which created the obvious risk that the person would be frightened without, however, giving any thought to the possibility of that risk existing, even though a reasonable man would have.

Similar problems arise when he stumbles forward and falls on Andy. This is certainly the actus reus of battery under the common law ie, a direct infliction of force. However, there would be no offence as there is no mens rea and he may be able to show that his actions were involuntary, thereby establishing a defence.

When Charles kicked Andy he may commit the offence of common law battery or an offence contrary to s47 of the Offences Against the Person Act 1861 providing there is some injury, however slight, as a consequence of his assault on Andy, although the difficulties of establishing sufficient mens rea for a s47 charge would be the same as those required in respect of Andy. However, he too would wish to claim self-defence under the common law or under s3 of the Criminal Law Act 1967. The right of self defence under the common law extends to immediate family *R* v *Rose* (1884) and *R* v *Duffy* (1967). Similarly the bystander who intervenes to stop the fight would be able to claim a defence under s3 of the Criminal Law Act 1967 if he used force that was reasonable in the prevention of a crime.

Question 2

C was walking near D's home. C knew that D and D's wife were on holiday. C saw movement in the house and thinking there were burglars, telephoned the police. C and two neighbours returned to D's house and entered with a key D had left with C. The lights were not working because the fuse had blown. C saw someone coming downstairs, shouted at him and grabbed him. He turned out to be E, D's 18 year old deaf son, who had unexpectedly returned from university. E was injured when he tried to avoid C and fearing C was attacking him E pushed C downstairs causing injury to C's back. E who was an epileptic had a fit and was ill for six weeks.

Advise C and E as to their criminal liability.

University of London LLB Examination
(for External Students) Criminal Law June 1985 Q2

General comment

A fairly straightforward question concerning primarily a range of possible assaults and the defences that may be available to C and E. Care is needed when considering what defence is appropriate because of the complications arising from the various mistakes of fact that take place.

Skeleton solution

Burglary - whether there is entry as a trespasser by either party - s47, s20 and s18 of the Offences Against the Person Act 1861 - the common law defence of self defence. Section 3 Criminal Law Act 1967 - mistake of fact as a defence - whether a mistake must be honest or honest and reasonable.

Suggested solution

When C, together with two neighbours. enters D's house with a key that D has left with him he does so for a lawful purpose and one undoubtedly within D's contemplation when the key was left with C. For this reason it cannot be realistically argued that C has entered the building as a trespasser. It is important to establish whether or not the entry is a trespassary entry under s9(1)(b) Theft Act 1968 because of the injuries caused to C. However E, as D's son would probably have permission to enter the building and unless it could be shown that he entered for a purpose in excess of the permission granted to him he would not have entered the building as a trespasser: *R v Jones and Smith* (1976). There is nothing to indicate that E had an intention to steal from the house, or commit rape, inflict grievous bodily harm or cause criminal damage and therefore not only does it seem that E did not enter as a trespasser but he had none of the necessary alternate specific intents required for an offence under s9(1)(a).

When C shouts and grabs at E he may commit the offence of common law assault and battery. A common law assault is committed when a person is put on fear of being then and there subjected to force. A battery under the common law is a direct infliction of force. The mens rea for common law assault and battery is either intention or recklessness: *R v Venna* (1975). A subjective test for recklessness should be applied because common law assault and battery is akin to those offences under the Offences Against the Person Act 1861 which have to be performed maliciously and an accused does not act maliciously unless he foresees the risk he is taking: *R v Cunningham* (1957).

When E has a fit and is ill for six weeks after the incident C could only be liable in criminal law if it could be shown that he was a substantial and operating cause of the illness. A victim's characteristics will not break the chain of causation that would otherwise be shown: *R v Blaue* (1975). Section 20 of the Offences Against the Person Act 1861 provides that it is an offence to unlawfully and maliciously wound or inflict grievous bodily harm.

The phrase grievous bodily harm means 'really serious bodily harm' *DPP v Smith* (1961). The word 'inflict' has been interpreted to mean a direct assault although in other cases an indirect assault has been *held* to be sufficient: *R v Clarence* (1888) and *R v Martin* (1881), however in *R v Wilson* (1984) the House of Lords held that direct application of force must be proved.

Possibly it could be argued that the initial battery did result in the illness but whether as a matter of causation that is the case for the jury to decide. A more difficult aspect of s20 to satisfy is the requirement for mens rea. It must be shown that an accused foresaw at least the risk of some harm before he can be *held* to be acting maliciously for the purposes of s20 Offences Against the Person Act 1861 *R v Mowatt* (1967), *W v Dolbey* (1983), *R v Parmenter* (1991).

Section 18 of the Offences Against the Person Act 1861 provides that any person who by any means whatsoever wounds or causes grievous bodily harm with intent to cause grievous bodily harm shall commit an offence.

Certainly the actus reus of s18 is more easily satisfied because injury may be 'caused' by any means whatsoever without there being a battery. Indeed, a jury may well find that C did 'cause' serious injury to E. However, s18 requires that there must have been an intention to cause grievous bodily harm. Recklessness is not sufficient; *R* v *Belfon* (1976), *R* v *Morrison* (1988).

When E pushes C downstairs he may commit offences contrary to s47 or s20 of the Offences Against the Person Act 1861. The actus reus of s47 would be satisfied if the injury was less serious but sufficient to interfere with health and comfort: *R* v *Miller* (1954). The actus reus of s20 would be satisfied if the harm was sufficient to amount to grievous bodily harm. However, it would seem unlikely that E would satisfy the requirements for mens rea as outlined above as the intention/recklessness required for either offence has recently been held to be the same: *R* v *Parmenter* (1991); *R* v *Spratt* (1990).

It should be noted that had a s20 offence been committed by either C or E and in addition if the accused had entered the building as a trespasser, an offence under s9(1)(b) TA 1968 might be established on the basis that the accused entered the building as a trespasser and inflicted grievous bodily harm on any person therein.

The defences that must be considered are s3 Criminal Law Act 1967 and the common law right of self defence in conjunction with the defence of mistake.

Where an accused makes a mistake of fact he may be able to claim the mistake as a defence if he can show that his conduct would not have amounted to a crime had the facts been as he believed them to be, or alternatively that his mistake negatives the particular mens rea necessary to prove the crime charged. In *DPP* v *Morgan* (1975) the House of Lords *held* that a mistake could be relied on by an accused if his mistake was honest, whether or not it was reasonable. In the Divisional Court decision of *Albert* v *Lavin* (1981) a distinction was drawn between a mistake in relation to an offence and a mistake in relation to a defence. In the former case the mistake need only be honest before it could be claimed as a defence, in the latter case it had to be both honest and reasonable. In *R* v *Williams* (1984) the Court of Appeal disapproved of the dicta in *Albert* v *Lavin* and considered that applying *DPP* v *Morgan* a mistake could be pleaded as a defence if it was honest whether or not it was reasonable. This was approved by the Privy Council in *Beckford* v *R* (1987).

Section 3 of the Criminal Law Act 1967 provides that a person may use such force as is reasonable in the circumstances in the prevention of crime or in effecting or assisting in the lawful arrest of offenders. Whether or not force is reasonable will depend on the type of crime involved. The more serious the offence the greater the force that would be viewed as reasonable. It is for the jury to decide in a particular case whether or not excessive force had been used.

The common law right of self defence overlaps with s3 of the Criminal Law Act 1967. It will be necessary for a jury to consider an accused's state of mind when considering self defence. An accused who acts aggressively or in retaliation would not be able to rely on the defence. However, a jury must also take into account the position of the accused at the time of the act and judge whether his acts were necessary applying ordinary commonsense principles: *R* v *Palmer* (1971). In the recent case of *R* v *Bird* (1985) the Court of Appeal *held* that while proof that an accused had tried to retreat was one method of rebutting any suggestion that the accused had acted aggressively it was by no means the only way and a jury must not consider that an accused who did not retreat was acting aggressively.

C may therefore be able to claim a defence under s3 Criminal Law Act 1967 providing his mistake was honest in which case he will be judged on the facts as he believed them to be. E may be able to claim a defence under s3 or alternatively the common law providing, of course, that his mistake was honest so that he is judged on the facts as he believed them to be.

Question 3(a)

I was a plain clothes police officer arresting a violent criminal. J saw the incident and decided to intervene as he knew the man being arrested and wished to help him. J hit I over the head with his bag. I who had a thick skull collapsed from the blow which fractured his skull. I was seriously ill for three months.

Advise I.

> Adapted from University of London LLB Examination
> (for External Students) Criminal Law June 1984 Q3(b)

General comment

This part of the question again requires knowledge of serious assaults and also the specific offence relating to assault on police.

Skeleton solution

I - battery - ss18 and 20 OAP 1861. Assault police - s51 Police Act 1964 obstruction.

Suggested solution

I should be advised that J has committed a battery which may fall under several headings.

First, under s51 of the Police Act 1964 a person who assaults a constable in the execution of his duty shall be guilty of an offence. It is not necessary that the accused knows that he is a constable provided the constable is acting in the execution of his duty.

Here I would appear to be so acting provided the arrest which he is trying to effect is lawful. His conduct would then fall within the general scope of preventing crime and catching offenders: *R* v *Waterfield* (1964).

Additionally J may be liable for wilfully obstructing a constable in the execution of his duty under s51(2) of the 1964 Act.

These offences are both summary offences and I should be advised to consider charging the following more serious assaults first.

I's injuries are serious enough to amount to grievous bodily harm: *DPP* v *Smith* (1961); *R* v *Saunders* (1985). Section 20 of the Offences Against the Person Act 1861 makes it an offence unlawfully and maliciously to wound or inflict any grievous bodily harm. The 'infliction', requiring direct application of force: *R* v *Wilson* (1984) is undoubtedly satisfied here and whether J is acting 'maliciously' will be determined on the subjective view of whether he foresaw at least the possibility of some harm: *R* v *Mowatt* (1968); *W* v *Dolbey* (1983). It is necessary to show that J intended to cause the particular kind of harm specified in the section or was subjectively reckless as to that consequence: *R* v *Parmenter* (1991).

Section 18 of the 1861 Act makes it an offence unlawfully and maliciously to cause grievous bodily harm with intent to do gbh or to prevent the arrest or lawful detainer of any person. Here J's intention appears to be to prevent the arrest in which case, provided that arrest is lawful, the more serious offence under s18 is complete.

Question 3(b)

R believed she was pregnant, and asked S, her boyfriend to help her 'to get rid of the baby'. S said he would, though he was only humouring R because in her depressed state S feared R might attempt suicide. S gave R some cough mixture telling her it would 'do the job'. In fact it could not produce a miscarriage. However, R proved allergic to the cough mixture and went blind. R became so depressed she attempted suicide. She failed, but her conduct prematurely induced a miscarriage. The child lived for two hours before dying from premature arrival.

Advise R and S as to their criminal liability.

University of London LLB Examination
(for External Students) Criminal Law June 1985 Q7

General comment

This was a difficult question and one that only a very competent student who enjoys a challenge should consider. The main difficulty would be to avoid getting bogged down in the technicalities of all the various offences.

Skeleton solution

Section 58 of the Offences Against the Person Act 1861 - Is the substance a 'noxious substance' - contrast R and S's liability under s58 - S's liability under s59 for procuring the noxious substance - S's liability for the injuries to R - the range of assaults under the Offences Against the Person Act 1861 - s47, s20, s18, s23 and s24 - could R be regarded as the legal cause of the injury to S - Suicide Act 1961 - Child destruction contrasted with murder or manslaughter.

Suggested solution

Section 58 of the Offences Against the Person Act 1861 provides that an offence shall be committed where a woman who is pregnant unlawfully administers to herself any poisonous or other noxious thing, or unlawfully uses any instrument or other means whatsoever with the intention of producing a miscarriage. Section 58 further provides that any person who administers to a woman or causes to be taken by her any poisonous or noxious thing or unlawfully uses any instrument or other means whatsoever with the intention of producing a miscarriage, whether or not the woman is pregnant but merely believes herself to be, shall commit an offence.

The section distinguishes between a 'poison' and a 'noxious thing'. Something other than a recognised poison may still be noxious. A substance that may be harmless when taken in normal quantities can be noxious if it is harmful when taken in excess: *R* v *Marcus* (1981). The fact that the substance may not be an abortifacient is irrelevant.

R is pregnant and therefore may be liable under this section if the cough mixture was a noxious substance. S, however, could not be liable as he lacks the necessary intention to produce the miscarriage. Because of his lack of mens rea there would not be an offence of conspiracy contrary to s1 Criminal Law Act 1967 because they are not truly in agreement.

If the substance was not noxious S might be liable for an attempt to commit a s58 offence if she administers a harmless substance believing it to be noxious. Section 1(2) of the Criminal Attempts Act 1981 states that a person may be guilty of attempting to commit an offence even though the facts are such that the commission of the offence is impossible.

Following the House of Lords' decision in *R* v *Shivpuri* (1987), R's belief that taking the cough mixture would procure her abortion is sufficient to make her actions amount to a criminal attempt.

Under s59 an offence of unlawfully and knowingly supplying or procuring a poison or noxious substance may be committed providing that the accused knows that it is intended to be unlawfully used with the intention of procuring the miscarriage of a woman.

In *R* v *Mills* (1963) it was *held* that to procure meant to get possession of something that the accused did not already have. Thus if S already had the mixture this element would not be satisfied.

Furthermore, S would argue that what he did was not unlawful because he thought it would be harmless.

The question of whether or not S can be liable for the injuries sustained by R will depend on whether or not he has sufficient mens rea to satisfy one of the assaults. Furthermore, it must be shown that his conduct is the legal cause of the injuries that resulted. It must be shown that S's conduct was a substantial and operative cause of R's blindness. The fact that R is allergic to cough mixture will not break the causal link because the characteristics of a victim cannot break the chain of causation: *R* v *Blaue* (1975). However, it could be argued that S's conduct was too remote. It is not clear whether S supplied the mixture or actually administered it to R. However, in *R* v *Dalby* (1982) it was *held* that an accused who supplied drugs to a person who administered them to himself was too remote from the death that resulted.

Even if S was *held* to be a substantial and operating cause of the blindness it is difficult to see what offence he may have committed: s47 of the Offences Against the Person Act 1861 (assault occasioning actual bodily harm) and s20 of the Act (wounding or inflicting grievous bodily harm) would not be appropriate as both require an assault against the victim. Furthermore, an accused must have foreseen the possibility of some harm resulting: *R* v *Parmenter* (1991). Similarly s18 of the Act is not appropriate because although S may have 'caused' grievous bodily harm within the section, he did not have the necessary intention to cause grievous bodily harm. Section 23 and 24 of the Offences Against the Person Act 1861 create offences concerning unlawfully administering poisonous or noxious substances. Section 23 provides that it is an offence to unlawfully and maliciously administer a poisonous or noxious substance so as thereby to endanger the life of such person or so as thereby to inflict upon such person any grievous bodily harm. Section 23 may be committed recklessly. In this context recklessness requires a subjective appreciation of the risk involved: *R* v *Cunningham* (1957).

No mens rea at all is required as to the second part of the actus reus. Section 24 requires a specific intent namely 'To injure, aggrieve or annoy such persons'.

On the facts in question S would not have committed any offence under s23 because he was not acting 'maliciously' and furthermore the phrase 'inflict grievous bodily harm' means that a direct assault is required: *R* v *Clarence* (1888), *R* v *Wilson* (1984).

Similarly, s23 is not satisfied because S does not have the necessary specific intent. It should be noted that had S met the necessary requirements under s58 of the Offences Against the Person Act 1861 the fact that the victim consented would be no defence. The consent of the victim would not negative the unlawfulness of his conduct.

When R attempts to commit suicide she commits no offence. The Suicide Act 1961 abolished the offences of suicide and attempted suicide. Furthermore, R will commit no offence under s1(1) of the Infant Life (Preservation) Act 1929 because the section only covers the situation where a child capable of being born alive dies, as a result of a wilful act of any person, before it has an existence independent of its mother. It is not clear on the facts how many weeks old the foetus was. Evidence that a woman was pregnant for a period of 28 weeks is prima facie proof that the child was capable of being born alive: *C* v *S* (1988). Whether or not this is the case s1 would not be appropriate because R's conduct was not done with the intention of destroying the child and furthermore the child did survive independent of its mother, albeit for a very short time.

The question of whether or not R could be liable for murder or involuntary manslaughter of the child must now be considered. In order to be a victim of murder the child must have had an existence independent of its mother. In *R* v *West* (1848) it was *held* that a person who injures a child while that child is in the mother's womb may be liable to murder or involuntary manslaughter. In *R* v *Senior* (1899) it was *held* that an injury inflicted before birth either with mens rea for involuntary manslaughter or by gross negligence a conviction for manslaughter was correct.

While this type of situation would not be one where generally the criminal law would intervene, theoretically R might be liable for murder or manslaughter depending on the mens rea present. Murder would only be satisfied if she intended to kill or intended to do grievous bodily harm. Arguably this is the case on the basis that by killing herself would involve killing the child. Alternatively, liability for manslaughter by gross negligence may be shown if R's conduct was grossly negligent, so much so that it amounted to a crime, although the *R* v *Bateman* test has been abolished: *R* v *Seymour* (1983) and *R* v *Kong Cheuk Kwan* (1985) and the test will be one of *Caldwell/Lawrence* recklessness.

Question 4(a)

A was engaged in rifle practice on a local firing range. A knew that B was 400 yards away in a trench below the target keeping score. A discharged six rounds at the target and B emerged from the protection of the trench. A decided to frighten him and fired a round over B's head. The round hit a concrete post and ricochetted and hit B who was seriously injured. Advise A of his criminal liability.

Adapted from University of London LLB Examination
(for External Students) Criminal Law June 1986 Q1

General comment

A question that requires detailed consideration of the assaults. Providing a student does not get bogged down in too much detail on the assaults, good marks could be achieved.

Skeleton solution

Common law battery - ss47, 20, 18 Offences Against the Person Act 1861.

Suggested solution

When A fired a round over B's head which ricochetted and hit B, causing a serious injury, he may commit a number of offences both at common law and under the Offences Against the Person Act 1861.

At common law the offence of assault is committed where the accused intentionally or recklessly does an act that makes the victim fear immediate personal violence. If B were not frightened then there could be an attempted assault, as A would have done an act more than merely preparatory to the full offence (s1 Criminal Attempts Act 1981) with full mens rea.

When A hit B causing him serious injury he may commit an offence contrary to s47 Offences Against the Person Act 1861. Section 47 provides that it shall be an offence to assault occasioning actual bodily harm. In *R* v *Miller* (1954) it was stated that actual bodily harm included 'any hurt or injury calculated to interfere with the health or comfort of the victim'. Intention of recklessness as to the assault must be shown, *R* v *Venna* (1975). As with a charge of wounding or inflicting grievous bodily harm (below) it will be necessary to shown that A intended to cause the particular kind of harm specified in that section of the Act or was subjectively

57

reckless as to that consequence: *R* v *Spratt* (1990) (the facts of which were similar to those in the question). Although in conflict with its own decision in *R* v *Savage* (1990) the Court of Appeal approved this test in *R* v *Parmenter* (1991).

The term 'assault' in this context does not mean simply frightening but includes the infliction of force (a physical assault). The old law was that a physical assault was only committed if the force was applied 'directly'. On the facts in question there would be a direct assault as there is no intervening act, as there would be if for example B had been injured when tripped over while trying to escape from A.

The injuries B sustains are serious. It may therefore be appropriate to charge A under s20 Offences Against the Person Act 1861. Section 20 provides that it is an offence to unlawfully and maliciously wound or inflict any grievous bodily harm. Grievous bodily harm means 'really serious bodily harm': *DPP* v *Smith* (1961).

The 'wounding' requires a break in the external skin, and not just bruising: *JJC* v *Eisenhower* (1984).

The term 'inflict' was interpreted to mean a direct assault in *R* v *Clarence* (1888), although in cases like *R* v *Halliday* (1889) indirect assaults were held to be within s20.

However, since the House of Lords' decision in *R* v *Wilson* (1984) it would appear that direct application of force is required.

The mens rea of s20 requires intention or recklessness as to the circumstances (in this case firing the gun) *R* v *Venna* (1975) together with foresight of the possibility of at least a little harm resulting: *W* v *Dolbey* (1983), *R* v *Mowatt* (1968). This foresight must be shown subjectively: *R* v *Morrison* (1988). An intention to frighten the victim is not sufficient to establish liability under s20 (*R* v *Sullivan* (1981)) unless there is the necessary foresight of the possibility of at least a little harm. On the facts this does not appear to be satisfied.

Section 18 Offences Against the Person Act 1861 provides that it will be an offence to unlawfully and maliciously wound or cause any grievous bodily harm by any means whatsoever with intent to do grievous or bodily harm. While the actus reus of s18 may be satisfied the necessary intention to do grievous bodily harm is not shown. In *R* v *Belfon* (1976) it was held that recklessness as to the grievous bodily harm was not sufficient.

In addition, A would commit various offences under the Firearms Act 1968.

Question 4(b)

L laced M's orange juice with a drug. M felt strange but was not sure that he had been drugged. He was travelling home on the underground train when he started to have hallucinations.

Advise L of his criminal liability.

Adapted from University of London LLB Examination (for External Students) Criminal Law June 1986 Q5

General comment

The question is a straightforward examination of knowledge of the relevant parts of the Offences Against the Person Act 1861.

Skeleton solution

Battery - ss23 and 24 OAP 1861 - 'noxious substance'.

Suggested solution

When L laced M's orange juice with a drug it will not amount to a battery as there must be some amount of force applied to the victim's body in order to constitute a battery, *R* v *Hanson* (1849). He may however be liable under ss23 or 24 Offences Against the Person Act 1861.

Section 23 provides that it is an offence to unlawfully and maliciously administer or cause to be administered any poisonous or noxious substance so as thereby to endanger the life of such person or to inflict upon him any grievous bodily harm. Section 24 provides that it is an offence to administer or cause to be administered any poisonous or noxious substance with intent to injure, aggrieve or annoy.

In *R* v *Marcus* (1981) the term noxious was broadly interpreted to include substances taken in small quantities if that quantity is administered with intent to injure, aggrieve or annoy. It was necessary to take into account quantity, quality and all circumstances to decide if a substance is noxious.

M suffers hallucinations. This may amount to an infliction of grievous bodily harm. Under s23 there is no need to show either a direct or an indirect assault for there to be an infliction of grievous bodily harm unlike s20 OAP 1861. The only mens rea required under s23 is intention or recklessness as to the administration of the noxious substance. No mens rea is required as to the consequence *R* v *Cato* (1976). For s24 there must be an ulterior intent to injure aggrieve or annoy.

Question 5

A, a religious zealot, seized B's son. He telephoned B telling him to collect and post a parcel to a leading churchman if he did not wish to see his son hurt. B posted the parcel as directed. B thought the parcel contained a bomb but he knew that the churchman's mail was being intercepted and therefore expected that no injury would occur. In fact, the postman handling the parcel was injured when it exploded in the sorting office where it had been delayed. Advise the parties of their criminal liability.

Adapted from University of London LLB Examination
(for External Students) Criminal Law June 1988 Q1

General comment

In order to decide which non-fatal offence against the person to consider first, assess the level of injury the facts indicate. One would expect more than slight harm to be caused, so start with the more serious offences, not the least serious offences. Obviously, a key issue here is the mens rea (or lack of it) of B.

Also, remember to consider A's criminal liability, as a secondary party to B's offence and as a principal offender, ie kidnapping and incitement.

Skeleton solution

Postman injured - non-fatal offences against the person - degree of injury - actus reus of s18 and s20 Offences Against the Person Act 1861 - definition of 'wound' - definition of 'grievous bodily harm' - mens rea - intention - *Cunningham* recklessness - s47 Offences Against the Person Act 1861 - actus reus - mens rea.

Defence of duress - was threat sufficiently serious - was it immediate - not directed at defendant - was it reasonable for B to give in to the threat.

Liability of A - secondary party to B's offences - principal offender - kidnapping - incitement.

Suggested solution

What offences has B committed in sending the parcel bomb and thereby causing injury to a postman?

It appears that the postman has suffered a non-fatal injury to the person.

Section 18 Offences Against the Person Act 1861 makes it an offence to wound or cause any grievous bodily harm.

To wound, the continuity of the whole skin must be broken: *Moriarty* v *Brooks* (1834); *JJC (A minor)* v *Eisenhower* (1984). It is not enough that the cuticle or outer skin be broken if the inner skin remains intact: *R* v *M'Loughlin* (1838); *R* v *Wood* (1830); *R* v *Waltham* (1849); *R* v *Jones* (1987). It is probably sufficient that the wound is directly inflicted whether by a battery or not: *R* v *Wilson* (1983); *R* v *Taylor* (1869); *R* v *Austin* (1973).

'Grievous bodily harm' must be given its ordinary natural meaning. 'Grievous' means 'really serious' and the word 'really' probably adds nothing but emphasis to the fact that the harm caused must be actually or really serious: *DPP* v *Smith* (1961); *R* v *Saunders* (1985).

'Cause' requires proof of a positive act: *Price* v *Cromack* (1975).

On the facts, it is not possible to decide whether the postman was wounded or suffered grievous bodily harm or both.

The mens rea required is either intention or *Cunningham* recklessness. It will be sufficient that a defendant intended or foresaw that some physical harm, but not necessarily amounting to a wounding or grievous bodily harm might occur: *R* v *Mowatt* (1968); *R* v *Sullivan* (1981).

If the charge is causing grievous bodily harm with intend to cause grievous bodily harm, then only intention will be sufficient mens rea. Smith and Hogan argue (in 'Criminal Law', 6th edition, p400) that if the charge is wounding with intent to do grievous bodily harm, then a defendant may intend to do grievous bodily harm *without* intending to wound so that if he in fact wounds, it must be proved that he intended to cause grievous bodily harm and that he foresaw that he might wound.

On the facts, as B knew that the mail was being intercepted and therefore expected no injury to occur, he cannot be said to have intended the injury or subjectively foreseen the consequences of his act. He would therefore appear to lack mens rea.

Section 20 Offences Against the Person Act 1861 makes it an offence to wound or inflict any grievous bodily harm.

'Wound' and 'grievous bodily harm' have the same meaning as in s18 Offences Against the Person Act 1861. 'Inflict' does not imply an assault but does imply the direct application of force: *R* v *Wilson* (1983).

The mens rea is either intention or *Cunningham* recklessness: *R* v *Parmenter* (1991).

Again, for the same reasons, whereas B may have caused the actus reus of the s20 offence, he would appear to lack the required mens rea.

Section 47 Offences Against the Person Act 1861 makes it an offence to commit an assault occasioning actual bodily harm. Actual bodily harm need not be really serious for it 'includes any hurt or injury calculated to interfere with the health or comfort of the' victim: *R* v *Miller* (1954).

On the facts, the injuries suffered by the postman whatever their nature would appear to come within the actus reus of this offence.

The mens rea, according to recent Court of Appeal rulings (*R* v *Spratt* (1990); *R* v *Parmenter* (1991)) is the same as that for s20. B's recklessness must not only extend to be assault but also to be actual bodily harm (cf *R* v *Savage* (1990)).

Again, B may well have caused the actus reus of this offence but would appear to lack the required mens rea.

However, if B was to be found liable for any of these offences, he may be able to plead the defence of duress.

The threat must be sufficiently serious to constitute duress. The threat must be one of death or serious personal injury to the person of the defendant or to a third person, ie the defendant's family, others to whom he owes a duty and even a complete stranger in some circumstances, eg a stranger held as a hostage to force the defendant to do a criminal act: *R* v *Steane* (1947); *R* v *Hudson* (1971). The gravity of the threat must be assessed against the enormity of the crime: *Abbott* v *R* (1977). The threat must be immediate or imminent: *R* v *M'Growther* (1746). There is now no longer any rule of law that the defendant must resort to the protection of the law if he is able to and is physically out of the range of his oppressors: *R* v *Hurley* (1967); *R* v *Hudson*.

The law applies an objective standard when considering the defendant's action. The defendant must have done what he did as a result of having reasonably believed what his oppressor had said or done, he had good cause to fear that he (or a person to whom he owed a duty) would suffer death or serious personal injury, and a sober person of reasonable firmness, sharing the characteristics of the defendant, would have also so responded: *R* v *Howe* (1987); *R* v *Graham* (1982). A person is expected to display the steadfastness reasonably to be expected of an ordinary citizen in the same situation.

Although B's son and, therefore, someone to whom he owed a duty, was seized it is not at all clear what the nature of the threats against the boy was, or whether it was reasonable for B not to seek police protection as he was not under the direct control of A.

A is liable for the false imprisonment of B's son and if the detention was accompanied with a taking away, force or fraud, it will also amount to kidnapping: *R* v *Brown* (1985).

A is also liable as a secondary party to any offence B may have committed with respect to the postman. Although A did not directly and must immediately cause the actus reus of the crimes, anyone who aids, abets, counsels or procures the commission of any offence is liable to be tried, indicated and punished as a principal offender: s8 Accessories and Abettors Act 1861, as amended by s1 Criminal Law Act 1967.

He also appears to have committed the offence of incitement in that by his threats he sought to reach and influence the mind of A to commit an act which, when done, would be a crime by the person incited: *R* v *Nkosiyana* (1966); *Race Relations Board* v *Applin* (1973); *R* v *Whitehouse* (1977).

Question 6

A disliked B, a well known local councillor. A believed that B was a rogue who had made secret profits from his office. A threw paint at B's car intending to frighten B as B was being driven past. A shouted, 'It is necessary to teach you a severe lesson and draw your behaviour to public notice.' The paint damaged the car and obscured B's driver's view and as a result the car crashed into a bus queue injuring a mother and her three children. B was slightly injured in the collision and B's driver suffered severe nervous shock.

Advise A of his criminal liability.

Adapted from University of London LLB Examination
(for External Students) Criminal Law June 1990 Q1

General comment

A complicated and lengthy question combining non-fatal assaults, criminal damage, and homicide. Note that both types of criminal damage require consideration. The nature of the injuries suffered by the children is not specified. It is suggested that they are merely discussed in general terms.

Skeleton solution

Common law assault. Words as an assault. Simple and aggravated criminal damage. Homicide, causation, disregard murder. Unlawful act manslaughter, whether unlawful act is dangerous. Non-fatal assaults.

Suggested solution

A may have committed common law assault in throwing the paint at the car. The actus reus of the offence requires proof that the victim apprehended immediate physical violence; see *Logdon* v *DPP* (1976). The determining factor will be the perception of the victim. The reasonable bystander would realise that the paint would not make physical contact with the victim, and that there was in fact no threat of direct physical violence. The victim, however, might have momentarily thought that the paint was going to hit him.

The mens rea for common assault is intention or recklessness; see *R* v *Venna* (1976). In *Venna* the court took recklessness to mean subjective recklessness, basing this decision on the earlier case of *R* v *Cunningham* (1957). Subjective recklessness requires proof that the defendant was aware of the risk that the victim would apprehend immediate physical violence. It would appear that the application of this form of recklessness to assault remains unaffected by developments in cases such as *MPC* v *Caldwell* (1982). *R* v *Spratt* (1990) and *R* v *Parmenter* (1991) both of which confirm that, as far as assault occasioning actual bodily harm contrary to s47 of the Offences Against the Persons Act 1861 is concerned, *Cunningham* type recklessness applies. It is submitted that the same reasoning should apply to the offence of assault at common law. On the facts it may be that A will say that, as he was throwing the paint at the windscreen of the car, he could not have foreseen any risk that the victim would apprehend physical contact, but it is submitted that he may have some difficulty in persuading any court to believe this.

A's act of shouting at B cannot of itself constitute the offence of common law assault. Words alone cannot constitute an assault; see *R* v *Meade and Belt* (1823) 'no words or singing could constitute an assault'.

It would appear that A has committed the offence of 'simple' criminal damage contrary to s1(1) of the Criminal Damage Act 1971. The car is clearly property belonging to another as against A. The paint has caused damage to the bodywork of the car. Damage can occur even where the effects can be rectified relatively easily; see *Hardman* v *Chief Constable of Avon* (1986). A appears to have had the necessary mens rea for the offence, either intention or recklessness.

A more difficult question is that of whether or not A could be convicted of the more serious offence of 'aggravated' criminal damage contrary to s1(2) of the 1971 Act. The aggravating factor lies in the mens rea. A must be proved to have had either an intention to endanger life, or at least to have been reckless as to whether life would be endangered. Following the House of Lords' decision in *R* v *Steer* (1988), the prosecution must establish that the defendant intended the criminal damage itself to endanger life, or that he was reckless as to whether it would endanger life. It is not sufficient, for example, merely to show that he was reckless as to whether the act causing the criminal damage might endanger life. On the facts of the problem, the minimum that the prosecution would have to establish in relation to the mens rea for the aggravated offence would be that A gave no thought to an obvious risk that obscuring the driver's view, by covering the car windscreen with paint would endanger the lives of others. The test for recklessness here is that laid down by the House of Lords in *MPC* v *Caldwell* (above). It is submitted that on the facts, the prosecution might be able to establish the necessary mens rea.

A has caused injuries to the woman's children. If causation is established in relation to the homicide it is submitted that it will be established in relation to these unspecified non-fatal offences. The precise charge brought against A will depend to a large extent on the nature of the harm done to the children. In any event it is unlikely that A will be convicted of anything more serious than malicious wounding, or maliciously inflicting grievous bodily harm contrary to s20 of the Offences Against the Persons Act 1861, since he appears not to have intended to cause any such harm.

The injuries to B and his driver are likely to constitute actual bodily harm contrary to s47 of the 1861 Act, in that they are injuries which interfere with the health and comfort of the victim; see *R* v *Miller* (1954). The mens rea for this offence is intention or recklessness as described above. The prosecution would have to prove that A was at least aware of a risk of the victims being frightened by his actions, which on the facts, seems likely.

5 HOMICIDE

5.1 Introduction

5.2 Key points

5.3 Recent cases and statutes

5.4 Analysis of questions

5.5 Questions

5.1 Introduction

Homicide, which covers the killing of one human being by another, forms a complex, fascinating and very important part of the criminal law syllabus. It is very important therefore that students are familiar with the varying types of homicide, both lawful and unlawful, together with the available defences.

5.2 Key points

a) *Homicides*

i) Homicides involve the killing - that is, the acceleration of the death of - a person under the Queen's peace within a year and a day of the accused's act which brought about that death: *R* v *Dyson* [1908] 2 KB 454.

ii) Murder is homicide with malice aforethought. Such malice aforethought, the mens rea, is an intention to cause the death, or a grievous bodily harm to another: *R* v *Moloney* [1985] AC 905. The apparent dual states of mind involving foresight expanded in *Hyam* v *DPP* [1975] AC 55 are no longer law.

Students **must** know the cases of *R* v *Hancock and Shankland* [1986] AC 455 and *R* v *Nedrick* [1986] 1 WLR 1025.

iii) A jury might infer an intention to kill or cause grievous bodily harm only if it appears to them that the accused foresaw such death/gbh as an 'overwhelming probability' (*R* v *Hancock and Shankland*) or, where those consequences were 'virtually certain' to occur and that they are satisfied that the accused knew that to be the case (*R* v *Nedrick*).

This does not abrogate s8 of the Criminal Justice Act 1967 which determines what amount of foresight a jury might impute to the accused in any case. Furthermore, the decisions in *R* v *Hancock and Shankland* and in *R* v *Nedrick* do not contradict *R* v *Moloney*: they uphold the rule that foresight is something from which intention **might** be inferred but restrict the scope of the *R* v *Moloney* direction.

b) *Manslaughter*

   i) Manslaughter is traditionally separated into voluntary and involuntary manslaughter. There is no requirement for malice aforethought.

   Voluntary manslaughter may be proved if certain mitigation is present in a case which would otherwise be murder:

   • provocation - Homicide Act 1957 s3;

   • diminished responsibility - Homicide Act 1957 s2;

   • suicide pact - Homicide Act 1957 s4.

   ii) If a jury finds that the accused was provoked (and thereby lost self-control) by things done or said he may be convicted, on a charge of murder, of manslaughter. The jury must decide whether the provocation would make a reasonable man lose self-control and in so deciding they must consider all the circumstances and the effect that those circumstances would have on a reasonable man. The test is therefore objective in nature.

   iii) A reasonable man may be viewed as having any characteristics peculiar to the accused: *DPP* v *Camplin* [1978] AC 705; *R* v *Raven* [1982] Crim LR 51; *Mancini* v *DPP* [1942] AC 1.

   iv) Diminished responsibility may similarly reduce a murder charge to one of manslaughter if the accused can prove he was suffering from an abnormality of mind which substantially impaired his mental responsibility for his acts.

   Note the restrictions on what will constitute an 'abnormality': *R* v *Gittens* [1984] QB 698; *R* v *Tandy* [1988] Crim LR 308.

   v) If a person kills another in pursuance of a common agreement having for its object the death of all of them (a suicide pact) then they shall be convicted of manslaughter. There must be an intention by the accused to die along with the other parties to the pact.

   It is still an offence to aid and abet another to commit suicide (Suicide Act 1961) and, if the accused cannot be shown to have done the killing of the other(s) this might be considered.

c) *Causation*

In homicide offences the question of causation is vital and students must know the leading cases dealing with causation and intervening acts: *R* v *Smith* [1959] 2 QB 35; *R* v *Blaue* [1975] 3 All ER 446; *R* v *Jordan* (1956) 40 Cr App R 152; see also *R* v *Cheshire* [1991] Crim LR 709 - question of medical treatment - even if such treatment falls well below that expected of competent medical staff that of itself does not necessarily break the chain of causation. The question is whether D's act caused death.

d) *Other forms of manslaughter*

i) Involuntary manslaughter - where the accused kills without sufficient mens rea for murder. Note killing by 'gross negligence': *R* v *Bateman* (1925) 19 Cr App R 8 and *Kong Cheuk Kwan* v *R* (1985) Cr App R 18; no distinction between gross negligence and recklessness tests. Also note recklessness, both *Caldwell* and *Cunningham: R* v *Stone and Dobinson* [1977] QB 354; *R* v *Lamb* [1967] 2 QB 981.

ii) Death by reckless driving s1 Road Traffic Act 1988: *R* v *Lawrence* [1982] AC 510; *R* v *Seymour* [1983] 2 AC 493. NB. This offence will be removed by the RTA 1991 and replaced by one of causing death by *dangerous* driving. Driving will be 'dangerous' if it falls below the standard of a careful and competent driver and it would have been obvious to such a driver that the driving involved a risk of harm or of serious damage to property (ie the test will be objective).

iii) Manslaughter by unlawful act/constructive manslaughter: *R* v *Larkin* [1943] 1 All ER 217; *R* v *Church* (1965) 49 Cr App R 206; *DPP* v *Newbury and Jones* [1977] AC 500.

Note that the 'unlawful act' need not be directed at the victim: *R* v *Pagett* (1983) 76 Cr App R 279 (cf *R* v *Dalby* [1982] 1 All ER 916); *R* v *Goodfellow* (1986) 83 Cr App R 23.

Note also transferred malice and constructive manslaughter: *R* v *Mitchell* [1983] QB 741.

5.3 Recent cases and statutes

R v *Barr, Kenyon and Heacock* (1989) 88 Cr App R 362 - murder - foreseeability - direction to jury should be that foreseeability only assists them to determine whether D had intention to kill or do serious harm.

R v *Donnelly* [1989] Crim LR 739 - murder - foresight - D struck security guard on head with loaded shotgun during robbery - gun discharged killing guard - probability of discharge did not entitle jury to conclude that D intended to fire it.

R v *Johnson (Christopher)* (1989) The Times 25 April - provocation brought about by behaviour which accused induced in another.

R v *Ali* [1989] Crim LR 736 - provocation - Not always necessary to direct jury on D's age.

R v *Sawyer* [1989] Crim LR 831 - provocation - not raised by defendant but evidence in police interview which may have supported it - judge not required to have left issue to jury.

McCluskey v *HM Advocate* [1989] RTR 182 - death by reckless driving can apply to destruction of child *in utero* if born alive.

R v *Lamb (Charles)* [1990] Crim LR 522 - death by reckless driving - jury should be directed that risk of causing damage or injury must be serious.

R v *Arobieke* [1988] Crim LR 314 - victim ran onto railway line and electrocuted, in fear of D. No assault by D. Manslaughter quashed.

R v *Watson* (1989) The Guardian 6 June - unlawful act, elderly occupant suffered heart attack during burglary - manslaughter appropriate despite accused's lack of knowledge of presence or condition of occupant.

R v *Reynolds* [1988] Crim LR 679 - premenstrual syndrome and post-natal depression - diminished responsibility.

R v *Slack* [1989] 3 WLR 513 - murder - joint enterprise. Express or tacit agreement that one of them would inflict serious harm or death if necessary.

R v *Wakely*; *R* v *Symonds*; *R* v *Holly* [1990] Crim LR 119 - express or tacit agreement as required by *R* v *Slack* - foreseeability of possibility of violence being used by one of group not enough - however in this case such foreseeability was indistinguishable from express/tacit agreement.

R v *Hyde and Others* [1991] Crim LR 133 - secondary party to murder - must be shown that he foresaw the consequence of killing/gbh which might follow from actions of principal.

R v *Cheshire* [1991] Crim LR 709 - causation - medical incompetence does not necessarily break chain.

R v *Ball* [1989] Crim LR 730 - In manslaughter arising from unlawful and dangerous act, the accused's state of mind is only relevant to establish: (a) that the act was committed intentionally; and (b) that it was an unlawful act. Once (a) and (b) were established the question whether the act was dangerous was to be judged not by the appellant's appreciation but by that of a sober and reasonable man.

R v *Jennings* [1990] Crim LR 588 - manslaughter arising from dangerous and unlawful act - carrying unsheathed knife in street not sufficient for 'unlawful act' - knife not offensive weapon per se therefore D's intent in relation thereto was relevant.

5.4 Analysis of questions

It is a safe bet that at least one question on the paper will be concerned with homicide in its various forms. There are usually several such questions, aimed particularly at one essential element eg causation or intention.

It cannot be stressed too much that a sound knowledge of this topic is vital to examination success and good overall marks can be attained by a student who has a strong grasp of the principles in this chapter.

5.5 Questions

Question 1

J had visited K, his hypnotherapist for treatment of relief of pain. After treatment J was still under the influence of hypnosis though he gave no signs of this. Whilst driving home J ran down and killed L, a child aged six years who had run out in front of J's car. Unaware of the accident, J walked away to his home nearby. J then went for a walk and met M who called him a 'thick idiot'. J lost his temper and hit M over the head with his walking stick. M had a thin skull and died from the blow.

Advise J and K as to their criminal liability.

Adapted from University of London LLB Examination
(for External Students) Criminal Law June 1985 Q4

General comment

A difficult question. The range of the question is wide, covering a number of fairly difficult aspects of the syllabus including recklessness. Furthermore, the difficulties are aggravated because of the need to consider the defence of automatism.

A student should take great care to ensure that his answer is clear and well planned. Although there is no one correct approach a student would probably find that the best approach would be to explain all the possible offences committed by J first and only then go on to consider and apply the defence of automatism.

Skeleton solution

The definition of recklessness following the decision in *MPC* v *Caldwell* (1982), s2, s3 of the Road Traffic Act 1988; s1 Road Traffic Act 1988 and involuntary manslaughter overlap - murder and the defence of provocation - alternative charge of constructive manslaughter - the defence of voluntary intoxication to crimes of specific intent and crimes of basic intent - the defence of non-insane automatism - limits on such a defence - *R* v *Bailey* (1983) whether K could be the legal cause of the deaths - liability of K for manslaughter by gross negligence - doctrine of innocent agency.

Suggested solution

When J drives the car while under the influence of hypnosis he may commit the offence of driving without due care and attention contrary to s3 of the Road Traffic Act 1988 (as amended) or the more serious offence of driving recklessly contrary to s2 of the Road Traffic Act 1988 (as amended). In *R* v *Lawrence* (1982) the House of Lords explained the distinction between the two offences by stating that driving without due care and attention dealt with driving that created the risk of inconvenience or annoyance to others while dangerous driving concerned driving which created a real risk of causing injury to persons or substantial damage to property.

The test for recklessness was also considered in *R* v *Lawrence* and the approach of the House of Lords in *MPC* v *Caldwell* (1982) was followed. To be driving recklessly a defendant had to be driving the vehicle in such a manner as to create an obvious and serious risk of causing injury to another or doing substantial damage to property. Furthermore, a defendant must have done so without having given any thought to the possibility of the risk or having seen the risk he had still gone on to take it. No details are given as to the competence or otherwise of J's driving. If the child was killed even though J was driving competently he would not be liable. However, if J could have saved the child had he been driving properly when in fact he was not he may still be liable: *R* v *Dalloway* (1847).

When J kills L, a six year old child who runs out in front of the car, he may commit the offence of killing by reckless driving contrary to s1 Road Traffic Act 1988. An alternative charge to this statutory offence would be the common law offence of causing death by gross negligence or recklessness. In order to satisfy this type of involuntary manslaughter it must be shown that in the opinion of the jury the negligence of the accused showed such a gross disregard for life and safety so as to amount to a crime. The former test of 'compensation and negligence' in *R v Bateman* (1925) has been disapproved and the objective test in *R v Seymour* (1983) will be applied: *Kong Cheuk Kwan v R* (1985).

In *R v Seymour* the House of Lords held that the offence of causing death by reckless driving contrary to s1 Road Traffic Act 1972 coexisted with the common law offence. Furthermore, while the definition of recklessness given on *R v Lawrence* was appropriate, the judge should point out to the jury that in order to constitute the common law offence of manslaughter the risk of death being caused by the manner of driving had to be very high: *R v Lamb (Charles)* (1990).

J may be liable for either murder or manslaughter when he strikes and kills M. He will not be able to claim that he did not cause the death because an accused must take his victim as he finds him and a characteristic like a thin skull will not break the chain of causation: *R v Blaue* (1975).

J will be liable for murder if he kills while intending to kill or intending to do grievous bodily harm. If he did the act foreseeing that it was highly probable that he would kill or do grievous bodily harm that may be evidence that he had the necessary mens rea but no more than that: *R v Moloney* (1985). If the judge considers it appropriate he may leave it to the jury to infer intention from J's foresight but they must only do so if J foresaw death or grievous bodily harm as 'virtually certain' per *R v Nedrick* (1986) or as being 'highly probable' per *R v Hancock and Shankland* (1986); *R v Barr, Kenyon and Heacock* (1989).

The jury is not bound to infer foresight of consequences by reason only of there being a natural and probable consequence of those actions - s8 Criminal Justice Act 1967.

If J had the necessary mens rea for murder but was provoked by M he may be able to claim the defence of provocation which would reduce murder to voluntary manslaughter. Provocation may be established if an accused can show that he lost his self control as a result of actions or words of the victim or a third party. Furthermore, it must be shown that a reasonable man would also have lost his self control and done as the accused did. In deciding the reasonable man test the jury must give a reasonable man the age, sex and other characteristics of the accused that affect the provocation: *DPP v Camplin* (1978), also *R v Doughty* (1986). In *R v Newell* (1980) 71 Cr App R 331 the Court of Appeal found that an accused's characteristics had to be permanent and directly relate to the provocation. Thus drunkenness and a hypnotic would obviously not be characteristics that could be imputed to the reasonable man.

An alternative charge to murder is that of constructive manslaughter. The prosecution must establish that J intended to do an unlawful act which was likely to subject the victim to at least the risk of some harm, albeit not necessarily serious harm: *R v Church* (1965). The unlawful act, which J must have intended, would be the striking of M on the head with a stick. It would not be necessary, however, to show that J foresaw the possibility of harm. It is sufficient if a reasonable man would have seen the risk involved.

It is now necessary to consider whether J can claim a defence resulting from his hypnotized state. Whatever offence under criminal law is being alleged it must be shown that an accused acted 'voluntarily' ie that his mind was in control of his body. If this is not the case he will be acting as an automaton. On the facts in question the automatism does not arise from a disease of the mind (insane automatism) and therefore non-insane automatism may be pleaded as a defence. It should, however, be noted that where the automaton state arose as a result of the accused's own recklessness he will be unable to claim it as a defence to a crime where recklessness is sufficient mens rea: *R v Bailey* (1983); *R v Hardie* (1985). The defence of automatism would therefore only be available to J if he can show that he has not acted 'voluntarily' through no fault of his own. While this might possibly be the case where L is killed it is not as easy to apply the principles where M's death is considered. Intoxication and automatism are acting in conjunction with each other. The need to protect the public would probably result in the principles relating to voluntary intoxication being applied.

K's liability would depend on whether or not his conduct rather than J's could be regarded as the legal cause of the deaths that occurred. If it could be established that K's conduct was a substantial and operating cause of death he might possibly be liable for manslaughter by gross negligence in respect of each victim. The type of conduct sufficient for such a charge has been detailed above: *R v Bateman* (1925); *R v Seymour* (1983).

It would not be appropriate to apply the doctrine of innocent agency because it does not appear that K had been acting intentionally. Had K been acting with the intention that J should perform such acts while under hypnosis K would be the principal offender while J would have been his innocent agent.

Question 2

P, an anti-hunt demonstrator, hid behind a fence in Q's field intending to startle horses and riders. In pursuit of a fox Q was galloping across his field preparing to jump a wall. P jumped out from his concealed position and startled Q's horse. Q was thrown to the ground. He was a haemophiliac and died as a result of the fall. P had foreseen that there was a possibility of a rider being dismounted but he had not desired death. Other hunt members, X and Y, picked P up, carried him out of the field and threw him into a lake.

Advise P, X and Y as to their criminal liability.

Adapted from University of London LLB Examination
(for External Students) Criminal Law June 1985 Q6

CRIMINAL LAW

General comment

A rather difficult question and one that requires careful consideration in order to recognize all the possible offences that may have been committed. A student must examine in detail the mens rea of murder and contrast it with involuntary manslaughter. A full range of assaults may have been committed against P and detailed consideration of those will be required.

Skeleton solution

Murder and involuntary manslaughter contrasted - ss47, 20 and 18 Offences Against the Person Act 1861 - defence contained in s3 Criminal Law Act 1967.

Suggested solution

The first point to consider in relation to Q's death is whether or not P can be regarded as the legal cause of the death ie 'a substantial and operating cause' of what occurs. There seems little doubt that this would be the case and it should be noted that the fact that Q was a haemophiliac will not break the chain of causation: *R* v *Blaue* (1975). P will be responsible for Q's death if it can be shown that he had the necessary mens rea for murder or came within involuntary manslaughter either constructive manslaughter or manslaughter by gross negligence.

The mens rea for murder is intention to kill or intention to do grievous bodily harm. It is not sufficient mens rea for murder to show that the accused foresaw that death or grievous bodily harm was highly probably going to occur, although such foresight *may* be evidence to show that an accused had the necessary mens rea: *R* v *Moloney* (1985). However, the jury must believe that P foresaw death or grievous bodily harm as being a 'virtually certain' consequence of his actions and virtually certain to occur: *R* v *Nedrick* (1986), or as being 'overwhelmingly probable': *R* v *Hancock and Shankland* (1986).

Applying these principles to the facts in question, P may not desire to kill Q but he could still have mens rea if he knew that death or grievous bodily harm was 'virtually certain' or 'overwhelmingly probable' but the jury must be sure that such an inference of intention is right. A conviction for murder carries with it a mandatory life sentence. Alternative charges to murder would be constructive manslaughter and manslaughter by gross negligence. A conviction for manslaughter carries a maximum life sentence.

Constructive manslaughter would be satisfied if it could be shown that Q died as a consequence of P's actions and that P had an intention to do an unlawful act which was likely to cause at least a little harm. The 'unlawful act' that an accused must intend must be more than a civil wrong. In *R* v *Franklin* (1883) the accused threw a box belonging to X into the sea killing P. It was held that such a civil wrong was not sufficient for constructive manslaughter. Applying this to the facts of the case undoubtedly P is committing the tort of trespass but this could not be relied on for constructive manslaughter. If it could be established that P intended to frighten Q and not just the horse when he jumped out he would have committed a common law assault in that he intended to put Q in fear of being then and there subjected to harm.

Terrifying an animal, contrary to s1(1) Animals Act 1911 would also amount to an 'unlawful act' here. The second limb of the test for constructive manslaughter requires that a reasonable man would have foreseen the possibility of at least a little harm, albeit not the serious harm that actually occurred *R* v *Church* (1965) and it could be argued that a reasonable man would foresee harm being caused to the rider of an animal which was deliberately terrorised. The 'act' need not be directed at the victim, *R* v *Pagett* (1983), provided there is no new intervening act - *R* v *Goodfellow* (1986). Once both limbs for constructive manslaughter have been established, the question of whether the act was dangerous will be judged against the appreciation of a reasonable and sober man and not that of P: *R* v *Ball* (1989).

Manslaughter by gross negligence is committed where an accused's actions show such a gross disregard for life and safety *R* v *Bateman* (1925) and that disregard is to be judged objectively: *R* v *Seymour* (1983); *Kong Cheuk Kwan* v *R* (1985).

When X and Y pick P up they could possibly be liable for false imprisonment or kidnap. False imprisonment is committed where a victim is detained against his will and without lawful excuse. Kidnap is committed where the victim is detained and carried away from the place he wishes to be without lawful excuse.

Undoubtedly X and Y would claim that they were entitled to detain P in view of what had just occurred and therefore they were acting with lawful excuse. They were not, however, entitled to throw him into the lake. Insufficient detail is given to establish exactly what offences X and Y have committed. They seem to be equally involved and would therefore be regarded as joint principals to whatever offences are shown.

The common law offence of assault and battery is committed if a victim is put in fear of immediate force being used against him (assault) and there is a direct infliction of force (battery). It must be shown that an accused acted intentionally or recklessly in his actions: *R* v *Venna* (1975).

If some injury is sustained by P an offence under s47 of the Offences Against the Person Act 1861 may have been committed. Section 47 contains the offence of assault occasioning actual bodily harm which is harm that interferes to some extent with health and comfort: *R* v *Miller* (1954). Section 47 requires the same mens rea as for s20 (below) ie intention or *Cunningham* recklessness as to the assault and the harm caused: *R* v *Spratt* (1990); *R* v *Parmenter* (1991).

Section 20 of the Offences Against the Person Act 1861 provides that it is an offence to wound or inflict grievous bodily harm. Grievous bodily harm is 'really serious' bodily harm: *DPP* v *Smith* (1960). The mens rea for s20 requires that the accused foresaw at least the possibility of some harm: *W* v *Dolbey* (1983). Section 18 of the Act contains the offence of wounding or causing grievous bodily harm with intention to cause grievous bodily harm. It is not sufficient to show recklessness as to causing grievous bodily harm: *R* v *Belfon* (1976).

The most serious charge of all would be attempted murder if it could be shown that X and Y had done an act more than merely preparatory to the full offence with intention to kill, s1 Criminal Attempts Act 1981, *R* v *Whybrow* (1951).

Depending on the state of mind of X and Y and the injuries, if any, that P sustained they could be liable for one or more of these offences.

X and Y would not be able to claim that they used reasonable force in the prevention of a crime within s3 of the Criminal Law Act 1967 because the crime (if any) has already occurred and in any event it would appear that they are acting aggressively and not defensively: *R* v *Palmer* (1971).

They have also gone beyond the use of reasonable force to make a citizen's arrest of P for an arrestable offence (under s24 Police and Criminal Evidence Act 1984) which might otherwise come under the s3 CLA defence.

Question 3(a)

E while driving along a road, saw a policeman step out in front of him and signal for him to stop. E, wishing to avoid apprehension drove at the policeman who was knocked down and killed. A pregnant woman who was crossing the road was also knocked down and, although uninjured herself, the woman lost her baby as a result.

Advise E of his criminal liabilities.

Adapted from University of London LLB Examination
(for External Students) Criminal Law June 1986 Q3

General comment

A straightforward question on homicide and the mens rea to support murder/ manslaughter charges. Also a consideration of 'killing a person'.

Skeleton solution

Murder/involuntary manslaughter, can foetus be victim?; death by reckless driving s1 RTA 1988 overlap with common law.

Suggested solution

Taking the case of the foetus first.

Whether E can be regarded as criminally responsible for the death of the child will depend on whether the child died in the womb or lived independent of the mother before it died. Only if the child has lived independent of the mother, for however short a time, can the child be a victim of unlawful homicide. The facts of the question would seem to indicate that the child had died in the womb in which case E has no criminal responsibility. If the child was born alive and then died it could be murder or manslaughter. Murder would be established by operating the doctrine of transferred malice whereby the mens rea that he had towards one victim transfers to the actus victim: *R* v *Pembliton* (1874). The mens rea for murder is intention to kill or intention to cause grievous bodily harm. As stated previously, 'intention' in criminal law includes not just desiring a consequence but knowing that it is certain to occur (oblique intent). Indeed if E is liable under s18 OAP Act 1861 the mens rea required for s18 - intention to cause grievous bodily harm, will be sufficient for murder if a death results, *R* v *Vickers* (1957). However, it must be shown that the child had been born alive before this would be appropriate. Furthermore, following the recent decisions of *R* v *Moloney* (1985) and *R* v *Hancock and Shankland* (1986), *R* v *Nedrick* (1986), it is not sufficient to show that he foresaw death or grievous bodily harm as a natural and probable consequence of what he did. While such foresight may be useful as evidence of intention it is not to be equated with intention.

Alternatively charges of constructive manslaughter or manslaughter by reckless conduct would be appropriate. Constructive manslaughter is shown where there is an intention to do an unlawful act which a reasonable person would foresee is likely to cause a little harm, albeit not the serious harm which actually results: *DPP* v *Newbury* (1976). The unlawful act must be a crime and cannot be sufficient for constructive manslaughter unless the act is invariably unlawful, not merely unlawful when it is badly done: *Andrews* v *DPP* (1937). It would not therefore be appropriate to allege that the unlawful act was for example reckless driving, because this would be an example of an act which became unlawful only when it was badly done. It would be sufficient to rely on one of the assaults.

Killing by reckless conduct is established where the accused causes the death by an act which creates an obvious and serious risk of causing injury to others and either he saw the risk and took it or gave no thought to the possibility of that risk: *R* v *Kong Cheuk Kwan* (1985). This common law offence is an alternative charge to the statutory offence of 'causing death by reckless driving' under s1 Road Traffic Act 1988 (as amended). As with common law manslaughter by reckless conduct, the test for recklessness is based on the test in *R* v *Lawrence* (1981). In *R* v *Seymour* (1983) the House of Lords considered that the common law co-existed with s1 RTA, killing by reckless driving. However, if both charges were found in a single indictment the trial judge had to require the prosecution to elect which of the two counts they wished to proceed. The jury should be directed that, if the s1 offence is to be made out, the risk of causing damage or injury by so driving must have been a serious one: *R* v *Lamb (Charles)* (1990).

In the Scottish case of *McCluskey* v *HM Advocate* (1988) it was held that, in circumstances such as these where a foetus is destroyed by reckless driving, that would be sufficient to support a conviction for 'causing death by reckless driving' if the child was born alive. It did not matter that the child had not been born at the time of the recklessness.

The less serious offence of driving recklessly under s2 RTA 1988 (as amended) may also be established. In *R* v *Lawrence* (1981) it was stated that reckless driving was shown where the accused drove in such a manner that it created an obvious and serious risk of causing physical injury to any other road user or substantial damage to property, without giving any thought to the risk or, having recognised that it existed, decided to take it.

In respect of the policeman, E could face charges of murder or manslaughter as previously outlined. On the facts it is quite possible that murder would be alleged as intention to kill or do grievous bodily harm may well be satisfied if E knew that death or grievous bodily harm was certain or virtually certain to occur as a result of what he did.

Question 3(b)

R's car broke down in an isolated part of Wales during a very severe winter storm. R's sick wife was with him and they started to walk through the snow after R failed to restart the car. After three hours they found a cottage and, as the door was unlocked, they went inside to shelter from the weather.

S who owned the cottage appeared and, although R asked him for assistance, S forced R and his wife to leave. R's wife died from the cold having walked as directed to the nearest village.

Advise R and S about their criminal liability.

Adapted from University of London LLB Examination
(for External Students) Criminal Law June 1986 Q7

General comment

Again a quite straightforward test of knowledge of homicide, particularly omission and intention.

Skeleton solution

Murder/involuntary manslaughter; causation; self-defence - s3 Criminal Law Act 1967.

Suggested solution

Considering the liability for the wife's death. Before either R or S can be liable it must be shown that one other was the legal cause of the death of the wife, ie a substantial and operating cause of the death that occurred. There is nothing on the facts to show that R was the cause of his wife's death. Furthermore it may not be easy to establish that S was the legal cause of death. Did his lawful act of turning R and his wife out of the house cause her death in legal terms?

In *R* v *Dyos* (1979) where there were two possible causes of death, as here, but the accused was responsible only for one of those causes, he was not liable for the death as it could not be established that his actions were the primary or continuing cause of death.

The principle that 'you take your victim as you find your victim' *R* v *Blaue* (1975), would mean that the wife's illness would not break the chain. It could however be argued that turning her out in such bad weather was a substantial and operating cause of her death. This is for the jury to decide.

In the event of S being found to be the legal cause of death he might be liable for manslaughter or possibly even murder.

Considering first a charge of murder, S could be liable for murder if he intended to kill or intended to inflict grievous bodily harm. Intention in this context means not just desiring the consequences but includes also oblique intent ie where an accused knows the consequence is certain or virtually certain to occur. This would not be an example of murder by omission as the prosecution could contend that it was his act of excluding the victim from the building that resulted in the death and not the failure to take proper care, by acting in such an inhumane way.

Murder can be committed by omission but only where there is a recognised duty to act and S's conduct does not appear to come within any recognised duty: *R* v *Dytham* (1979).

It is arguable, on the strength of Lord Diplock's speech in *R* v *Miller* (1983) that S's failure to act may attract some liability for the woman's death.

Alternatively a charge of manslaughter may be appropriate. At common law there are two main categories of manslaughter - constructive manslaughter (unlawful act doctrine manslaughter) or manslaughter by reckless conduct. Constructive manslaughter would be inappropriate on the facts as there is no unlawful act shown.

Manslaughter by reckless conduct would be established if S's conduct created an obvious and serious risk of injuring a person and either he gave no thought to that risk or alternatively recognised the risk existed and decided to take it: *R* v *Kong Cheuk Kwan* (1985). In this case the *Bateman* test, with its references to compensation and negligence, was disapproved, and the objective test in *R* v *Kong Cheuk Kwan* of 'recklessness (or gross negligence)' may suffice to support a charge of manslaughter against S.

It would probably not be open to S to claim the defence of self defence either under the common law or s3 Criminal Law Act 1967. At common law it must be shown that he used reasonable force to protect himself. Under s3 CLA 1967 he may use such force as is reasonable to prevent a crime. It must be shown that he was acting defensively and not aggressively: *R* v *Shannon* (1980). However the offences, if indeed there be any have already occurred therefore it would have to be shown he was acting to protect his property from future offences.

Question 4

X kissed Y, his girlfriend, good night. He kissed her so vigorously that she had a bleeding lip. The lip became infected but Y refused medical treatment because of her irrational fear of doctors. Eventually she became unconscious and her parents called a doctor. He mistakenly administered an anti-viral drug. Y died from the drug.

Advise X and the doctor about their criminal liability.

University of London LLB Examination
(for External Students) Criminal Law June 1986 Q9

General comment

A good question to do as it involves a progression through the assaults and the homicides without too many diversions to lead a student astray.

Skeleton solution

CL battery - s47 Offences Against the Person Act 1861 consent as a defence - s20 Offences Against the Person Act 1861 - s18 Offences Against the Person Act 1861 causation - murder/involuntary manslaughter - constructive manslaughter - manslaughter by reckless conduct.

Suggested solution

When X kissed his girlfriend so vigorously that he caused her lip to bleed he may commit an assault occasioning actual bodily harm within s47 Offences Against the Person Act 1861 and common law battery.

A common law battery is an unlawful infliction of force against the victim committed intentionally or recklessly. Recklessness in this context requires the accused to have appreciated the risk of force against the victim but nonetheless gone on to take the risk ie - *Cunningham* recklessness as opposed to *Caldwell* recklessness, *R v Morrison* (1988).

Section 47 of the Offences Against the Person Act 1861 provides that it shall be an offence to assault occasioning actual bodily harm. 'Actual bodily harm' includes any hurt or injury calculated to interfere with the health and comfort of the victim: *R v Miller* (1954).

The mens rea for s47, as the law now stands, is the same as that required for s20 (below) ie an intention to cause the harm or subjective recklessness as to that consequence: *R v Spratt* (1990); *R v Parmenter* (1991).

For both common law battery and s47 there will only be an offence if the act was unlawful ie without consent. The onus of proving lack of consent is on the Crown: *R v Donovan* (1934).

On the facts in question there would appear to be a valid consent and only if there was for example an intention to injure does it seem likely that this conduct would be within the criminal law. As this does not appear to be the case it seems likely that consent operates to negative what would otherwise be a crime: *R v Muir* (1986).

When the lip became infected arguably that could be regarded as grievous bodily harm, grievous bodily harm being really serious bodily harm: *DPP v Smith* (1961). However s20 Offences Against the Person Act 1861 would not be appropriate on the facts because X has not acted 'maliciously' in the sense of foreseeing a little harm, *W v Dolbey* (1983), and there would not be an 'infliction' of grievous bodily harm as there is no assault either direct or indirect because there is consent.

Similarly for s18 of Offences Against the Person Act 1861 although he may have 'caused' grievous bodily harm he does not have the necessary intention to do grievous bodily harm: *R v Belfon* (1976).

In order to decide whether X or the doctor can be liable for Y's death it must first be shown that one or other of them was the legal cause of the death. Causation is a question of fact and law. The act must be a sine qua non of the event (in this case the death). This is a question of fact for the jury to decide. However certain acts which are the sine qua non of the event cannot be regarded as the legal cause of the event.

It is not necessary to show that an accused is the sole or even the main cause of death. It is sufficient that the accused is a substantial and generating cause of the death without any subsequent act breaking the chain of causation between what the accused did and the death that resulted.

Applying these principles to the facts of the question only if X can be regarded as a substantial and operating cause of the death will he regarded as the legal cause of death. Y's refusal to obtain treatment will not break the chain of causation: *R* v *Holland* (1841) and *R* v *Blaue* (1975). X must take his victim as he finds him and the neglect of the victim will not break the chain. Less easy to deal with is the question of whether the medical treatment breaks the chain of causation. Medical evidence may be introduced to show that the medical treatment of the injury was the cause of death and not the injury itself: *R* v *Jordan* (1956). If the original injury can only be regarded as the setting in which another cause generates can it be said that the death does not result from the injury: *R* v *Smith* (1959). The doctor administered the wrong drug from which Y died - if this can be regarded as wrong and abnormal treatment ie treatment that no competent doctor would give, then it may break the chain of causation. However, the fact that such treatment fell below that which a competent doctor might be expected to provide will not of itself break the chain of causation: *R* v *Cheshire* (1991). If however the treatment was treatment that a competent doctor would have given then it will not break the chain of causation: R v *Malcherek and Steel* (1981).

If X is found by the jury to be the cause of the death then it is necessary to consider what crime he may have committed. On the facts there is nothing to indicate the mens rea for murder ie intention to kill or to do grievous bodily harm. Preferable charges to murder would be constructive manslaughter or manslaughter by reckless conduct.

Constructive manslaughter is only established where it can be shown that there was an intention to do an unlawful act which a reasonable person would foresee as likely to cause at least a little harm: *DPP* v *Newbury* (1976). On the facts this does not appear to be satisfied because it is doubtful that there is an unlawful act. Furthermore it is not an act that a reasonable man would foresee as likely to cause a little harm: *R* v *Church* (1965).

Manslaughter by reckless conduct would be established if the prosecution could show that X did an act that created an obvious and serious risk of causing physical injury to Y and either X saw the risk and took it or gave no thought to the possibility of the risk: *Kong Cheuk Kwan* v *R* (1985). In that case the *Bateman* test of gross negligence manslaughter with its reference to compensation and negligence was disapproved of. On the facts it would seem unlikely that X would be liable under this head.

If the doctor broke the chain of causation between what X did and the death that resulted then it may be that he may be liable for manslaughter on the ground that he killed by reckless conduct as outlined above.

Question 5(a)

During a wrestling match between E and F, E bit F's ear infecting him with AIDS. Subsequently E threw F out of the ring onto Miss G's lap. Both F and G died from their injuries.

Advise E of his liability in respect of the deaths.

Adapted from University of London LLB Examination
(for External Students) Criminal Law June 1987 Q2

General comment

The question of AIDS and causation is a topical one and provides a useful vehicle for testing a number of concepts in homicide cases.

Skeleton solution

Murder/involuntary manslaughter; causation; recklessness; ss47, 20, 18 OAP 1861

Suggested solution

In respect of F, it is necessary to consider E's possible liability for unlawful homicide. However this would only be necessary if F died within a year and a day of being infected by E. If F died after this period of time then as a matter of law E will not be regarded as the legal cause of F's death: *R v Dyson* (1908). If F dies within a year and a day E could be liable for murder or one of the involuntary manslaughters. Murder is established if E kills F intending to kill or intending to do grievous bodily harm. This is a very high mens rea and on the facts would be difficult to establish unless for example E knew he had AIDS and he knew that by biting he was certain or virtually certain to cause grievous bodily harm or kill. It was not sufficient that E foresaw that grievous bodily harm was high probable: *R v Moloney* (1985); *R v Hancock and Shankland* (1986); *R v Barr, Kenyon and Heacock* (1989). It must be established that E either desired to kill or do grievous bodily harm or knew that it was certain or virtually certain to occur. Furthermore a jury should be directed that they are not entitled to infer the necessary intention unless they feel sure that death or grievous bodily harm was virtually certain as a result of E's actions and that E knew this to be the case: *R v Nedrick* (1986).

Even if E did know that he had AIDS, it would be difficult to show that E knew of the 'virtual certainty' of F's dying or suffering grievous bodily harm from the bite.

On the facts it seems unlikely E would be liable for murder. Constructive manslaughter would be established if there is an unlawful act that kills and E had intention to do an unlawful act which a reasonable man would foresee is likely to cause at least a little harm: *DPP v Newbury* (1976); *R v Church* (1965).

Only if E's acts against F were held to amount to a crime would there be the necessary intention to do the unlawful act.

Assuming the wrestling match itself is not unlawful as otherwise any assault during the match would be 'unlawful' (*R v Coney* (1882)), an assault likely to occasion actual bodily harm or more serious harm will be unlawful: *R v Donovan* (1934).

80

Moreover, F's 'consent' to the wrestling will not negative the 'assault' by E as E has gone outside the bounds of the game.

Alternatively E could be liable for killing by reckless conduct. The *Bateman* test for gross negligence manslaughter has recently been much criticised. In its place the *Lawrence* test for recklessness has been applied so that E could be liable if he did an act which created an obvious and serious risk of causing injury to a person and at the time he did the act he gave no thought to the possibility of that risk or having recognised that the risk existed decided to take it: *R* v *Kong Cheuk Kwan* (1985).

Similar considerations would apply to E's liability for the constructive manslaughter of Miss G. In relation to the 'unlawful act', when E threw F out of the ring there would be a common law battery - a use of force intentionally or recklessly applied. When F lands on Miss G causing her serious injury it seems very unlikely that F could have any criminal responsibility for her injuries as he lacks mens rea and at this time he is not acting voluntarily. Indeed F would be regarded as simply the means whereby the actus reus is achieved against Miss G. E could be liable under s47, s20 or even s18 but only if the doctrine of transferred malice is applied, so that the mens rea E has towards F transfers to Miss G: *R* v *Latimer* (1886). Mens rea may be transferred providing the mens rea coincides with the actus reus of the same type of crime. An alternative approach would be the objective test of E's recklessness as above: *R* v *Kong Cheuk Kwan* (1985).

It does not appear that there is evidence of the high degree of mens rea required to prove murder of Miss G.

Question 5(b)

K was attacked in a street by a group of youths. L, who was the leader caused K to be thrown to the ground where several of the gang kicked him until he became unconscious. They then left the scene. Whilst K was on the ground M passed by and removed K's wallet to see if there was anything worth stealing. M took five pounds from the wallet and kicked K twice before leaving causing severe bruising. N who was next to pass the scene saw that K was seriously ill but did nothing, deciding that he did not want to become involved. O, a doctor, also passed by without rendering assistance. P finally came over to K's aid but because of his inexperience in such matters, he moved K which in turn caused K's internal injuries to become severe.

K subsequently died within a few days.

Advise the parties of their criminal liability in relation to the death of K.

Adapted from University of London LLB Examination
(for External Students) Criminal Law June 1987 Q4

General comment

Although there are numerous offences disclosed in the question - indeed it is used elsewhere in the book to illustrate other aspects of the subject - the primary concern here is with causation, omission and duty of care in homicide.

Skeleton solution

Murder/involuntary manslaughter; recklessness; omission and duty to act; causation; mens rea.

Suggested solution

It is necessary to consider who was the legal cause of the death of K in order to assess the culpability of each of the actors.

It is most likely that the youths who killed K unconscious would be the legal cause of his death. They would only be liable for murder if they had a very high mens rea - intention to kill or intention to do grievous bodily harm. Intention means desiring a result or knowledge that it is certain or virtually certain to occur: *R v Moloney* (1985). In *R v Hancock and Shankland* (1986) the House of Lords emphasised again that foresight of a consequence is not the same as intending that consequence. It may be useful as evidence but only if it can be established that the accused foresaw the consequence as at least highly probable. Even then it is not conclusive evidence.

In *R v Nedrick* (1986) it was stated that a jury are only entitled to infer the necessary intention if they are sure that death or grievous bodily harm was virtually certain as a result of the defendant's actions and the defendant appreciated this.

Constructive manslaughter is established where a person kills as a result of an unlawful act. The unlawful act must be a crime (*R v Franklin* (1883)) and a positive act (*R v Lowe* (1973)). Furthermore it must be one that a reasonable man would foresee is likely to cause at least a little harm: *DPP v Newbury* (1976).

This would appear to be appropriate on the facts as the assaults already outlined would constitute the unlawful act.

Killing by reckless conduct is a further type of involuntary manslaughter. This is established if the accused did an act which created an obvious and serious risk of causing injury and when he did the act he either has not given any thought to the possibility of the risk or having seen the risk he took it: *R v Lawrence* (1981). This test was approved of by the Privy Council in *R v Kong Cheuk Kwan* (1985) where the '*Bateman* test' for liability for gross negligence manslaughter was criticised as being outmoded and unnecessary.

All the youths could be liable for manslaughter if it were shown that their acts were within the common design. Liability for murder would be more difficult with a number of joint principals. It is the cumulative acts and circumstances that lead to the death. It is not possible to show one particular act that kills therefore the parties are equally involved and best regarded as joint principals. Therefore individually there would have to be established mens rea for murder. If this were only present in one or some but not others those that lacked such mens rea would be liable for manslaughter.

L who may be an accomplice to the assaults could not be an accomplice to murder unless he had contemplated one of his gang was going to inflict grievous bodily harm: *Chan Wing Siu v R* (1984); *R v Slack* (1989).

M's kicking caused severe bruising but it is not clear whether this attack had any contributory effect upon K's death. In *R* v *Grundy* (1989) it was held, in relation to gbh, that a jury should look at all the injuries together to decide if they amount collectively to gbh.

However, the difficulty here is that M acts alone in kicking K after the other youths have gone. He may be liable under the reckless/gross negligence test in *R* v *Kong Cheuk Kwan*.

N would appear to have no liability in this matter. Undoubtedly certain crimes may be committed by omission. But there can be no liability by this means unless there is a duty to act in law. In these circumstances N has no duty to act in law and therefore would have no liability. It should be noted in relation to matters already discussed that an assault cannot be performed by omission. It must invariably take place by means of a positive act: *Fagan* v *MPC* (1969).

It is arguable that O, being a doctor, has a duty by virtue of his office to preserve and sustain life and that his omission to act makes him liable in the same way that a police officer would be: *R* v *Dytham* (1979).

When P moves K causing his internal injuries to become severe, he would not become liable in criminal law for as a matter of law he would not be regarded as the *legal* cause of the injuries. The chain of causation will not be broken in these circumstances - P would be regarded as an innocent or non-responsible intervener. Where such a person intevenes by an act instinctively done to assist someone he would not break the chain of causation and the harm resulting would not be in law attributable to him but rather to those who started the chain of causation.

However, it may be argued that, having apparently undertaken to care for K he thereby attracts a duty of care towards him per *R* v *Stone and Dobinson* (1977).

Question 6

U, who was 22 years but with a mental age of ten years, had a terrible temper, which he did his best to control. Also, because of a motoring accident he had only one leg. He was in the playground when a fellow pupil, V, abusively called him, 'Peg-leg'. U lost his temper and pushed V to the ground. V, who had a thin skull, was concussed by the fall. X, who was U's best friend, tried to pull U away from V whom U was trying to kick. Released U ran and kicked V on the ground.

Advise the parties of their criminal liability on the basis that V had died as a result of concussion and internal injuries.

Adapted from University of London LLB Examination
(for External Students) Criminal Law June 1987 Q7

General comment

A good question to tackle. Core elements of the syllabus were examined and all the main aspects were easily recognisable on the facts.

Skeleton solution

U assault - s47, s20 OAP 1861 - causation - murder; diminished responsibility; constructive manslaughter

X battery - lack of MR - accomplice role - s3 CLA 1967

Suggested solution

When U, having lost his temper, pushes V to the ground he may commit a number of assaults contrary to the Offences Against the Person Act 1861.

Section 47 OAP 1861 provides that it will be an offence to assault occasioning actual bodily harm. 'Actual bodily harm' includes 'any hurt and injury calculated to interfere with health or comfort': *R v Miller* (1954). The mens rea for s47, following recent developments in the Court of Appeal, is the same as that required for s20, namely an intention to do the harm specified in the charge or a subjective recklessness as to that consequence: *R v Spratt* (1990); *R v Parmenter* (1991). It is no longer sufficient simply to show recklessness as to the assault. The prosecution must also show such recklessness as to the bodily harm: *R v Spratt* (cf *R v Savage* (1990)).

Section 20 OAP 1861 provides that it is an offence to unlawfully wound or inflict grievous bodily harm. 'Grievous bodily harm' means really serious bodily harm. The term 'inflict' requires an assault either direct or possibly indirect: *R v Martin* (1881); *R v Wilson* (1984). Undoubtedly this is satisfied in the facts in question as U uses direct force on V. The mens rea for s20 is intention or recklessness as to circumstances (as for s47). Furthermore the accused must foresee the possibility of at least a little harm: *W v Dolbey* (1983).

Both s47 and s20 are 'result crimes', that is crimes where a consequence must be shown as part of the actus reus.

V who had a thin skull was concussed by the fall. In order to establish the actus reus of either s47 or 20 it must be shown that U is the legal cause of the injury sustained by V. However U must take his victim as he finds him *R v Blaue* (1975), and therefore the chain of causation will not be broken because of the victim's special characteristic of a thin skull.

When U later returns to kicking V he will commit further assaults within s47 or s20 depending on his state of mind. If he has the necessary foresight he may be liable under s20. If he lacks this he will be liable under s47.

The victim dies as a result of concussion and internal injuries. V's possible liability for murder must be considered. In order to established this very serious offence it must be shown that U is the legal cause of V's death. Furthermore it must be shown that U had the necessary mens rea for murder at the time of the actus reus. The mens rea for murder is very high. The prosecution would have to establish that U killed V intending to kill or intending to do grievous bodily harm. 'Intention' includes both desiring to kill or do grievous bodily harm (direct intent) or knowing that death or grievous bodily harm is certain or virtually certain to occur (oblique intent). Where the prosecution rely on oblique intent it is not sufficient to establish the accused foresaw the result as highly probable. While this may be useful as evidence it is no more than that: *R v Barr, Kenyon and Heacock* (1989). Foresight is not to be equated with intention. A jury should be directed that they are not entitled to infer the necessary intention unless they are satisfied that death or grievous bodily harm was virtually certain as a result of the defendant's actions *and* the defendant appreciated that this was the case: *R v Moloney* (1985); *R v Hancock and Shankland* (1986); *R v Nedrick* (1986).

On the facts in question there seems little doubt that U is the legal cause of death. If he has intention to kill or intention to do grievous bodily harm at any time when the actus reus is continuing he may be liable for murder.

The offence of murder carries a mandatory life sentence. Provocation is a limited defence available to murder which, if successful, will reduce murder to voluntary manslaughter thus avoiding the mandatory life sentence. Provocation is a common law defence available to a charge of murder where by words or acts an accused is so provoked by the victim or a third party that he suffers a sudden and temporary loss of self-control, which would have caused a reasonable man to lose his self-control and so act as the accused did, ie kill *R v Duffy* (1949), as amended by s3 Homicide Act 1957. Section 3 also provides that the question of whether a reasonable man would have lost control and killed must be left to the jury. Also *R v Gilbert* (1977).

The jury must attribute to the reasonable man the power of self control to be expected of an ordinary person of the same age and sex of the accused and also sharing such of the accused's characteristics as would affect the provocation: *DPP v Camplin* (1978).

Moreover, the judge must bring any peculiarities of U to the jury's attention, provided those peculiarities are relevant: *R v Burke* (1987).

In *R v Newell* (1980) it was stated that, in addition to age and sex, only permanent characteristics where there was some real connection between the nature of the provocation and the particular characteristic of the offender could be attributed to the reasonable man.

Applying these cases to the facts in question U's bad temper could not be attributed to the reasonable man as it is a temporary state that came from time to time, furthermore the provocation does not relate to it. However his disabilities could be attributed to the reasonable man as that is permanent and the provocation does relate to it. U has a physical age of 22 but a mental age of ten. Applying *R v Raven* (1982), the jury should be directed to consider the reasonable man test on the basis of a person aged 22 but with retarded development and a mental age of ten.

The fact that shouting abuse may not of itself be unlawful does not prevent it amounting to provocation provided it would have provoked a reasonable person with U's characteristics to lose self-control: *R v Doughty* (1986).

There was a time lapse between the provocation and the ultimate killing of V. The longer the time lapse the more difficult it is to establish provocation because the accused will have had opportunity to recover control: *R v Ibrams and Gregory* (1982).

However on the facts the period of time involved is not sufficient to discount provocation as a defence.

In addition to the defence of provocation, the statutory defence of diminished responsibility under s2 Homicide Act 1957 may be available. Section 2 provides that where a person kills he shall not be convicted of murder if he was suffering from such abnormality of mind (whether arising from arrested or retarded development or any inherent causes or induced by disease or injury) as substantially impaired his responsibility. Thus murder will be reduced to voluntary manslaughter. On the facts in question this may well be available.

If U lacked mens rea for murder he could be liable for constructive manslaughter. This is established where a person kills as a result of an unlawful act - in this case one of the assaults. Furthermore in addition to an intention to do the unlawful act it must be shown that a reasonable man would foresee the possibility of at least a little harm from the act: *DPP* v *Newbury* (1976).

X has no criminal responsibility on the facts as given. Undoubtedly he uses force against U when pulling him away and this could amount to a common law battery - a direct use of force, intentionally or recklessly committed. However, under s3 Criminal Law Act 1967, a person may use reasonable force in the prevention of a crime. It must be established that X was acting defensively and not aggressively: *R* v *Shannon* (1980). The question of whether the force used was reasonable must be considered by reference to the circumstances the accused found himself in *R* v *Palmer* (1971); *R* v *Whyte* (1987). There seems little doubt on the facts that this would be available to X as a defence.

Question 7

'Infecting another when one knows one has AIDS is murder.'

Discuss.

Adapted from University of London LLB Examination
(for External Students) Criminal Law June 1988 Q6

General comment

This question is more of an essay type question than a problem question and requires a thorough knowledge of the offence of murder. You must be systematic and carefully identify the actus reus and mens rea of this offence. It is not as easy as it looks. Furthermore, remember that you are asked by the question *only* to consider murder, not any other form of homicide.

Skeleton solution

Homicide - murder - voluntary manslaughter - involuntary manslaughter

Murder - actus reus - mens rea

Voluntary manslaughter - mens rea.

Suggested solution

The actus reus of homicide is committed when a person of sound mind and discretion unlawfully kills any reasonable creature in being and under the Queen's peace, the death following within a year and a day: Coke, 3 Inst 47.

A person is 'of sound mind and discretion' if he is not insane within the meaning of the M'Naghten Rules: 10 Cl & F 200, or under ten years of age at the time the act was committed.

'Unlawfully' means without legal justification or excuse.

The defendant must 'kill' the victim, ie he must be the factual and legal cause of the death of the victim. A defendant's act cannot be held to be the cause of death if death would have occurred without his act. The defendant's act must be a sine qua non of the death and whether it is so is a question of fact. However, even if an act is the sine qua non of homicide, it may not be the cause of the homicide in law. Whether a particular act which is a sine qua non of an alleged actus reus is also the cause of it is a question of law.

'Any reasonable creature in being' means a person who has had an existence independent of its mother: *R v Poulton* (1832).

The person killed must be 'under the Queen's peace'. The killing of any person, even an alien, not in the actual heat and excise of war would be murder: *R v Page* (1954).

Death must occur within a year and a day of the date when the defendant inflicted his injury upon the deceased. If a victim dies more than a year and a day from that time, the law conclusively presumes that death was *not* caused by the defendant's act: *R v Dyson* (1908).

Therefore, in so far as the actus reus of homicide is concerned, the difficult issue in an AIDS case may well be that death does *not* occur within a year and a day of a defendant infecting his victim. Secondly, as the AIDS virus can be transmitted to a foetus, the issue would be whether the foetus had an independent existence *before* its death (from AIDS) and whether death occurred within a year and a day of it being infected.

Homicide can take one of three forms: murder, voluntary manslaughter and involuntary manslaughter.

Homicide is murder when the defendant has the mens rea of an intention to kill or an intention to cause grievous bodily harm. 'Grievous bodily harm' means injury which is serious but not necessarily dangerous to life: *R v Cunningham* (1982); *R v Vickers* (1957).

'Intention' in the crime of murder must be distinguished from motive or desire. Foresight by the accused of death or causing grievous bodily harm as a probable consequence of his voluntary act, where that probability can be defined as exceeding a certain degree, cannot be equated or considered to be an alternative to the mens rea required for murder, ie an intention to kill or an intention to cause grievous bodily harm. A man is *not* to be *presumed* to *intend* the natural and probable consequences of his acts: s8 Criminal Justice Act 1967 and a jury is to have regard to all the circumstances in deciding whether an accused intended those consequences or not: *DPP* v *Smith* (1961); *R* v *Steane* (1947).

In cases where the defendant's motive or purpose was *not* primarily to kill or seriously injure then it must be shown that the defendant did the act which caused death knowing that he was doing and intending to do it, and if he did, then the defendant's act must be of a kind which was highly likely to cause death or serious bodily injury. If it was, then the defendant must have appreciated that what he did was highly likely to cause death or serious bodily injury. The fact that he may not have desired the result will be irrelevant for 'desire' and 'intent' are two different things: *R* v *Hancock and Shankland* (1986); *R* v *Moloney* (1985).

The decision of the House of Lords in *R* v *Hancock and Shankland* emphasised that *R* v *Moloney* clarified the law with respect to the mens rea of murder in three respects.

It restated that the mental element in murder is a specific intent - an intention to kill or an intention to cause grievous bodily harm. Nothing less will suffice.

Secondly, foresight of consequences is no more than evidence of the existence of intention; it must be considered and its weight assessed together with all the evidence of the case: *R* v *Barr, Kenyon and Heacock* (1989). Foresight does not necessarily imply the existence of intention, though it may be a fact from which, when considered with all the other evidence, it may be right to infer the necessary intent.

Thirdly, the probability of the rest is an important matter and can be critical in determining whether the result was intended. Where foresight of consequences is an issue, the greater the probability of a consequence the more likely it was that the consequence was foreseen and that if it was foreseen the greater the probability that it was also intended.

In *R* v *Nedrick* (1986), the Court of Appeal endeavoured to crystallise the effect of the speeches in *R* v *Moloney* and *R* v *Hancock and Shankland.*

A jury should be told that a defendant might intend to achieve a certain result while at the same time not desiring it to come about. Because the greater the probability of a consequence, the more likely that it is that the consequence was foreseen and the greater the probability is that that consequence was also intended, the jury could helpfully ask themselves how probable was the consequence which resulted from the defendant's voluntary act.

Then, they should ask themselves whether the defendant foresaw that consequence.

If he did *not* appreciate that death or grievous bodily harm was likely to result from his act, he could *not* have intended to bring it about.

If he *did* appreciate that death or grievous bodily harm was likely to result from his voluntary act *but* thought that the risk to which he was exposing the person killed was only *slight*, it is open to a jury to conclude that he did *not* intend to bring about that result.

If however, the jury are sure beyond reasonable doubted that at the material time the defendant recognised that death or grievous bodily harm was virtually certain (barring some unforeseen intervention) to result from his voluntary act, then it would be open to a jury to infer that the defendant intended to kill or cause grievous bodily harm, *even* thought he might not have had the desire to achieve that result.

A jury would *not* be entitled to infer intention *unless* they feel sure that death or grievous bodily harm was a virtual certainty as a result of the defendant's actions *and* that the defendant appreciated that such was the case.

Therefore, it is not possible to say that knowingly infecting a person with AIDS is the equivalent to the mens rea of murder or that a jury would, in every case, infer such mens rea.

Question 8

O entered P's circus tent to release animals which O believed were being ill-treated. O let out a lion and a tiger. The lion attacked and killed a person nearby.

Advise O of her criminal liability in relation to the death of the passer-by.

Adapted from University of London LLB Examination
(for External Students) Criminal Law June 1988 Q8

General comment

A brief examination of causation and mens rea for homicide.

Skeleton solution

Murder/involuntary manslaughter; causation - remoteness; mens rea.

Suggested solution

The possible offences arising from the killing of the passer-by are murder or involuntary manslaughter. O requires a high degree of mens rea to satisfy murder - ie an intention to kill or an intention to cause grievous bodily harm to any person *R* v *Moloney* (1985). O's intention here appears to be simply to release the animals for their own welfare.

Intention *may* be inferred from O's foresight of the consequences of her actions but only if the judge considers it appropriate to leave the matter before the jury who may only make the inference of intention if they believe that O foresaw death or gbh as 'highly probable' or 'virtually certain' per *R* v *Hancock and Shankland* (1986) and *R* v *Nedrick* (1986).

The fact that releasing a lion may have serious harm or death as a natural and probable consequence does not allow a jury to infer that O intended those consequences and they must look at all the circumstances in determining the question of O's intention s8 Criminal Justice Act 1967.

Grievous bodily harm here would be serious bodily harm: *R* v *Saunders* (1985).

When the lion attacked and killed a man, the possible offences are either murder or involuntary manslaughter.

On the facts, O does not appear to have the mens rea of murder, ie an intention to kill any person or an intention to cause grievous bodily harm to any person: *R* v *Moloney*; *R* v *Hancock*; *R* v *Nedrick*. 'Grievous bodily harm' means serious bodily harm: *DPP* v *Smith* (1961); *R* v *Saunders* (1985).

If O does not have the mens rea for murder she cannot, a fortiori, be guilty of voluntary manslaughter which requires the *same* mens rea as for murder.

O appears to have committed an unlawful act of involuntary manslaughter which consists of an intention to do an act which, whether O knows it or not, is unlawful and dangerous in the sense that it is likely to cause direct personal injury, though not necessarily serious injury.

There must be an intention to do an act which is in fact unlawful and dangerous. If the defendant knows all the relevant facts, it will be irrelevant that he did not know that the act was unlawful or dangerous. The defendant's ignorance that the act was unlawful will be irrelevant for ignorance of the criminal law is no defence *Grant* v *Borg* (1982).

A material mistake of fact or of civil law might, if reasonable, be a defence. The test of dangerousness is objective not subjective, ie irrespective of whether the defendant knew that his act was dangerous, would all sober and reasonable people have recognised its danger: *DPP* v *Newbury* (1977).

There must be an unlawful act which was unlawful for some reason other than the negligent manner of its performance: *Andrews* v *DPP* (1937).

The act must also be one which all sober and reasonable men would realise was likely to cause harm, which need not be serious but must involve some degree of pain or injury. The harm caused need not be directed at the victim: *R* v *Goodfellow* (1986).

Therefore, on the facts, O appears to be guilty of involuntary manslaughter with respect to the person killed. Her act was unlawful and dangerous; it was unlawful other than because of its negligent performance and was one which was likely to cause harm. Her unlawful and dangerous act appears *not* to have been directed at any specific person but this, on present case law, would not prevent her from being liable.

O's act also appears to be objectively reckless in that it created an obvious and serious risk of causing injury and O either saw the risk and took it, or gave no thought to the risk occurring, in which case an offence of involuntary manslaughter may again be made out: *R* v *Kong Cheuk Kwan* (1985).

6 THEFT, BURGLARY AND DECEPTION

6.1   Introduction

6.2   Key points

6.3   Recent cases and statutes

6.4   Analysis of questions

6.5   Questions

6.1   Introduction

These areas are of crucial importance in understanding the criminal law and make up a large part of the syllabus.

Students will be examined closely on the different elements of the Theft Acts and a clear understanding of each individual offence and its relationship to other and crimes of 'dishonesty' is required.

6.2   Key points

a) *Defining 'theft'*

The definition of theft under s1 of the Theft Act 1968 must be known by heart and the meaning of each element must be clear in a student's mind. 'Dishonestly', 'appropriates', 'property', 'belonging to another', 'intention of permanently depriving' must all be known along with the leading cases. The occasions on which a person will be deemed by the Theft Act 1968 to have acted 'dishonestly' or to have 'appropriated' property, or to have intended permanently to deprive the owner must be learnt (eg ss2, 6 etc): *R* v *Feely* [1973] QB 530; *R* v *Ghosh* [1982] QB 1053; *R* v *Morris* [1983] 3 WLR 697; *R* v *McPherson* [1973] Crim LR 191; *R* v *Gilks* [1972] 1 WLR 1341.

b) *Burglary offences*

   i)   The two separate burglary offences under ss9(1)(a)and (1)(b) must be learnt by heart and the distinction between them clearly appreciated. Note in particular the meaning of 'building' *R* v *Walkington* [1979] 2 All ER 716 and the fact that a person may, by entering another part of a building in which he lawfully find himself, become a trespasser for the purposes of this section. Note too the extent of 'entry' required and the need to be a 'trespasser': *R* v *Collins* [1973] QB 100.

ii) It is useful to remember that, although a person is granted permission (express/implied) to enter, if he harbours a secret intention of eg stealing property therein then that secret intention may have be effect of negativing the invitation. This is because the owner/occupier would not have extended that permission had he known of the intention to steal and under such circumstances the accused could be a 'trespasser': *R v Jones and Smith* [1976] 3 All ER 54.

iii) It should be noted that, having entered without the requisite mens rea for a s9(1)(a) charge, it is only a commission of either theft/attempted theft or inflicting/attempted inflicting of grievous bodily harm on a person therein that will constitute burglary under s9(1)(b).

It can be argued that, having entered a building and committed a s9(1)(b) offence, the accused's entering another part of the building with the requisite intent (theft/gbh/rape/damage) would amount to a separate s9(1)(a) offence.

iv) The offence of aggravated burglary must be known and the aggravating feature may usefully be remembered as his WIFE ie Weapon of offence, Imitation firearm or Firearm, or Explosive. The accused must 'have it with him' at the time: *R v Russell* [1985] Crim LR 231.

c) *Other definitions*

i) Again, the definitions of obtaining property by deception, (s15 TA 1968) and obtaining a pecuniary advantage must be learnt and the concept of a 'deception' understood.

The deception may be deliberate or reckless, by words or conduct, as to fact or law. It must be operative on the 'victim' *DPP v Ray* [1974] AC 370 If they are not deceived there is only an attempt, and any deception must take place before or at the time of the property being obtained *R v Collis-Smith* [1971] Crim LR 716 and must also be the cause at the parting with the property.

ii) The offence of obtaining a service by deception (s1 TA 1978) must similarly be learnt. The more difficult offences of s2 should be known, particularly in relation to the 'time' of the liability which it is sought to evade, subs(1)(a) involves an existing liability, subs(1)(b) involves stalling in payment an existing liability, intending never to pay and subs(1)(c) can cover a deception practised now in order to reduce/avoid a future liability (eg doubling self-reading on gas meter just before prices go up thereby getting future gas supply at cheaper, present-day rate) and may be committed by commission or omission: *R v Firth* (1989) The Times 29 December.

iii) Section 3 of the 1978 Act should be learnt and note that no deception is required. The offence again involves 'time' if the intention not to pay is formed before the service/goods are supplied then a charge under s15 TA 1968 is appropriate. This offence of making off is more a 'spur of the moment' offence.

It should be noted that, in *R v Allen* [1985] AC 1029 it was held that there must be: a 'making off' without payment; knowledge that payment on the spot was required; dishonesty and an intention permanently to avoid payment.

6.3 Recent cases and statutes

Theft:

R v Davis [1988] Crim LR 762 - cheques received under mistake - duty to restore to issuer.

R v Shadrokh-Cigari [1988] Crim LR 465 - bank error credited account by 1,000 times the intended amount - duty to restore - choses in action.

DPP v Huskinson [1988] Crim LR 620 - housing benefit cheque cashed, only part of proceeds given to landlord - obligation to deal with remainder 'in particular way'?

R v Davis (1989) 88 Cr App R 347 - person received two housing benefit cheques in error - cashed both - cash amounted to proceeds of property got by mistake per s5(4) Theft Act 1968 - no need to identify which cheque was stolen.

R v Hamilton [1990] CL 150 - person presenting withdrawal slip at bank to withdraw funds from account which had been opened with stolen cheque - held to be representing to cashier that bank was indebted to him that amount - therefore deception was made out.

Chan Man-Sin v Attorney-General of Hong Kong [1988] Crim LR 319 - cheques forged by accountant, drawn on company - appropriation?

R v Philipou (1989) The Times 6 April - sole directors and shareholders of company - can be guilty of appropriation of company's assets.

R v McHugh; R v Tringham (1989) 88 Cr App R 385 - appropriation by officer or agent of company means 'misappropriation' - cannot involve acts which are expressly/impliedly authorised by company.

R v Bagshaw [1988] Crim LR 125 - 'borrowed' property - 'virtue' test.

R v Wille (1988) 86 Cr App R 296 - director drawing cheque on company for own purposes - theft? - authority given to bank?

R v Velumyl [1989] Crim LR 299 - 'borrowed' from employer intending to restore.

R v Governor of Pentonville Prison, ex parte Osman [1989] 3 All ER 701 - appropriation prima facie takes place where property situated - however, sending telex can be appropriation and can be committed where dispatched and where received.

R v Small [1988] Crim LR 777 - unreasonable belief that property abandoned - misdirection to tell jury such belief cannot be honest - *Ghosh* direction needed.

R v Wise (1990) The Times 10 July - counsel's advice that using brass tokens in gaming machine was not illegal did not save subsequent actions from being dishonest.

R v *O'Connell* [1991] Crim LR 771 - D deceived building society to advance loan against mortgaged property. D averred that he intended to pay back money after selling property. Judge should have given *Ghosh* direction to jury.

Dobson v *General Accident, Fire and Life Assoc plc* (1989) The Guardian 5 October - goods obtained with worthless cheque were 'stolen'.

R v *Spencer and Turner* (1989) unreported - a *Ghosh* direction is not to be given mechanically in every case where 'dishonest' appears in the indictment - only needed where accused accepts certain facts as true but then goes on to raise defence in terms of his own subjective assessment of those facts (Archbold 43rd edition, November supplement).

R v *Price* [1990] Crim LR 200 - *Ghosh* direction only needed where D might have believed actions to be in accordance with ordinary person's idea of honesty.

R v *Wootton and Peake* [1990] Crim LR 201 - claim of right under s2(1) Theft Act 1968 - *Ghosh* direction is not always sufficient - jury should be directed on provisions of subsection.

R v *Holden* [1991] Crim LR 471 - where D claims to have honestly held belief that he had a right in law to take property the issue for the jury is the honesty of that belief and not whether such a belief was reasonable.

Deception:

R v *Kassim* [1988] Crim LR 372 - execution of valuable security procured by deception.

Dearlove v *Drucker* [1988] Crim LR 323 - false representation that purchase of 'oxo' cubes was for export - dual pricing was breach of EC law - was such breach defence?

R v *Firth* (1989) The Times 29 December - dishonestly obtaining exemption/ abatement of liability by deception s2(1)(c) Theft Act 1978 - can be committed by omission and before any liability has come into existence (NB Times report refers to Theft Act 1968).

R v *Melwani* [1989] Crim LR 565 - *Feely* and *Ghosh* not restricted to cases of theft - apply to deception as well - not correct to direct jury that genuine belief as to ultimate repayment could never be defence.

Burglary:

R v *Stones* [1989] 1 WLR 156 - no need to prove intention to use weapon in course of burglary.

6.4   Analysis of questions

As with the chapter on homicide, this forms an essential part of the syllabus and one can expect several property - based questions in the examination. Occasionally there will be questions which are purely based on offences against property, some of which have recently appeared in three parts (as at Q10). More commonly, questions will include other theft related offences (see Chapter 7) and/or elements of criminal damage (see Chapter 8).

6.5 Questions

Question 1

Dan, a young Maori, arrived in England with no knowledge or understanding of property interests. He had always lived communally, in which everything was owned by everyone. He moved into a room in a boarding house in London and, feeling hungry, entered a neighbouring room to take anything he found appetising. He rummaged through his neighbour's drawers but found nothing to eat and so left the room. He became friendly with a group of communists who explained to Dan the nature of individual property interests and, as they saw it, the injustice of these. Convinced by their arguments, Dan entered a large country mansion intent upon taking anything of value therein to give to the poor. He placed some items in a sack but was disturbed by the houseowner. Dan produced an imitation gun and said, 'I am here to help the poor and to punish the rich. Don't make trouble.' The houseowner realised Dan's gun was an imitation one and calmly got down a rifle which was hanging on a wall. Dan ran off.

Dan travelled home on the underground train. He forgot to buy a ticket. He waited in the queue outside the 'excess fare' ticket office at his destination, intending there to pay for his trip. He became irritated at the delay and shouted, 'I'm not waiting here forever!' and ran off through the ticket barrier. He intended to return the next day to pay, but in fact never did so.

Discuss Dan and the houseowner's criminal liability.

Adapted from University of London LLB Examination (for External Students) Criminal Law June 1981 Q6

General comment

A typically complex question testing the candidate's knowledge of many different Theft Act offences but one where good marks are attainable by the well-prepared.

Skeleton solution

Burglary ss9(1)(a) and 9(1)(b): theft ss1-7 TA 1968 aggravated burglary; deception; making off.

Suggested solution

Dan may commit an offence contrary to s9 of the Theft Act 1968 when he enters his neighbour's room. Section 9(1)(a) provides that a person commits burglary if he enters any building or part of a building as a trespasser with intent to steal, cause grievous bodily harm, rape or do criminal damage. Section 9(1)(b) provides that a person will commit an offence where having entered any building or part of a building as a trespasser, he steals or attempts to steal anything in the building or that part of it, or inflict or attempt to inflict on any person therein any grievous bodily harm. However, there would be a number of problems in showing that Dan had indeed committed burglary. Most of these problems concern the mens rea necessary in order to prove the offence. Under s9 it is immaterial that Dan has a room in the boarding house as the section will be satisfied if he enters a part of the building as a trespasser. Therefore, by going into a room where he is not entitled to go, he will have entered that part as a trespasser.

He may also be a trespasser if he harboured a secret intention to steal: *R v Jones and Smith* (1976).

However, in *R v Collins* (1972), it was stated that simply being a civil trespasser is not sufficient to satisfy s9. It is necessary to show that the accused was intentional or reckless as to the facts which make him a trespasser. If Dan is charged under s9(1)(a), it must be shown that at the time of entry, he intended to steal. The offence of theft is contained in s1 of the Theft Act 1968, which states that a person will be guilty of theft if they dishonestly appropriate property belonging to another with the intention of permanently depriving the other of the property. The question of whether or not Dan was dishonest is one to be left to the jury: *R v Feely* (1973).

The jury should apply the standard of the ordinary decent person, although, they must take into account the accused's own view as to whether or not he was dishonest: *R v Ghosh* (1982). In determining Dan's dishonesty, regard will be had to s2 of the 1968 Act which states that where the accused believes he has a right *in law* to take property he will not be dishonest, and that belief need not be reasonable and the jury should be specifically directed on the provisions of that section: *R v Wootton and Peake* (1990); *R v Holden* (1991). However, Dan's belief, based on communism, appears to be a moral one and therefore s2 will not help him, neither will his ignorance of the law *ignorantia juris non excusat*.

It may be that Dan can claim the benefit of s2 of the Theft Act 1968, which states that the person will not be dishonest if he believes that the owner would consent to the taking, or if he believes he had the right in law to the property. The belief must be an honest one, even though it may be unreasonably held. The fact that Dan finds nothing to eat and leaves the room without taking anything will not preclude a charge under s9(1)(a), as it is immaterial that nothing at all is stolen providing that at the time of entry, there was an intention to steal. The fact that Dan found nothing to steal, therefore, will not in itself mean that he is not liable under s9(1)(a): *R v Walkington* (1979) and *Attorney-General's References (Nos 1 and 2 of 1979)* (1979).

Dan may commit a separate offence of burglary when he enters the country house with the intention of taking anything of value to give to the poor. Once again, there may be problems in showing dishonesty but in this situation, it is unlikely that he will be able to claim the benefit of s2 and therefore, the test of dishonesty will be entirely for the jury to decide: *R v Feely*. There will be a complete offence contrary to s9(1)(a), at the moment when he enters the building as a trespasser with intent to steal. The crime is complete as soon as there is a substantial and effective entry accompanied by the necessary mens rea: *R v Collins* (1973); *R v Brown* (1985).

There may be a further offence contrary to s9(1)(b) when he places some items in a sack. The question at that stage is whether there is a theft or an attempted theft of the items. It could be argued that the appropriation is complete in that he has fulfilled the requirements of s3 of the Theft Act 1968, which states that there will be an appropriation where there is an assumption of the rights of an owner.

Dan may have completed the appropriation notwithstanding that the articles had not yet been removed from the house. If this were indeed held to be an appropriation, it would be in line with the cases of *Anderton* v *Wish* (1980) and *R* v *Monaghan* (1979). Indeed, Dan may not simply be liable under s9, he may be liable under s10 of the Theft Act 1968, which provides that a person is guilty of aggravated burglary if he commits any burglary and at the time he has with him any firearm or imitation firearm. The section provides that Dan must have the article with him at the time of the commission of the burglary where the charge is of committing a particular offence after having entered the premises at the time of the commission of that particular offence. It is not necessary to show that Dan intended to use the weapon in the course of the burglary: *R* v *Stones* (1988). Moreover Dan may be guilty of 'going equipped' contrary to s25 of the Theft Act 1968 in that he is not at his place of abode and has with him an article for use in the cause of, or connection with a burglary or theft (see Chapter 7).

When Dan fails to wait in the queue outside the excess fare ticket office at his destination, he will be avoiding an existing liability. However, he will not commit an offence under s2 of the Theft Act 1978, as there is no deception which operates to enable him to avoid payment of the existing liability. To come within this section, he would have had to deceive intentionally or recklessly and as he is blatant in his evasion, there will be no offence under this section.

Neither is there an offence contrary to s1 of the Theft Act 1978, as he did not obtain any services by deception. It may be that there is an offence contrary to s3 of the Theft Act 1978, where knowing that payment on the spot is required or expected of him for goods supplied or services done, he dishonestly makes off without paying, intending not to pay. Once again, it will be necessary to show that he is acting dishonestly.

'Dishonestly making off' requires no special direction to a jury and bears its ordinary natural meaning *R* v *Brooks and Brooks* (1982). It must be shown that Dan made off without paying, that he knew payment on the spot was required and that he was dishonest and intended permanently to avoid payment: *R* v *Allen* (1985). Therefore, given Dan's intention to return and pay later, the requirements under *R* v *Allen* are not met and the offence does not appear to be made out.

Question 2

Peter was a house painter. He was contracted to paint a house for a particular fee and was given £50 with which to buy materials. Believing he had £50 at his home, Peter spent the £50 he was given on a suit. However, he discovered that his wife had spent the £50 at his home. Furious, he took his wife's favourite ring and threw it into a nearby river.

Peter visited his bank manager and told him that his wife was expecting their first baby, and he requested an overdraft facility of £50 to purchase some garments for the baby. The story was entirely untrue. His bank manager, however, readily agreed to the overdraft and added that there was no need for any explanation as to why it was required when the amount was so small. Peter cashed a cheque for £50 and bought the materials.

Peter met a friend, Brian, and told Brian that he was painting a house for charity and wondered whether Brian would like to assist him although, being a charitable work, there was no payment. Brian agreed to help and did do half the painting. Unknown to Peter, when the work was finished, Brian saw Peter being paid by the householder.

Brian kept silent but went around to Peter's house that evening, intent upon taking goods to the value of half what Peter had been paid. Peter's wife, Anne, let Brian in. Peter was out. Anne poured Brian a brandy and left the drawingroom to make some sandwiches for Brian. Whilst she was out of the room Brian finished off the bottle of brandy.

Discuss the criminal liability of Peter and Brian.

Adapted from University of London LLB Examination
(for External Students) Criminal Law June 1981 Q7

General comment

A straightforward examination of knowledge of the various elements of theft and burglary, and also deception.

Skeleton solution

Theft - 'appropriates', 'belonging to another', 'dishonestly' ss1-7 TA 68; burglary - enters as trespasser s9 TA 68; deception - obtaining property/services 15 TA 68 - s1 TA 78; obtaining pecuniary advantage s16 TA 68.

Suggested solution

Peter may have committed offences contrary to the Theft Act 1968 and the Theft Act 1978.

When Peter used the £50 given to him to buy materials in purchasing a suit he may have committed an offence contrary to s1 of the Theft Act 1968 which states that it will be an offence to dishonestly appropriate property belonging to another with the intention of permanently depriving the other of it. However, on the facts of the question, there may be difficulty in showing first of all that Peter was dishonest and secondly, that the property did belong to another. Section 5(3) states that where a person receives property from or on account of another and is under an obligation to the other to retain and deal with that property in a particular way, the property shall be regarded as belonging to the other. Therefore, s5(3) will be useful in showing that prima facie, there is the actus reus of theft. To come within the section it would have to be shown that there was an obligation to deal with that particular property in a certain way. If Peter received the payment as a straightforward advance of remuneration, it would be unlikely that he would come within the scope of the section. However, the money has been received to buy materials and it is therefore submitted that this will bring his act within the scope of the actus reus of theft. However, it should be noted that in *R v Hall* (1972) it was stated that the obligation had to be a legal obligation, although this appears to be satisfied on the facts in question. The requirement for a legal obligation was reiterated in *DPP v Huskinson* (1988).

As to the question of dishonesty, it would be open to Peter to claim the benefit of s2 of the Theft Act 1968 on the basis that he believed that he would have had the owner's consent if the owner knew of the appropriation and the circumstances of it. However, it has to be shown subjectively that Peter did have such a belief. If this cannot be shown then the usual rule will apply. In *R v Feely* (1973), it was stated that the question of dishonesty was one always to be left to the jury and the jury would apply the standard of the ordinary decent person. However if Peter raises his own subjective belief in the honesty of what he was doing the *R v Ghosh* (1982) direction must be given (*R v Price* (1990)), ie did Peter regard himself as dishonest by his own standards and are those standards shared by the community, or has he been dishonest by the standards of the ordinary man and is he aware of that standard?

At the time when he spent the £50 on the new suit, he may have committed a further offence contrary to s15 of the Theft Act 1968 in that he dishonestly obtained the property (the suit) by deception with intention to permanently deprive the other of it. The same test for dishonesty would apply as for s1 of the Theft Act except that in relation to an offence other than theft, he would not be able to claim the benefit of s2. To come within s15, it would have to be shown that he intentionally or recklessly deceived the vendor of the suit. The deception may be by words or conduct as to fact or as to law including his deception as to the present intention of the person using the deception or any other person s15(4). Furthermore, it is not just enough to show that there was a deception as to the ownership of the money, it has to be shown that the deception was the operative factor in him obtaining the goods: *R v Kovacs* (1974) The question of whether it was the operative cause is one of fact to be left to the jury: *R v King and Stockwell* (1987). Therefore, on the facts of the question, it would have to be shown that Peter intentionally or recklessly deceived by implying that the money was his and that the deception enabled him to obtain the suit ie, that the vendor would not have sold the suit to him if he had known that the money was not Peter's to use in this particular way.

Peter may have committed a further offence of theft when he threw his wife's favourite ring into a river. By virtue of s30(1) of the Theft Act 1968 husband and wife can steal or indeed, do any other offence within the Theft Act 1968 and 1978 in relation to the property of the other. The proceedings may be instituted by the injury spouse and therefore, on this basis, Peter's wife may prosecute him for stealing her property. Furthermore, she may give evidence for the prosecution at every stage of the proceedings. The elements necessary to show theft of the ring appear to be satisfied. There is an appropriation when he takes the ring and throws it into the river in that he will have assumed the right of an owner at that stage. The property belongs to another and therefore the actus reus is complete. Once again, the question of dishonesty is to be left to the jury: *R v Feely*. Furthermore, his conduct evidences an intention to permanently deprive in that he treats the ring as his own to dispose of regardless of the other's rights: s6(1).

Peter may commit an offence contrary to s16 of the Theft Act 1968 when he asks his bank manager for an overdraft facility. Section 16(1) provides that a person who by any deception dishonestly obtains for himself or another any pecuniary advantage shall commit an offence. A pecuniary advantage obtained by Peter is that within s16(2)(b) in that he was allowed to borrow by way of overdraft. However, once again there may be problems in showing that there was a complete offence. Certainly there is a deception within s15(4) made intentionally by Peter. Furthermore, he does obtain a pecuniary advantage within s16. However, there may be problems in showing that Peter does indeed obtain an overdraft by deception. It has to be shown that there is a causal link between the deception and the obtaining of the overdraft: *R v Kovacs* (1974) and *R v Collis-Smith* (1971). If he would have obtained the overdraft without the deception, then there cannot be an offence within s16 although there may be an attempt under the Criminal Attempts Act 1981 s1(3).

When Peter persuades Brian to assist in the painting of the house for charity, there is prima facie an offence within s1 of the Theft Act 1978 which states that a person who by any deception dishonestly obtains services from another, shall be guilty of an offence. However, there would be problems within s1(2) because it provides that there will only be an obtaining of services within s1(1), where the other is induced to confer a benefit by doing some act or causing or submitting some act to be done on the understanding that the benefit has been or will be paid. Because Brian has agreed to receive no renumeration, there will be no offence within the section.

Brian may be liable for attempted theft when he enters Peter's house intending to take property to the value of half what Peter had been paid. However, once again, there would be a number of problems in showing such an offence. First of all, it would have to be shown that Brian had mens rea within s1 of the Theft Act 1968, which defines theft as dishonestly appropriating property belonging to another with intention of permanently depriving that other. There is certainly an intention to permanently deprive but it would not be so easy to show that Brian was dishonest.

It may be that he could claim the benefit of s2 of the Theft Act 1968 in that he believed that he had the right in law to the property. If he cannot claim the benefit of s2, then the question of dishonesty is one to be left to the jury *R v Feely* (1973) and the *R v Ghosh* (1982) direction given. In *R v Woolven* (1983) it was held that such a direction should cover all occasions where a claim of a right in law was made although in *R v Wootton and Peake* (1990) the sufficiency of a *Ghosh* direction in such cases was questioned. It is the honesty of Brian's belief in such a case by which his 'dishonesty' will be determined and not the reasonableness of such a belief: *R v Holden* (1991).

As to the actus reus of theft, it would have to be shown that Brian had done an act which was more than simply an act of preparation and was so proximate to the commission of the offence that it would amount to an attempt. The question of whether an act is or is not proximate, is one always to be left to the jury: *DPP* v *Stonehouse* (1978). However, as Brian has not got in mind to steal particular items, but simply stating that Brian attempted to steal from the contents of the house, the charge should be successful: *R* v *Easom* (1971); *Attorney-General's References (Nos 1 and 2 of 1979)* (1979).

It is necessary to consider whether s9 of the Theft Act 1968, is applicable. Section 9 of the Theft Act 1968, provides that a person is guilty of burglary, if:

1) he enters the building or part of the building as a trespasser with intent to steal, causing grievous bodily harm, rape or do criminal damage; or

2) having entered any building or part of a building as a trespasser, he steals or attempts to steal anything in the building or inflict or attempt to inflict on any person therein any grievous bodily harm.

The most obvious problem here would be whether Brian had entered as a trespasser or as an invitee. It could be argued that because Brian had the intention of taking property when he came into the building, he did indeed enter as a trespasser. If this view is correct, then providing what he intended to do would have amounted to theft, then he would commit an offence within s9(1)(a) in that he entered, as a trespasser, with intent to steal: *R* v *Jones and Smith* (1976).

If the entry were established as trespassary then, having so entered, Brian may commit a further offence of theft by drinking the contents of the bottle of brandy while Anne was out of the room. Certainly, he has appropriated property belonging to another with intention to permanently deprive. However, once again, it would have to be shown that there was dishonesty and Brian may be able to invoke s2 again, based on the fact that Anne has already given him some of the brandy.

Question 3

Lionel was blind. He drew his old age pension from the post office and Nina, the village postmistress, by mistake gave him £1 too much. Lionel was unaware of this fact till later when shopping he discovered the additional note. He used it to buy extra meat.

Lionel purchased groceries from Morgan's market stall. The bill came to £4 and Lionel presented a £10 note saying, 'This is a fiver. Don't forget my change.' Morgan gave Lionel £1 change.

When talking home Lionel stopped for a rest in the park. He put his basket on the park bench beside him. Orlando, aged 13 years, who was sitting on the seat removed one of Lionel's apples and threw it to his friend Paul, who was playing nearby. Lionel suspected that something had happened when he heard Orlando laugh.

Advise Lionel, Orlando and Paul.

Adapted from University of London LLB Examination
(for External Students) Criminal Law June 1982 Q6

CRIMINAL LAW

General comment

Although the question requires the student to 'advise Lionel, Orlando and Paul' it is necessary to include in the answer the possible liability of Morgan as this would be included as part of the advice to Lionel.

The issues involved are fairly straightforward and primarily concern offences against property. In view of the case law on the point a student should be able to give a very detailed explanation of the controversy surrounding the test to be applied in ascertaining 'dishonesty'.

Skeleton solution

Theft - ss1-7 TA 1968; 'dishonestly', 'appropriates', obtaining property by deception s15 TA 1968.

Suggested solution

When Lionel uses the £1 given to him by mistake he may commit an offence contrary to s1 of the Theft Act 1968. Section 1 states that 'a person is guilty of theft if he dishonestly appropriates property belonging to another with the intention of permanently depriving the other of it'. The two elements of theft which require particular consideration in this instance are: 'belonging to another' and 'dishonesty'.

Under s5(4) where a person gets property by another's mistake, and is under an obligation to make restoration of the property, then to the extent of that obligation the property shall be regarded as belonging to the person entitled to restoration, and an intention not to make restoration shall be regarded as an intention to deprive that person of the property. In *R* v *Gilks* (1972) it was stated that the word 'obligation' in s5(4) means a legal obligation. it is not sufficient simply to show a moral or social obligation. However, on the facts of the question it would seem that the £1 paid in error still belonging to Nina, and at the time when he used the money to purchase extra meat, he 'appropriated property belonging to another'. If this were so there would be no need to rely on s5(4).

The question of 'dishonesty' is one to be left to the jury unless Lionel can claim to have held one of the beliefs contained in s2. Section 2 outlines three situations where an accused would not be dishonest. However, it does not give any positive guidance as to what will amount to dishonesty. In *R* v *Feely* (1973) the Court of Appeal held that it was for the jury to decide in each case what the accused's state of mind was and whether or not that amounted to a dishonest state of mind. However, there has been much debate as to whether a jury, in making that decision, should apply an objective standard, ie that of the ordinary, decent person, or whether they should take into account the subjective views of the accused as to whether or not he is dishonest. In *R* v *McIvor* (1982) the Court of Appeal stated that dishonesty could be established independently of the knowledge or belief of the defendant, ie they supported an objective test although the jury could consider the defendant's evidence as to his state of mind at the time of the alleged offence in making their decision.

The question of dishonesty was again considered by the Court of Appeal a few weeks after *R* v *McIvor* in the case of *R* v *Ghosh* (1982). Judgment in this case was given by the Lord Chief Justice who took a rather different approach from that in *R* v *McIvor*. The Lord Chief Justice considered that by seeking to reconcile an objective and a subjective approach, *R* v *McIvor* was seeking to reconcile the irreconcilable. It was, therefore, necessary to choose between the two alternative views, and the test to be applied was subjective.

'In determining whether the prosecution had proved the person charged was acting dishonestly, a jury had first of all to decide whether, according to the ordinary standards of reasonable and honest people, what was done was dishonest. If it was not dishonest by those standards, that was the end of the matter and the prosecution failed.

If it was dishonest by those standards then the jury had to consider whether the person charged himself must have realised that what he was doing was by those standards dishonest. In most cases, where the actions were obviously dishonest by ordinary standards there would be no doubt about it. It would be obvious that the person charged himself knew that he was acting dishonestly.' However the Court of Appeal has stated that the *Ghosh* direction need not be given in every case where dishonesty is in issue: *R* v *Spencer and Turner* (1989), and that in some cases it may even be misleading to do so: *R* v *Price* (1990). It is only necessary where D is saying in his defence 'I thought that what I was doing was honest but other people and the majority of people might think that it was not honest' (per Lord Lane CJ in *Price*).

It could be argued that there is a further offence under s15 of the Theft Act 1968 when by deception Lionel dishonestly obtains property belonging to another with the intention of permanently depriving that other of the property. Section 15(4) defines 'deception' to include any deception (whether deliberate or reckless) by words or conduct, as to fact or as to law. The question to be considered here was whether Lionel impliedly deceived by using the money which was not his to use to purchase meat. Furthermore, it must be shown that the deception was 'operative', ie that he would not have obtained the property had it not been for the deception: *R* v *Clucas* (1949); *R* v *Rashid* (1977).

Lionel should be advised that when Morgan keeps the extra £5 change which belonged to Lionel, he has committed an offence contrary to s1 of the Theft Act 1968 providing that the jury are satisfied that the taking was a dishonest appropriation. Certainly, there is a mistake on Lionel's part, and it will be possible to argue that s5(4) is applicable in this situation also. However, it may be unnecessary in this case to apply s5(4) as it could be argued that property in the £5 never passed to Morgan at all, and therefore, irrespective of s5(4), he was appropriating property belonging to another.

It is unlikely that Morgan's silence will amount to a 'deception' and his moral duty to tell Lionel that the note is actually a ten pound note will probably not be translated into a legal duty, although it is arguable on the principles of *DPP* v *Ray* (1974) that his actions in giving Lionel change for a £5 note may well support a charge of deception.

When Orlando removes the apple from Lionel's basket he is committing the actus reus of theft, in that he is appropriating property belonging to another. 'Appropriation' is defined in s3 of the Theft Act 1968 and requires an assumption of the rights of an owner. Certainly this has been satisfied in this situation, although it is possible that Orlando was not dishonest and/or did not have an intention to permanently deprive. It is unclear from the question whether Orlando and Paul are taking part in a prank. Obviously, this would be important in deciding whether or not they were dishonest. If the jury were satisfied that Orlando did have the necessary dishonest intention to permanently deprive, then the elements of theft are satisfied. It could be argued that Paul was also involved in the theft in that he aided and abetted the offence committed by Orlando who was the principal offender. To be an aider and abettor, he has to be present, assisting or encouraging at the scene of the offence: *R* v *Coney* (1882). Furthermore, he must have full knowledge of all the circumstances of the offence: *Johnson* v *Youden* (1950).

It could be argued that Paul was not involved in the initial theft. However, he may still commit an offence contrary to s22 of the Theft Act 1968 if he dishonestly receives stolen goods for his own benefit, knowing or believing them to be stolen. Providing that Orlando has satisfied all the necessary elements of theft, then the apple that he removed will be within the definition of 'stolen goods' which includes goods taken contrary to s1 of the Theft Act 1968. However, before there could be any liability under s22, it must be shown that the original theft is complete.

Orlando is 13 years old, and therefore, before he may be liable for any criminal offence the jury must be satisfied that as well as having the ordinary mens rea necessary for the particular offence involved, that he has the extra element of 'mischievous discretion'. Indeed, children over ten and under 14 years of age are exempt from criminal responsibility unless it is proved that they have this additional element of mischievous discretion which involves a comprehension of right and wrong. There is no information given as to Paul's age. However if he were to be between ten and 14, the same principles would apply. If he were under ten years old, then in no circumstances could he be liable for a criminal offence. If he was 14 years or more, then he would be liable as an adult although the sentences in respect of juvenile offences may be different.

Question 4

Stan got out of his friend's car and walked up to the front door of a house which he believed to be his. In fact he was in the wrong street although the houses were identical. Failing to make the key work, Stan attempted to climb a drain pipe but finally opened an insecure window and let himself in. When inside Stan realised that he was in the wrong house. He picked up a coat hanging in the hallway because it had started to rain and walked home. Stan left the door wide open and a group of teenagers saw this and entered the house. Once in the house, they drank the alcohol and played the records which were on the premises.

One of the teenagers was Stan's 13 year old daughter Tina who had played most of the records and now felt guilty about what she had done.

Advise Stan and Tina of their criminal liability if any.

Adapted from University of London LLB Examination
(for External Students) Criminal Law June 1982 Q7

General comment

The question is a straightforward test of the elements of burglary and having only two defendants, is uncomplicated in comparison with some other examination questions.

Skeleton solution

Burglary s9(1)(a) and (b) TA 1968; Theft ss1-7 TA 1968; conditional intention; mistake.

Suggested solution

When advising Stan of his criminal liability it is necessary to consider burglary under s9(1)(a) and 9(1)(b) of the Theft Act 1968.

Under s9(1) of the Theft Act 1968 a person is guilty of burglary if:

a) he enters any building or part of a building as a trespasser with intent to steal, or to rape or to cause grievous bodily harm or to do criminal damage; or

b) having entered any part of a building as a trespasser he steals or attempts to steal anything in that building or part of it or inflicts or attempts to inflict on any person therein any grievous bodily harm.

Certainly Stan performs the actus reus of the offence contained in s9(1)(a) when he enters the building as a trespasser. There is no doubt that he has performed a 'substantial' entry as required by *R* v *Collins* (1973). However, in *R* v *Collins* it was stated that it was not sufficient that the accused was a trespasser in civil law. The accused must know or be reckless as to the facts which make him a trespasser for the purposes of s9. Certainly Stan does not 'intend' to enter the building as a trespasser as he believes it to be his own. However, it could be argued that he is 'reckless' as to the facts which make him a trespasser. Under the definition of 'recklessness' contained in *MPC* v *Caldwell* (1982); a person may be reckless notwithstanding that they are unaware of the particular risk that their actions have created. However, even though these elements of burglary may be satisfied, Stan does not have any of the necessary particular intentions under s9(1)(a), ie to steal, to rape, to inflict grievous bodily harm or to do criminal damage.

Stan's mistake may in fact negative any mens rea required for the offence and, if so, then it is a defence: *DPP* v *Morgan* (1976); *Beckford* v *R* (1987).

This is not so much a defence but more of a failure to meet the basic requirements of mens rea for the offence.

Once Stan enters the house and realises his mistake he may commit an offence contrary to s9(1)(b) of the Theft Act 1968 when he removes the coat from the hallway. He will commit such an offence if it can be shown that having entered the building as a trespasser he steals.

Section 1 of the Theft Act states that a person is guilty of theft if he dishonestly appropriates property belonging to another with the intention of permanently depriving the other of it. Certainly there is the actus reus of theft because by picking up the coat and using it he has assumed the rights of an owner over it s3 Theft Act 1968. However, he must be acting dishonestly and with an intention to permanently deprive. Dishonestly is partially defined under s2 of the Theft Act 1968 so that if he believes that the owner would consent or if he believed that he had a right in law or, if he believed that the owner could not be found taking reasonable steps, then he will not be dishonest. However, it seems unlikely that Stan would come within any of these situations and therefore, it would be for a jury to decide whether or not he was dishonest: *R* v *Feely* (1973). In *R* v *Ghosh* (1982) the Court of Appeal stated that the test to be applied by the jury in making their decision was the subjective test. Nevertheless, a person would be dishonest notwithstanding that he believed that he was morally justified in acting as he had acted if he realised that ordinary people would consider his actions to be dishonest.

Providing all the elements of theft are satisfied then it would seem that s9(1)(b) burglary is shown. The fact that he did not realise that he was a trespasser until after he had gained entry is immaterial because he performed the necessary actus reus of entry as a trespasser and at the time when the theft occurred he had all the necessary mens rea as to the trespass.

Tina should be advised that she may be liable for the offences of burglary and theft under 9(1)(a) of the Theft Act 1968 the offence of burglary is committed if a person enters a building as a trespasser with intent to steal. It is not necessary that the accused has a particular item in mind or that the item that he intended to steal was not in fact there: *R* v *Walkington* (1979) and *Attorney-General's References (Nos 1 and 2 of 1979)* (1979). All that must be shown is that there is a general intention to steal and the indictment may be drafted in broad terms without particularising any item. On this basis, if Tina went into the house intending to take anything that she liked, then she may commit an offence contrary to s9(1)(a). Similarly, an offence could be committed under s9(1)(a) if she had the necessary mens rea to commit criminal damage as she went into the house.

An offence contrary to s9(1)(b) of the Theft Act 1968 may be shown when having entered the building as a trespasser, she stole or attempted to steal. On the facts in question it appears that by drinking the alcohol she has appropriated property belonging to another with the intention of permanently depriving the other of the property. Certainly, by drinking the substance, she has 'assumed the rights of an owner' over it. However, it would be for the jury to decide whether or not her appropriation was dishonest. It should, however, be noted that the fact that Tina felt guilty during the intrusion may indicate that she recognised that the ordinary person would find her conduct dishonest and if this were the case, then she would be dishonest under the principles outlined in *R* v *Ghosh* (1982).

By playing the records, Tina has assumed the rights of an owner over them, furthermore, it may be a dishonest appropriation. Nevertheless on the facts it would appear there is no offence of theft contrary to s1 of the Theft Act 1968 because she lacks the necessary intention to permanently deprive the owner.

Unlawfully using the householder's electricity will not amount to theft, either to support the substantive offence or to show a s9(1)(b) burglary. It is however a separate offence of abstracting under s13 of the Theft Act 1968.

Tina is 13 years old and may therefore be able to claim the defence of infancy. Children under ten years old are entirely exempt from criminal responsibility, however, children between the ages of ten and under 14 may be criminally responsible but only if it can be shown that that child has 'mischievous discretion'.

Proof of mischievous discretion involves showing that the child comprehends the difference between good and bad, right and wrong, at the time of the committing of the offence. The fact that Tina felt guilty during the time of the intrusion was being committed is an indicator that she did indeed have 'mischievous discretion'.

Question 5

Xeres took a spear from Zepher's house. Zepher was not at home when Xeres removed it. Whilst using the spear, Xeres broke it. Till then Xeres had intended to return it.

Xeres went to a public baths where he was bathed by slaves. He left without paying as was the usual custom. From Berclay, Xeres borrowed £100 intending never to repay it.

Advise Xeres. Would your advice differ if he had decided not to repay Berclay after receiving the money?

Adapted from University of London LLB Examination
(for External Students) Criminal Law June 1982 Q9

General comment

This question involves a number of offences under the Theft Act 1968 and the Theft Act 1978. It is quite a straightforward question but it does require detailed knowledge and explanation of the definitions of the various offences together with supporting case law.

Skeleton solution

Burglary - s9(1)(a) and (b) TA 1968; theft - ss1-7 TA 1968 'appropriates'; making off without payment s3 TA 1978; obtaining a service by deception s1 TA 1978; obtaining property by deception s15 TA 1968.

Suggested solution

When Xeres removes a spear from Zepher's house he may commit offences contrary to s9(1)(a) and s9(1)(b) of the Theft Act 1968.

107

Under s9 a person is guilty of burglary if:

a) he enters any building or part of a building as a trespasser with intent to steal, or inflict grievous bodily harm, or rape any woman therein, or do criminal damage; or

b) having entered any building or part of a building as a trespasser he steals or attempts to steal anything in the building or part of it or inflicts or attempts to inflict grievous bodily harm on any person therein.

There are two aspects of burglary which would have to be particularly considered in relation to the facts in the question. Firstly, was Xeres a trespasser and did he have the necessary intention or recklessness as to the facts which made him a trespasser? *R v Collins* (1973). If he believed on reasonable grounds that Zepher would have consented to him entering to remove the article, then he may not have the necessary mens rea as to the trespass which is required for an offence contrary to s9.

Secondly, for an offence under s9(1)(a) it must be shown that Xeres had intention to steal as he entered and s9(1)(b) it must be shown that the taking of the spear amounted to theft or attempted theft.

Section 1 of the Theft Act 1968 states the person is guilty of theft if he dishonestly appropriates property belonging to another with the intention of permanently depriving the other of it. Certainly, Xeres had appropriated property belonging to another in that he has assumed the rights of an owner over that property. There may be more difficulty in showing that he has the necessary mens rea. 'Dishonesty' is not defined for the purposes of the Theft Acts although s2 states that a person's appropriation of property belonging to another is not to be regarded as dishonest if he appropriates the property in a belief that he would have the owner's consent if the other knew of the appropriation and the circumstances of it. This is a subjective test and providing Xeres honestly held that view it is immaterial that it turned out to be incorrect. In the event of s2 not applying, then it is for the jury to decide whether or not the taking was dishonest: *R v Feely* (1973). In the case of *R v Ghosh* (1982) the Court of Appeal stated that a subjective test was to be applied by the jury in deciding dishonesty, nevertheless a person should be regarded as being dishonest if that person subjectively appreciated that the ordinary person would find the conduct dishonest even though he himself did not believe it as such. The element of theft which appears not to be satisfied is that of 'intention to permanently deprive'. As with dishonesty, there is no definition of an intention to permanently deprive under the Theft Acts. It is for the jury to decide whether an accused has the necessary intention. Section 6 of the Theft Act 1968 gives two examples of what can amount to an intention to permanently deprive. Under s6(1) a person appropriating property belonging to another without meaning the other permanently to lose the thing itself is nevertheless to be regarded as having an intention to permanently deprive the other of it if his intention is to keep the thing as his own to dispose of regardless of the other's rights, and the borrowing or lending of it may amount to so using, if, but only if, the borrowing or lending is for a period and in circumstances making it equivalent to an outright taking or disposal. On the facts of the question it seems unlikely that Xeres had the necessary intention to treat it as his own when he removed the spear because at that time he intended to return it. When Xeres decided not to return it, it could be argued that there is no offence because the mens rea and actus reus do not coincide. However, by s3(1) Theft Act 1968 a later assumption of rights after an initial innocent taking may amount to theft.

The next situation to be considered is when Xeres goes to the public bath and leaves without paying. It is unclear whether the usual custom was to pay or to leave without paying. Obviously, if the usual custom was to leave without paying then Xeres will perform no offence by following what was the usual custom. However, if the usual custom was to pay on leaving then Xeres may commit an offence contrary to s3 of the Theft Act 1978 when he dishonestly makes off without having paid knowing that payment on the spot for goods supplied or services done is required or expected of him, intending not to pay.

Xeres must know that such payment is required and he must be shown to be dishonest and also shown to have intended permanently to avoid paying: *R v Allen* (1985).

Furthermore, if Xeres had decided not to pay before he went into the baths then he may commit an offence contrary to s1 of the Theft Act 1978 in that he dishonestly obtained services by deception. Section 1(2) states that there will only be an obtaining of services where the other is induced to confer a benefit by doing some act on the understanding that the benefit has been or will be paid for. If Xeres had decided not to pay before he went into the public baths then he will be impliedly deceiving by conduct within the definition of deception contained in s15(4) of the Theft Act 1968: *DPP v Ray* (1974).

However, it must be shown that the deception was operative, ie that he would not have been provided with the service had it not been for the deception: *R v Clucas* (1949).

Both ss1 and 3 of the Theft Act 1978 require the action of the accused to be 'dishonest'. The test to be applied has been previously outlined. However, s2 of the Theft Act 1968 is not applicable to offences other than theft, and therefore, the question of dishonesty is to be left entirely to the jury in all circumstances.

When Xeres borrows money from Berclay intending never to repay it, he may commit an offence contrary to s15 of the Theft Act 1968 in that he has by deception dishonestly obtained property belonging to another for the intention of permanently depriving the other of it.

Under s15(4) the term 'deception' means any deception (whether deliberate or reckless) by words or conduct as to fact or as to law. There is an intentional implied deception on the part of Xeres as he clearly had no intention of carrying out his promise at the time he made it. Furthermore, it seems that there is no doubt that deception was the operative factor in obtaining the property. The fact that the property is money creates no problem under s15 as the definition of 'property' contained in s4 of the Theft Act 1968 includes money.

It is necessary to consider the overlap between s15 and s1 of the Theft Act 1968. In *Lawrence v Metropolitan Police Commissioner* (1971) the Court of Appeal stated that whenever the defence contained in s15 was shown there was automatically an offence contrary to s1 of the Theft Act at the same time. This view was not altogether reflected in the House of Lords judgment in *Lawrence v MPC* where it was stated that in certain circumstances there would be an overlap between s15 and s1 but it would not occur in all situations. It has been suggested that the overlap between s15 and s1 would only occur where ownership remained in the original party and that it would not be a direct overlap where by deception the accused claimed ownership, possession and control. On the facts of the question it seems that ownership of that money had passed to Xeres there being no intention that that particular £100 be repaid to Berclay. If this were the case then s15 would apply on its own, although if the Court of Appeal judgment were to be applied literally then a s1 offence would also be shown.

If Xeres decided not to pay Berclay until after receiving the money then there would be no offence contrary to s15 at the time when the money was borrowed. However, an existing liability had been created and if Xeres used any deception to avoid repaying the liability, then he may commit an offence contrary to s2 of the Theft Act 1978.

Section 2(1) states that a person commits an offence when by deception he:

a) dishonestly secures the remission of the whole or part of any existing liability; or

b) with intent to make permanent default in whole or in part of any existing liability to make payment dishonestly induces the creditor to wait for the payment or to forego the payment.

Section 2(1)(a) requires the deception to induce Berclay to consent to the remission of the whole or part of the existing liability, ie it requires the consensus.

Section 2(1)(b) can be satisfied where a party does an unilateral act which does amount to a deception for example, where he gives a cheque which he knows is not going to be met.

Until there is a further deception after Xeres has decided not to repay the money there will be no offence on the facts as given.

Question 6

Russell went to his local self-service garage and filled his car with ten gallons of petrol. On the pump was a notice that property in the garage was not to pass till the petrol was paid for. Russell who had only limited cash with him, saw that the forecourt attendant's attention was elsewhere, so he started to drive off to avoid payment. Before leaving the forecourt he changed his mind, stopped the car and went to the attendant. He explained the position and the attendant reluctantly agreed to accept a cheque without a banker's card in full settlement. The cheque was dishonoured because of insufficiency of funds due to the fact that Russell's wife had drawn out a lot of money from their joint account without telling Russell.

Russell decided to purchase some oil and offered the attendant a £1 note. The attendant gave Russell change for a £5 note. Russell realised this but because of the assistant's unhelpful attitude he decided to say nothing. He resolved not to spend the excess change and left in his car. Had he been asked for it, he would have given it up.

Advise Russell about his criminal liability.

University of London LLB Examination
(for External Students) Criminal Law June 1983 Q9

General comment

A detailed but straightforward question on the Theft Acts in which a well-prepared student could obtain very good marks.

Skeleton solution

Making off without payment s3 TA 1978; obtaining property by deception s15 TA 1968; Deception - evasion of liability s2 TA 1978; Theft ss1-7 TA 1968.

Suggested solution

Russell should be advised that by starting to drive off from the garage without having paid for the petrol he may have committed an offence contrary to s3 of the Theft Act 1978. Under s3 a person who knowing that payment on the spot for any goods supplied or service done is required or expected from him dishonestly makes off without having paid as required or expected and with intent to avoid payment of the amount due shall be guilty of an offence.

Under s3 there is no requirement that any party be deceived in order to enable an accused to make off, but it must be shown that the accused acted dishonestly and intended to avoid payment, not simply to delay it: *R* v *Allen* (1985).

The question of dishonesty is always for the jury to decide: *R* v *Feely* (1973). In *R* v *Ghosh* (1982) the Court of Appeal considered the various cases concerning dishonesty and concluded that the test to be applied in all cases was subjective. However, it was not subjective in the sense that if an accused felt he was not dishonest he would not be liable. The test was whether firstly the jury was satisfied that according to the standards of the ordinary man, what was done was dishonest. If it was not dishonest by those standards that was the end of the matter and the prosecution failed. If, however, it was dishonest by those standards then the jury had to consider whether the person charged must himself have realised that what he was doing by those standards was dishonest. Furthermore, it is dishonest for a person to act in a way which he knows ordinary people consider to be dishonest, even if he genuinely believes that he is morally justified in acting as he does.

Applying those cases to the facts in question it would seem that the mens rea required under s3 may well be satisfied. However, the actus reus of the offence may not be made out because it could be argued that Russell had not 'made off' but merely attempted to make off. In *R* v *McDavitt* (1981) it was held that as the accused had not actually left the spot he had not 'made off' although the jury could return a verdict of attempt.

The need to show a 'making off' was reiterated in *R* v *Allen* (1985). In *R* v *Brooks and Brooks* (1982) the Court of Appeal considered that the words 'dishonesty makes off' were easily understandable by any jury and therefore in the majority of cases required no elaboration in summing up. However, in a case where an accused was stopped before passing the spot where payment was required a jury should be directed that that might constitute an attempt.

On the facts in question, although Russell was not stopped but rather had a change of heart, it could be argued that until he had left the premises he had not 'made off' but had merely attempted the offence. Under s1 of the Criminal Attempts Act 1981 there will be an attempt to commit an offence provided an accused has done an act 'more than merely preparatory' to the full offence accompanied by the necessary full mens rea for the offence. It is for the jury to decide whether the accused's conduct has satisfied the test contained in s1: *DPP* v *Stonehouse* (1977). Furthermore, the fact that Russell has a change of heart will in no way negative his liability providing the attempt elements were satisfied.

Although s3 of the Theft Act 1978 is the most likely offence to be shown on the facts in question Russell may commit other offences under the Theft Act. If he intended not to pay before he went into the garage he may have committed an offence contrary to s15 of the Theft Act 1968. Under s15 it is an offence dishonestly by any deception to obtain property belonging to another intending to permanently deprive. The deception may be intentional or reckless by words or by conduct, express or implied, s15(4). However, it must be shown that the deception was the operative factor (in obtaining the property here) and that the deception operated on a human mind. Therefore unless the attendant saw Russell coming into the self-service garage to take petrol and therefore assumed that he was going to pay, there would be no operative deception.

The fact that on the pump there was a notice saying that property was not to pass until the petrol was paid for means that Russell should be advised that he may face a charge of theft contrary to s1 of the Theft Act 1968. The general rule in relation to self-service garages is that property in the petrol passes to the customer on delivery: *Edwards* v *Ddin* (1976).

If Russell had the necessary dishonest intention permanently to deprive the garage at that stage, the offence of theft may be complete. The fact that Russell was doing something he was authorised by the garage to do would not relieve him of responsibility: *Lawrence* v *Metropolitan Police Commissioner* (1971) and *R* v *Morris* (1984). However, it would have to be shown that he had the necessary mens rea at the time of putting the petrol in the car. If he formed the mens rea after the petrol was put into the car and if the notice were effective, then it could be argued that at the time he drove off there was an appropriation of property belonging to another with a dishonest intention permanently to deprive. Under s3(1) of the Theft Act 1968 there is an appropriation where there is any assumption by the person of the rights of an owner and this includes a later assumption where that person had originally come by the property (innocently or not) without stealing it. In *R* v *Morris* the court considered that it was unnecessary for the prosecution to prove that the defendant had assumed all the rights of the owner.

When Russell gives a cheque to the attendant which later is dishonoured it seems probable that he commits no offence under s15. At the time when he gives the cheque he is impliedly warranting that the cheque will be met on presentation: *Metropolitan Police Commissioner* v *Charles* (1977). However, on the facts in question it seems that Russell believes that it would be met. Under s2(1)(b) of the Theft Act 1978 it is an offence dishonestly by deception to induce a creditor to wait for payment or forego payment of an existing liability with intent to make permanent default. On the facts this offence is not shown as there is no intention to default. Under s15(4) Theft Act 1968 'deception' means any deception (whether deliberate or reckless) by words or conduct as to fact or as to law including the deception as to the present intentions of the person using the deception.

It is arguable that Russell does not obtain the petrol by his presentation of the cheque and that any deception in relation thereto would more appropriately fall under s2 of the 1978 Theft Act as the deception comes after the liability to pay has been incurred.

Certainly it appears that Russell is not intentional in his deception. However, it could be argued that perhaps he was reckless as to whether or not the cheque would be met. Recklessness would be shown if he knew there would be a risk, or closed his eyes to what would to the ordinary man be an obvious risk that the cheque might not be met. However, even if this element to the offence were found to be satisfied, it seems very unlikely on the facts in question that he would have satisfied the necessary 'dishonest' state of mind.

When Russell keeps the excess change given to him by the garage assistant he may commit a further offence of theft contrary to s1 of the Theft Act 1968. As already stated the actus reus of the theft is an 'appropriation of the property belonging to another'. The problem here is whether the property belongs to another or whether ownership has passed to Russell. If the mistake were 'fundamental' then it could be argued that there had been no intention to pass ownership to Russell. However, it would appear more likely that the attendant had intended to give that amount of money to Russell acting on a mistake of fact. If this is the case then ownership will have passed to Russell.

A charge of theft may still be satisfied if it is possible to apply s5(4) of the Theft Act 1968. This subsection provides 'where a person gets property by another's mistake and is under an obligation to make restoration (in whole or in part) of the property then to the extent of that obligation the property or proceeds shall be regarded (as against him) as belonging to the person entitled to restoration, and the intention not to make restoration shall be regarded accordingly as an intention to permanently deprive that person of the property or proceeds'.

A most difficult point to decide is when there is 'an obligation to make restoration of the property'. This is decided according to principles of civil law, although an important aspect of quasi-contractual liability is that of repaying money where it is received as a result of the payer's mistake of facts and therefore it could be argued that there is an obligation to make restoration on the facts in question. It would seem that in order to amount to an obligation under s5(4) it must be a legal obligation to make restoration not simply a moral obligation: *R* v *Gilks*(1972).

It seems therefore that Russell, simply by keeping the excess change given to him, which indeed may belong to him in law, may commit the actus reus of theft by appropriation of property which because of the application of s5(4) belongs to another. It must now be considered whether he has the necessary mens rea to satisfy s1. The test for dishonesty has already been outlined, see *R* v *Feely* (1973) and *R* v *Ghosh* (1982). However, it should be remembered that in certain circumstances where there is a charge of theft, the jury must find that an accused is not dishonest. These circumstances are outlined in s2 of the Theft Act 1968 and include a situation where an accused believes he has the right in law to deprive the other of the property. If Russell believed he had a right to keep the property then he will not be dishonest and must be acquitted of any charge of theft. Such a belief must be honestly held and the reasonableness or otherwise of that belief is irrelevant to the issue of 'dishonesty': *R* v *Holden* (1991). However, if that belief is not present it is for the jury to decide in accordance with the case law already outlined and the jury must be directed on the specific provisions of s2: *R* v *Wootton and Peake* (1990).

There is no definition of 'an intention permanently to deprive' under the Theft Act. Under s6 of the Theft Act 1968 there are two examples of circumstances which would amount to an intention permanently to deprive. However, it would seem likely that on the facts in question even though Russell had no intention to spend the excess change and indeed would have given it up had he been asked for it, simply by keeping it when he could have returned it he is in effect treating it as his own and so long as he intends to keep it over a period then he may well have satisfied this element of theft. Ultimately, however, it would be for a jury to decide on this point.

Question 7

A who was 15 years old represented he was 14 years old and as a result obtained half-price admission to a local cinema. The ticket seller knew that A was 15 years old but despite instructions from her employer did not insist on full payment.

In the cinema, B an ice-cream vendor, gave A incorrect change. A had presented a £1 note but B believed that A had given a £5 note for his ice-cream. A thrust the change - which was all in coins - into his pocket without looking at them. It was only later he realised he had excess change.

A found a sealed box on the floor of the cinema. He put it in his pocket and forgot about it.

Advise A of his criminal liability.

Adapted from University of London LLB Examination (for External Students) Criminal Law June 1984 Q8

General comment

A more general question and one from which a reasonably well prepared student should be able to pick up good marks. The scope of the question includes the Theft Act 1968 s1 and s9, the Theft Act 1978 s1 and s2.

Skeleton solution

Deception - obtaining services s1 TA 1978; evading liability s2 TA 1978; attempted deception Criminal Attempts Act 1981; burglary s9 TA 1968.

Suggested solution

When A aged 15 represents that he is 14 years old in order to gain half-price admission to the local cinema there is a deception for the purposes of s1 and s2 of the theft Act 1978. Under s15(4) of the Theft Act 1968 'deception' means any deception (whether deliberate or reckless) by words or conduct as to fact or as to law including a deception as to the present intention of the person using the deception or any other person. On the facts in question there is a deliberate deception by words as to facts. Section 1 of the Theft Act 1978 provides that where a person by any deception dishonestly obtains services from another he shall be guilty of an offence. Under s1(2) of the Theft Act 1978 it is an obtaining of services where the other is induced to confer a benefit by doing some act or causing or permitting some act to be done on the understanding that the benefit has been or will be paid for.

Under s2(1)(c) of the Theft Act 1978 a person commits an offence where by any deception he dishonestly obtains any exemption from or abatement of liability to make a payment.

On the facts in question the ticket seller is not deceived and therefore the full offence will not be shown. However, it seems that A will have satisfied the requirements for an attempt to commit a s1 and a s2(1)(c) offence under the Theft Act 1978. In *R v Hensler* (1870) the accused wrote a begging letter to P containing a number of lies. P was not deceived but nevertheless sent some money. The accused was convicted of an attempt to obtain the money by false pretences.

Under the Criminal Attempts Act 1981 the jury must be satisfied that A has done an act 'more than merely preparatory': *DPP v Stonehouse* (1977). The mens rea for an attempt is generally the same as for the full offence. However, to result in crime it is necessary to show that the accused intended the consequences contained within the actus reus of any particular offence. Therefore on the facts in question it would have to be shown that as well as having the necessary mens rea towards the deception he intended to obtain the service by deception or to evade liability by deception. Also it is necessary to show that he was acting dishonestly.

It is for the jury to decide whether or not the accused is acting dishonestly *R v Feely* (1973) and the test to be applied is that stated in *R v Ghosh* (1982). The jury has first of all to decide whether according to the ordinary standards of reasonable, honest people what was done was dishonest. If it was not dishonest by those standards that is the end of the matter and the accused must be acquitted. If it was dishonest by those standards then the jury has to go on to consider whether the person charged must have realised that what he was doing was by those standards dishonest. Furthermore, a person will still be dishonest if he knew the ordinary person would consider his conduct to be dishonest even if he asserted or genuinely believed that he was morally justified in acting as he did.

When A gained entry into the cinema it is necessary to consider in the light of what happens later whether or not he enters as a trespasser. In order to be a trespasser for the purposes of s9 of the Theft Act 1968 it is insufficient to show that the accused is a trespasser in civil law; it is also necessary to show that he knew or was reckless as to the facts which made him a trespasser. The point is not clear on the facts in this question as theoretically the ticket seller has permitted A to enter the building even though he has not paid the proper ticket price. However, as the ticket seller was acting contrary to her employer's instructions it may be that her permission would be insufficient and that A still entered as a trespasser for the purposes of s9: *R* v *Collins* (1973).

When A realises he has excess change he may commit an offence under s1 of the Theft Act 1968. The actus reus of theft provides that there must be an appropriation of property belonging to another. Under s3 of the Theft Act 1968 any assumption by a person of the rights of the owner amounts to an appropriation and this includes where he has come by the property (innocently or not) without stealing it and makes any later assumption of a right to it by keeping or dealing with it as the owner, as this would amount to an innocent taking. However, there would be a later assumption of a right by keeping it when he realises he has the excess change.

Section 5(1) and s5(4) of the Theft Act 1968 should be examined when considering whether or not the property 'belongs' to another. Under s5(1) property shall be regarded as belonging to any person having possession or control of it or having any proprietary right or interest to or in it. If the ice cream vendor retained ownership of the money then s5(1) would be the appropriate section to consider in relation to property 'belonging to another'. However, on the facts it would seem that ownership of the money has passed to A and therefore the appropriate section to consider is s5(4) which provides that where a person gets property by another's mistake and is under an obligation to make restoration (in whole or in part) of the property then to the extent of that obligation the property or proceeds shall be regarded (as against him) as belonging to the person entitled to restoration, and an intention not to make restoration shall be regarded accordingly as an intention permanently to deprive that person of the property or proceeds. 'Obligation' means a legally enforceable obligation: *R* v *Gilks* (1972). This would seem to be the appropriate section in relation to the facts of the question. It would therefore seem that at the time of keeping the excess change he would have satisfied the necessary actus reus of theft and have an intention permanently to deprive. The question of 'dishonesty' will be left to the jury in the absence of A having a belief within s2 of the Theft Act 1968. The test for dishonesty as stated in *R* v *Ghosh* (1982) has been outlined above.

If A has entered the building as a trespasser and stolen it should be noted that he has committed an offence under s9(1)(b) of the Theft Act 1968.

Where A finds the sealed box on the floor of the cinema, picked it up and puts it in his pocket, he may commit an offence of theft contrary to s1 of the Theft Act 1968 in that he appropriated property belonging to another with an intention permanently to deprive the other of it. The question of dishonesty is the aspect that may create difficulties in that it is possible that A would claim he believed the owner could not be found taking reasonable steps. This is one of the defences contained with s2 of the Theft Act 1968. In the absence of the application of s2 the question of dishonesty is left to the jury applying the test as stated in *R* v *Ghosh*.

Question 8

D, a doctor engaged in medical research, used to remove organs from dead bodies as part of his transplant experiments.

He removed the liver from E's dead body even though E before his death had said that neither he nor his family wanted his body to be so used.

D removed the left lung from E's dead body and transferred it to G. When F's executor discovered this he demanded the return of the lung because F and his executor belonged to a religious sect which believed that spiritual peace was not obtainable unless the whole body was buried. G would not return the lung.

What is D's criminal liability?

Adapted from University of London LLB Examination
(for External Students) Criminal Law June 1984 Q9

General comment

This question is a very difficult one as it covers an area where the criminal law is as yet unclear. A student could very easily get bogged down in an area where lack of any clear rules would lead him to generalise too greatly.

Skeleton solution

Theft - ss1-7 TA 1968 - 'property' - 'belonging to another'.

Suggested solution

A person commits theft contrary to s1 of the Theft Act 1968 where he dishonestly appropriates property belonging to another with an intention permanently to deprive that other of it. Section 4(1) gives a basic definition of 'property' as including money and all other property real or personal including things in action and other intangible property. However, this is by no means an all-embracing definition and on occasions substances have been held not be property for the purposes of the Theft Act: *Low* v *Blease* (1975) where electricity was held not to be property.

This problem concerns whether or not E's dead body is 'property belonging to another' for the purposes of the Theft Act so that removal of the liver from it would amount to theft. The traditional rule at common law is that there is no property in a corpse and therefore it was not larceny to remove a corpse. It is generally thought that this same rule applies to theft. Indeed, evidence of the rule in areas other than

117

criminal law can be seen by the fact that a person's body, not being regarded as property, is not part of his estate passing to his personal representatives on death.

It should be noted that in certain circumstances a proprietary interest in a corpse could be acquired by one who expended work and skill on the corpse with a view to its preservation. In *Doodeward* v *Spence* (1908) such a right existed where embalmers had spent time mummifying a corpse.

It can be argued that, under s5(1) of the 1968 Act which states that property shall be regarded as belonging to any person having (inter alia) possession or control of it, D may be the owner of the body. Alternatively, it could belong to the hospital or undertakers when argued along the same lines.

In recent years there has been some case law to support the contention that certain products of the human body are capable of being the subject matter of theft. In *R* v *Welsh* (1974) the accused was convicted of theft when he disposed of a urine sample he had given in compliance with s9 of the Road Traffic Act 1972. In *R* v *Rothery* (1976) a driver who had provided a blood specimen was convicted of stealing the capsule and its container although he was not charged with theft of the contents. However it would seem logical that had he been so charged he would have been liable. None of the decided cases have actually involved the removal of organs from a corpse and it would seem that the common law rule in this area would still prevail.

However, it could also be argued that D has received the 'property' (if property it be) under an obligation (that is, a legal one *R* v *Hall* (1973) to retain and deal with it in a particular way, in which case the property will be treated as belonging to another (s5(3)).

Undoubtedly by removing a liver in these circumstances from E's body D would have committed offences contrary to the Human Tissue Act 1961 and other pieces of legislation concerning the removal of organs from a corpse.

The same considerations apply to removal of the left lung from F's dead body. However, D should be advised as to the difficulties involved when G refuses to return the lung. In that event any action by D to recover the lung would amount to an assault. Indeed, in view of the nature of the operation that would have to be performed and the resulting condition that G would be left in, it would seem quite possible that D would be laying himself open to a charge of causing grievous bodily harm with intent to cause grievous bodily harm contrary to s18 of the Offences Against the Person Act 1861. It should be recalled that under s18 intention as to the consequence is required: *R* v *Belfon* (1976). 'Intention' includes not just desiring that a consequence be brought about but knowing that it is certain to occur. In the event of the jury not being satisfied that D had the necessary mens rea required under s18 then a verdict for the lesser offence contained in s20 could be returned providing the jury is satisfied that he inflicted grievous bodily harm. The term 'inflict' requires an assault of some kind although not a direct assault as originally stated in *R* v *Clarence* (1888).

Question 9

B decided to steal a diamond from a local jewellery exhibition. In order to 'case' the exhibition B bought an entry ticket. After inspection B decided it would be too difficult to steal the jewel. On the way out from the exhibition he took a coat from a staff cloakroom. B was challenged by a commissionaire whom B pushed aside before running away.

Advise B of his criminal liability.

Adapted from University of London LLB Examination
(for External Students) Criminal Law June 1985 Q1

General comment

A straightforward question testing the broad elements of theft and burglary with particular regard to trespassary entry.

Skeleton solution

Attempted theft - burglary under s9(1)(a) Theft Act 1968 - burglary under s9(1)(b) Theft Act 1968 - theft - robbery - assault and battery.

Suggested solution

It must be borne in mind that, although the jewel is at an exhibition, any theft of it (ie taking with an intention of permanently depriving the owner) will still be theft and not an offence under s11 of the Theft Act 1968 - removal of articles on display to the public. It is all too easy to assume that the question concerns s11 at first glance.

When B buys the ticket in order to 'case' the exhibition he may commit an offence contrary to s9(1)(a) of the Theft Act 1968. Under s9(1)(a) the offence of burglary is committed where there is entry by an accused into a building as a trespasser with intent to steal. The entry must be 'effective and substantial' and the accused must have intention or at least recklessness as to the facts which make him a trespasser: *R v Collins* (1972). Considering the facts in question there are two main difficulties.

Firstly, B has bought himself a ticket and therefore it could be argued that he has not entered the building as a trespasser. However, B's permission to enter was not given to help plan a theft. B has entered the building for a purpose other than the purpose for which he was given permission and therefore he may have entered 'as a trespasser': *R v Jones and Smith* (1976).

Secondly, it seems doubtful that B entered with intent to steal. B's entry was done with the purposes of assisting him in planning the burglary and therefore the requirement of an intention to steal would not appear to be satisfied unless B had a more general intention to steal anything that took his fancy while in the building: *Attorney-General's References (Nos 1 and 2 of 1979)* (1979).

B could not be liable for an attempt to steal the diamond because he must have done an act which is more than merely preparatory to the full offence with full mens rea, s1(1) Criminal Attempts Act 1981. His acts seem to be just that - ie acts which are preparatory to the theft - and so this would seem unlikely on the facts here, although it is for the jury to decide. If there was an attempt to steal the diamond there may be a further offence under s9(1)(b).

When B removes a coat from the cloakroom he commits the offence of theft contrary to s1 Theft Act 1968. Under s1 a person is guilty of theft if he dishonestly appropriates property belonging to another with the intention of permanently depriving the other of it.

Section 3 provides that an assumption by a person of the rights of an owner will amount to an appropriation. In *R* v *Morris* (1983) the House of Lords held that it was not necessary for the prosecution to prove that an accused assumed all the rights. It is sufficient to prove that he assumed any of the rights.

Furthermore, the concept of appropriation involved an act by way of 'adverse interference with or usurpation of those rights'. The question of dishonesty must be left to the jury who should apply the test as stated in *R* v *Ghosh* (1982).

Additionally, we are told that it is a staff cloakroom and therefore, even if B's ticket were sufficient authority to negative an original trespass, the room is beyond that permission to enter and therefore he would be guilty of entering a part of a building either intending to steal (s9(1)(a)) or having so entered, stealing property (s9(1)(b)).

When B pushes the commissionaire aside he may be liable for assault and battery. Assault is shown where a victim is put in immediate fear of force. A battery is a direct infliction of force. They may be performed either intentionally or recklessly: *R* v *Venna* (1975). There is nothing to indicate that the victim is injured so the more serious assaults under the Offences Against the Person Act 1861 will not be considered. The offence of robbery is committed under s8 of the Theft Act 1968 where a person steals and immediately before or at the time of the theft he uses force on any person in order to steal.

There are two possible problems arising from the definition of robbery. Firstly, it is not entirely clear whether the force was used immediately before or at the time of the theft. While an appropriation of the property may continue for a period of time while the process of stealing is taking place: *R* v *Hale* (1978), on the facts in question it would seem that the theft is over.

Secondly, the force must be 'in order to steal'. It is not sufficient that force is used in order to escape, which seems to be what happened in the facts.

We are not told of any injuries to the commissionaire and, unless he suffers grievous bodily harm, the assault upon him will not suffice to support a charge of burglary (s9(1)(b)) under this head.

Question 10

C was in D's self service store.

a) She decided to help herself to a tin of salmon which she put in her coat pocket, but whilst in the check-out queue she decided to pay for the salmon and placed it in her basket before doing so.

b) C received excess change from the checkout girl. She put it in her pocket without examining it. She discovered the excess only when she was at home.

c) C decided to take out life assurance on her son and in two proposal forms she described her son as a non-smoker. This C knew to be incorrect. From company X, C obtained additional cover and from company Y a reduced premium because her son was thought to be a non-smoker.

Advise C about her criminal liability.

University of London LLB Examination
(for External Students) Criminal Law June 1986 Q2

General comment

A new type of question with three distinct and separate parts but all concerned with particular aspects of property offences. Parts (a) and (b) were straightforward. Part (a) in particular could have been anticipated in view of recent case law. Part (c) was not without its difficulties and a careful approach was required in order to deal with the two policies in their different ways.

Skeleton solution

a) Section 1 Theft Act 1968 - s3 Theft Act 1968 - *R* v *Morris* (1983): appropriation - *R* v *McPherson* (1973).

b) Section 1 Theft Act 1968 : later appropriation - ss5(1) and 5(4) Theft Act 1968.

c) Sections 16(1) and 16(2) Theft Act 1968 - s15(4) Theft Act 1968 - operative deception.

Suggested solution

a) Section 1 Theft Act 1968 provides that 'a person is guilty of theft if he dishonestly appropriates property belonging to another with the intention of permanently depriving the other of it'.

The question to be decided on the facts as given is whether the offence of theft is satisfied or whether there is merely an attempted theft.

When C puts the tin of salmon in her pocket intending not to pay for it every element of theft as defined above appears to be satisfied with the possible exception of 'appropriation'. The question of dishonesty must always be left to the jury in these circumstances: *R* v *Feely* (1973) and the jury must apply the test as stated in *R* v *Ghosh* (1982): (1) Was C dishonest according to the standards of reasonable honest people. If no, C will not be guilty. If yes, (2) Did C realise that reasonable and honest people would regard what she did as dishonest. If yes, she is guilty. If no, she is not guilty. On the facts as given there would appear to be little doubt that C was acting dishonestly.

Section 3 of the Theft Act 1968 provides that 'any assumption by a person of the rights of an owner amounts to an appropriation'.

In *R* v *Morris* (1983) s3 was considered by the House of Lords. The facts of *R* v *Morris* involved label-switching rather than concealment as here. However, the House considered that in order to satisfy s3 there had to be an act by way of 'adverse interference with or usurpation of an owner's rights'. Furthermore it is not necessary for there to be an assumption of all the rights of an owner, it is sufficient if a right is assumed.

In *R* v *Morris* the House confirmed as correct the case of *R* v *McPherson* (1973) where D removed items from the supermarket shelf and concealed them in her own shopping bag. In their view there was a plain case of appropriation effected by a combination of the acts of removing the goods from the shelf and concealing them in the bag. On the facts in question there would appear to be an appropriation in the same manner ie by concealment.

When C changes her mind, decides to pay and places the item in the basket this will make no difference to an already complete offence.

In the unlikely event that this was found not to be a full appropriation then an attempted theft would be established if C had done an act 'more than merely preparatory' to the full offence s1(1) Criminal Attempts Act 1981.

b) When C receives excess change from the checkout girl no offence is shown when she put it in her pocket because at that stage she has no mens rea. Later when she discovers the excess she may be liable for the offence of theft as defined above.

Section 3 of the Theft Act 1968 which defines appropriation as any assumption of the rights of an owner further provides that there can be an appropriation where a person has come by the property (innocently or not) without stealing it, any later assumption of a right to it by keeping and dealing with it as owner can amount to an appropriation. On the facts in question C had appropriated by keeping the money.

The next point to consider is whether the money 'belongs to another' for the purposes of s1 Theft Act 1968.

Section 5(1) provides that property shall be regarded as belonging to any person having possession or control of it or having in it any proprietary right or interest (other than certain equitable interests).

Section 5(4) further provides that where a person gets property by another's mistake, and is under an obligation to make restoration (in whole or in part) then to the extent of that obligation the property shall be regarded as belonging to another, and an intention not to make restoration shall be regarded as an intention to deprive that person of the property.

If ownership of the money remains in someone other than C it is not necessary to rely on s4(4), s5(1) would be appropriate. However if ownership has passed to C then s5(4) will apply but only if the 'obligation to make restoration' is a legal obligation: *R* v *Gilks* (1972).

The last point that requires brief consideration is that of dishonesty. Usually it is for the jury to decide whether a person is or is not dishonest (*R* v *Feely* (1973)) applying where necessary the test as stated in *R* v *Ghosh* (1982). However s2 Theft Act 1968 lists three instances where a jury must acquit. The only one that might be available on the facts in question would be if C believed she had the right in law to keep the property. If this were the case the jury must find that she was not dishonest however unreasonable the belief was.

c) Section 16(1) Theft Act 1968 provides that a person who by any deception dishonestly obtains for himself or another any pecuniary advantage shall commit an offence. Section 16(2) details the type of pecuniary advantages within s16(1) and provides (inter alia) that a pecuniary advantage within the meaning of the section shall be regarded as being obtained for a person where he is allowed to take out any policy of insurances or annuity contract or obtains an improvement of the terms on which he is allowed to do so. This particular aspect of s16(2) would appear to cover exactly the situation where C obtains insurance cover with a reduced premium from company Y but it is less clear whether the additional cover obtained from company X would be within s16(2) as the section appears to apply only where the cover is being taken out and not where it already exists.

In any event it must be remembered that it is still necessary to show that there was a deception which was the effective cause of the obtaining of the pecuniary advantage. Section 15(4) of the Theft Act 1968 defines a 'deception' as any deception (whether deliberate or reckless) by words or conduct as to fact or as to law, including a deception as to the present intentions of the person using the deception or any other person. The false statements in the proposal forms would come within s15(4) and certainly in the case of company Y the deception is the operative reason for the reduced premium being allowed.

There seems little doubt on the facts as given that C is dishonest although, as stated previously it is always for the jury to decide.

Question 11

P entered O's self-service garage intending to pay for petrol with his credit card. Having filled his tank with petrol P discovered that he did not have his card with him and went to explain to the attendant what had happened. The attendant said that P should leave the car till P returned to pay either with cash or the card. This P refused to do because he needed the car so he drove home and was unable to find his credit card. Later P decided not to pay.

Advise P about his criminal liability. Would it make any difference to your advice if there had been a notice on the pump stating 'Property in the petrol shall not pass till paid for'?

University of London LLB Examination
(for External Students) Criminal Law June 1986 Q6

General comment

Another 'property' question and a type of question that has appeared before. Providing a student has a firm grasp of basic criminal law principles very good marks could be obtained.

Skeleton solution

Section 1 Theft Act 1968: actus reus and mens rea not coinciding - s3 Theft Act 1978: *R* v *Allen* (1985) - s2 Theft Act 1978: why not available.

Effect of notice: s5(1) - Theft Act 1968: later appropriation within s3 Theft Act 1968.

Suggested solution

Section 1 Theft Act 1968 defines theft as a dishonest appropriation of property belonging to another with an intention to permanently deprive the other of the property. When P fills his tank with petrol he commits no offence because, although he may satisfy the actus reus of theft, he lacks the mens rea. He would not be regarded as dishonest on the facts as given. When he later decides not to pay at that time a jury would almost certainly regard him as dishonest. However he commits no offence under s1 Theft Act 1968 as mens rea and actus reus do not coincide. The actus reus is complete and the property has passed to P before he becomes dishonest.

When P, having explained the situation to the attendant, refuses to leave the car at the petrol station but drives it home he commits no offence. Undoubtedly there is an existing liability within s2 Theft Act 1978. However it would only be an offence to avoid payment of such existing liability if he did so dishonestly by deception. On the facts as given there is no deception at all.

Section 3 Theft Act 1978 provides that a person who, knowing that payment on the spot for any goods supplied or services done is required or expected from him, dishonestly makes off without payment as required or expected of him and with intent to avoid payment of the amount due commits an offence.

This offence seems the most appropriate to the facts as given. Undoubtedly P has 'made off' for the purposes of s3 because he has passed the spot where payment is required: *R* v *Brooks and Brooks* (1982). Furthermore goods have been supplied to him for which he knows that payment on the spot is required. However two points required further consideration. Firstly is P dishonest and secondly does he intend to avoid payment for the purposes of s3?

P must be dishonest at the time he makes off and it is not sufficient that he becomes dishonest later. It is for the jury to decide whether or not P is dishonest: *R* v *Feely* (1973). The test to be applied is as stated in *R* v *Ghosh* (1982):

1) was P dishonest by the standards of an ordinary person. If no, he is not guilty. If yes;

2) did P realise that he was dishonest by their standards. If yes, he is dishonest. If no, he is not dishonest.

The last requirement under s3 that requires consideration is that of the intent to avoid payment of the amount due. In *R* v *Allen* (1985) the House of Lords considered that these words meant that D must intend to avoid payment altogether and not merely to avoid payment for a short period of time. This would mean that P could not be liable under s3 because at the time he makes off he does intend to pay at a future time and he only later forms the intention never to pay.

If there was a notice on the pump stating that property in the petrol would not pass until it was paid for a different result might occur. However this would only be the case if the notice were effective. In that event ownership of the petrol would remain in someone else until it was paid for and therefore for the purposes of s1 Theft Act 1968 the property would still belong to another. Section 5 of the Theft Act 1968 provides that property shall be regarded as belonging to any person having possession or control of it or having in it any proprietary right or interest. Thus even though P has possession of the petrol someone else has ownership. The initial taking of the property would not amount to theft because, as stated previously, there is no mens rea. However s3 Theft Act 1968 provides that an appropriation of property occurs within s1 where there is any assumption by a person of the rights of an owner and this includes, where he has come by the property (innocently or not) without stealing it, any later assumption of a right to it by keeping or dealing with it as owner. When P drove off without paying at that time there could be a 'later appropriation' within s3 Theft Act 1968. Undoubtedly there is an intention to permanently deprive the owner of the property. The only question is that of dishonesty - he does intend to pay at some time. None of the defences within s2 Theft Act 1968 are available so it is for the jury to decide the question of dishonesty as previously outlined.

At the latest P would most likely come within s1 when he keeps the petrol or uses it after he has decided not to pay for it, providing of course that it has not been fully used by that time.

Question 12

H went into I's self-service store intending to steal salmon. In fact there was no salmon because it had all been sold. H went to the meat counter where her friend J, was serving. H placed an order and J weighed the specified meat before pencilling in a lower price than should have been charged. H, who was not paying attention, did not notice that the price was lower than it should have been. At the checkout the shop girl rang up the lower amount and then it dawned on H that it did seem a little on the low side. However, she said nothing. The cashier gave £5 excess change to H who did not notice this till she arrived at her car. H decided to keep it.

Advise H and J of their criminal liability, if any.

University of London LLB Examination
(for External Students) Criminal Law June 1987 Q3

General comment

An averagely difficult question. Most of the important aspects of the question are regularly examined and therefore a student who prepared by reference to past papers would have had few difficulties with this question.

Skeleton solution

H Attempted theft - impossibility - s9(1)(a) and s9(1)(b) - conspiracy - lack of agreement - s15 TA 1968 - s1 TA 1968 - dishonesty - theft of excess change. Section 5(4) contrast s5(1) TA 1968 - coincidence of AR and MR.

J Section 1 TA 1968 - s17 TA 1968 - accomplice to offences by H.

Suggested solution

When H enters the self-service store intending to steal salmon she may become liable for attempted theft.

Theft is defined in s1 Theft Act 1968 and is established where there is a dishonest appropriation of property belonging to another with intention to permanently deprive the other of the property. The actus reus of attempted theft will be established where there is an act more than merely preparatory towards the full offence, s1 Criminal Attempts Act 1981. It is for the jury to decide whether the act of the accused is more than merely preparatory: *DPP* v *Stonehouse* (1977).

The mens rea for attempted theft is the same as the full offence ie a dishonest intention to permanently deprive. The fact that the salmon has all been sold will not preclude liability. Section 1(2) Criminal Attempts Act 1981 provides that a person may still be liable for attempt notwithstanding that the offence is impossible. Furthermore in deciding whether a person has the necessary mens rea he should be judged on the facts as he believed them to be ie that the salmon was in the store. Section 1(3) CAA 1981.

The more serious offence of burglary requires some consideration. Although in practice this type of factual situation described in the question is not prosecuted as such technically the offence of burglary may be satisfied.

Under s9(1)(a) Theft Act 1968 a person commits burglary if he enters a building or part of a building as a trespasser. H must make a 'substantial and effective' entry and must know or be reckless as to the facts which make him a trespasser: *R* v *Collins* (1973).

It could be argued that H does not enter as a trespasser as she has the implied consent of I to enter the self-service store. However I only gives permission to enter the store to shop and for such other lawful purposes. H enters to steal and therefore she enters for a purpose in excess of the permission granted to her and could be regarded as entering as a trespasser: *R* v *Jones and Smith* (1976).

Under s9(1)(a) H must have the necessary intent to steal (or commit rape, grievous bodily harm or criminal damage) at the time of entry. It is immaterial that she never achieves the offence. Furthermore if as here the prosecution would rely on intent to steal all that is required under s9(1)(a) is a general intention to steal - it is immaterial that there turns out to be nothing she wants or that the object that she wants is not there: *R* v *Walkington* (1978); *Attorney-General's References (Nos 1 and 2 of 1979)* (1979). However if the indictment refers to an intention to steal particular items the prosecution must establish that H had mens rea towards those items.

Section 9(1)(b) provides a further offence of burglary where a person having entered a building or part of a building as a trespasser steals or attempts to steal. Technically this would be satisfied only if the prosecution established that what H did was sufficient to amount to attempted theft.

When J places a lower price on the order J may commit theft. The actus reus is established where there is an 'appropriation of property belonging to another'. Section 3 Theft Act 1968 provides that 'any assumption by a person of the rights of an owner amounts to an appropriation'. In the case of *R* v *Morris* (1983) the House of Lords held that there could be an appropriation even though all the rights of an owner had not been assumed. It was sufficient to prove that any of the rights had been assumed. Furthermore the concept of appropriation involves an act by way of 'adverse interference with or usurpation of an owner's rights'.

On the facts it would seem that by writing a lower price on the goods the actus reus of theft is satisfied. The mens rea is a dishonest intention to permanently deprive. Considering dishonesty first, J cannot claim any of the limited defences contained in 2 Theft Act 1968. Therefore the question is for the jury to decide. In most cases the jury will not require direction but where there are difficulties the test as stated in *R* v *Ghosh* (1982) should be applied. The jury must first consider where the person charged was acting dishonestly by the ordinary standards of reasonable and decent people. If it was not dishonest by those standards the prosecution fails. If it was dishonest by those standards the jury must consider whether the person charged realised that what he was doing was dishonest by those standards. If he does he will be dishonest. Furthermore it would be dishonest to act in a way that he knew ordinary people considered to be dishonest even if he believed that he was justified in acting as he did.

A further offence which may be committed by J is that of false accounting. Section 17 Theft Act 1968 provides that where a person with a view to gain for himself and another and with intent to cause loss to another:

'a) Destroys, defaces, conceals, or falsifies any account or any record or document made or required for any accounting purposes shall commit an offence.'

The actus reus of s17 would only be satisfied if the paper on which the lower price was marked could be regarded as an account record or document made or required for any accounting purpose: *Edwards* v *Toombs* (1983).

It should be noted that as H is unaware of what J is doing there is no question of a conspiracy or of H being an accomplice to any offences committed by J at this stage.

When H takes the article at the cash desk she realises that the price marked may be on the low side but says nothing. If J has committed a s17 offence by putting a lower price on the goods H may commit a further s17 offence when she makes use of any account, or record or document which she knows to be misleading, false, or deceptive in a material particular.

Furthermore H could commit a more serious offence under s15 Theft Act 1968 in that she dishonestly by deception obtains property belonging to another with intention to permanently deprive the other of it. The most important question in relation to s15 is whether or not there is a deception by H.

Section 15(4) provides that 'deception' means any deception (whether deliberate or reckless) by words or conduct as to fact as to law, including a deception as to the present intentions of the person or any other person. It could be argued that H recklessly deceived because she knows that there is a risk that the price of the goods is wrong but says nothing.

If there is a deception it must be shown that the deception precedes the obtaining of the property (in this case the point when ownership passes) and that the deception is the operative reason for the obtaining.

It could also be argued that H commits the offence of theft when continuing to purchase the goods realising that the price may be wrong. However, this could only be established if ownership had not passed when she realised that the price could be wrong. Furthermore H must be dishonest both for s15 and for s1. On the facts this is by no means clear and therefore the jury should be directed to approach the question of dishonesty by reference to the test in *R* v *Ghosh*.

Undoubtedly s15 and s1 can overlap on occasions: *Lawrence* v *MPC* (1971). There is a certain amount of confusion as to when this overlap occurs and unfortunately although the House of Lords had opportunity on the *R* v *Morris* (1983) case to consider the relationship between s15 and s1 they failed to consider this point.

If H does commit any offences at the cash desk J may be liable as an accomplice, either as an aider and abettor or as a procurer. An aider and abettor must be present or constructively present at the crime, assisting or encouraging: *R* v *Coney* (1882); *R* v *Clarkson* (1971). Whether this is satisfied on the facts is unclear. Certainly J could only be liable as such if quite a wide interpretation of 'presence' were allowed. Alternatively she could be a procurer. A procurer is a person who assists a principal offender before the crime occurs. A person who is an accomplice is to be treated as a principal offender for the purposes of trial and punishment. Section 8 Accessories and Abettors Act 1861.

When H receives the excess change there is no offence at that time because she has no mens rea. However when later she decides to keep it at that point mens rea and actus reus may coincide and she could be liable for theft. There seems little doubt that H would be regarded as dishonest: *R* v *Ghosh*. Furthermore, there is an intention to permanently deprive. The actus reus of theft requires further consideration. Section 3(1) provides that an appropriation may take place at a later stage where a person comes by property (innocently or not) without stealing it but later assumes a right to it by keeping or dealing with as owner. Applying this H would appropriate at the time she decides to keep it.

The next question to be considered is whether the money belongs to another. Obviously this depends on whether ownership of the money has passed to H as a result of the mistake. If it has not then the property will still belong to another within s5(1) because H will not own the money even though she has possession and control of it. If ownership of the money has passed to H it is necessary to consider s5(4) which provides that where property is got by another's mistake, and is under an obligation to make restoration of the property to the extent of that obligation the property shall be regarded (as against him) as belonging to the person entitled to restoration and an intention not to make restoration shall be regarded accordingly as an intention to deprive that person of the property. It must be noted that under s5(4) it is not sufficient that property passes by mistake. The obligation within s5(4) must be a legally enforceable obligations: *R* v *Gilks* (1972).

If the actus reus were satisfied then at the time H decided to keep the money the offence of theft would be complete.

Question 13

L entered M's supermarket intending to take some bottles of Brecon beer. When L arrived at the beer counter she found that Brecon beer was out of stock. L did the rest of the shopping and noticed that there was a tin of salmon which had obviously been underpriced. L put it in her basket. L removed a 24p label from a tin of beans and put it on a £3 tin of asparagus before placing it in her basket. Before going to the checkout L decided to return the tin of asparagus to its shelf. At the checkout the shop girl rang up the incorrect price for the salmon. Also she gave L too much change though L did not notice this until later.

Advise L of her criminal liability.

Adapted from University of London LLB Examination
(for External Students) Criminal Law June 1988 Q5

General comment

You will need to consider both theft and burglary in this question, but note especially that the facts do not indicate beyond reasonable doubt that L had the required mens rea, ie dishonesty and an intention to permanently deprive, and the mens rea of a trespasser.

When she switches labels on the tin, the issue is whether that constitutes an appropriation and whether it was done with the required mens rea, and when the offence is complete.

The underpriced tin of salmon raises the issue of deception, and the excess change the issue of appropriating property belonging to another.

Skeleton solution

Entering supermarket - burglary contrary to s9(1)(a) Theft Act 1968, mens rea of theft and trespasser, offence committed at time of entry - irrelevant that supermarket was out of stock.

CRIMINAL LAW

Underpriced tin of salmon - when was there an appropriation - was there a deception - was there dishonesty.

Switching labels - act of appropriation - did she have mens rea.

Given excess change - when did L appropriate it - did it at that point still belong to another - did she have mens rea.

Suggested solution

When L entered M's supermarket intending to take some bottles of Brecon beer, L may be guilty of burglary, contrary to s9(1)(a) Theft Act 1968, which states that a person is guilty of burglary if he enters a building or any part of a building as a trespasser and with intent to commit theft.

The actus reus of burglary consists of an entry, as a trespasser, of any building or part thereof.

Whether a person can be properly described as being outside a building or in the process of entry or as being inside the building must be determined in a commonsense way by the jury, who must determine whether the defendant had made an 'effective entry': *R* v *Brown* (1985); *R* v *Collins* (1973).

A defendant must enter as a trespasser. Trespass is a legal concept and the law of tort must be considered. As a matter of civil law any intentional, or reckless or negligent entry into a building would constitute a trespass if the building was in the possession of a person who did not consent to the entry. If there is no civil trespass there can be no burglary but liability in tort is not sufficient for the criminal law. To commit burglary requires mens rea, ie the defendant must know or be reckless as to the facts which make him a trespasser: *R* v *Collins*. Once a defendant has entered as a lawful visitor, he cannot commit burglary thereafter for the criminal law does not accept the civil law doctrine of trespass ab initio: *R* v *Collins*. Burglary requires entry as a trespasser of a building or part thereof. If a person is authorised to enter premises for one purpose but enters with another, he enters as a trespasser so that a shoplifter could be guilty of burglary as soon as he has entered a shop as he enters for a purpose alien to the shopkeeper's invitation: *Barker* v *R* (1983).

To constitute a 'building' for the purposes of burglary, the structure must have some degree of permanence: *R* v *Manning and Rodgers* (1871).

On the facts, the relevant ulterior offence which L appears to have intended to commit is theft, contrary to s1 Theft Act 1968. An offence under s9(1)(a) Theft Act 1968 is committed at the time of entry so that it would be irrelevant that there was no Brecon beer to steal - this would not be a case of attempting the impossible as the full crime would have been committed. However it is not clear that L had the mens rea of theft, ie dishonesty and an intention of permanently depriving the owner of his property.

Section 2 of the Theft Act provides a partial definition of dishonesty by stating that a belief in legal right or a belief in the owner's consent or a belief that the property had been lost is not to be regarded as dishonest. Apart from this guidance, the matter is one entirely for the jury who must find a defendant dishonest if his conduct would be regarded as dishonest by the ordinary standards of reasonable and honest people and if the defendant realised that his conduct would be so regarded: *R v Ghosh* (1982).

There must be an intention to permanently deprive and the best evidence of this will usually be what the defendant did with the goods.

Therefore, L will be guilty of burglary contrary to s9(1)(a) Theft Act 1968 if, when she entered, she entered with the mens rea of a trespasser and the mens rea of theft.

When L removed a 24p label and placed it on a £3 tin, she appears to have committed theft contrary to s1 Theft Act 1968. The fact that she put the tin back onto the shelf cannot affect her then existing liability.

The actus reus of theft consists of an appropriation of property belonging to another. Clearly, the tin is property: s4 Theft Act 1968. It clearly belongs to another: 5(1) Theft Act 1968. By s3(1) Theft Act 1968, an appropriation is 'any assumption by a person of the rights of an owner'.

In *R v Morris* (1983) Lord Roskill said that 'in the context of s3(1) Theft Act 1968, the concept of appropriation involves not an act expressly or impliedly authorised by the owner but an act by way of adverse interference with or usurpation of those rights': [1983] 3 All ER 288 at 293. Therefore, the theft was complete when the appropriation was complete, ie when the label was switched.

However, L will also require the mens rea of theft, ie dishonesty and an intention to permanently deprive the owner of his property.

When L purchases a tin of salmon which she knows was underpriced, she does not appear to be guilty of theft because she has not committed an essential element of the actus reus of theft, namely an appropriation. If the essence of appropriation lies in the conduct of the defendant which is observable as conduct which is inconsistent with or is an usurpation of the owner's rights, then L has done nothing which was she was not authorised by the owner of the tin to do: *Dip Kaur v Chief Constable for Hampshire* (1981). As L had not put the label on the tin, there can be no deception offence for there is generally no liability for deception by omission to undeceive where the defendant has not caused the misapprehension.

L was given too much change by the shop girl but found this out after the event. The actus reus of theft does not appear to have been committed as when and if L decided to keep the excess change (and thereby appropriate it), it was no longer property belonging to another. The shop girl's mistake did not prevent ownership in the money passing immediately upon delivery: *Moynes v Cooper* (1956). By s5(4) Theft Act 1968, where property is got by mistake, a defendant can steal if if he dishonestly appropriates it if he is under a legal obligation to make restoration, despite being the owner of it. Whether a defendant is under a legal obligation to make restoration depends on the civil law.

Therefore, L can only steal the excess change if it still remained property belonging to another when she discovered that she had it and if she decided to keep it dishonestly and with an intention to permanently deprive the owner of it.

By having the basket with her for use in the course of or connection with the burglary or theft L may also commit the offence of 'going equipped' under s25 of the Theft Act 1968 (see Chapter 7).

Question 14

C entered the local antique shop to make enquiries about a clock he had seen in the shop window. Inside the shop he decided to look round to see if there was anything worth stealing. He saw a Swansea teapot and decided to try to steal it. While the shopkeeper was serving another customer, C put the teapot in his bag. He felt guilty and replaced it before the shopkeeper returned. C left the shop having purchased the clock. C had paid the price requested by the shopkeeper which was less than on the price label because, as C knew, the shopkeeper by mistake had misread the price label.

Advise the parties. What difference, if any, would it make to your advice if the teapot had been kept behind the shop counter?

University of London LLB Examination
(for External Students) Criminal Law June 1990 Q2

General comment

The question clearly requires a sound grasp of the law of theft, not least the current debate as to the nature of appropriation, and the complexities of s5(4) of the 1968 Act.

It is necessary to consider burglary, if only to explain why such a charge could not be sustained. Given the difficulties in establishing liability for theft of the clock, it is suggested that alternatives such as deception ought to be considered.

Skeleton solution

Attempted theft of items unknown. Theft of the teapot - consider intent to deprive. Burglary, no liability. Theft of the clock on alternative assumptions. Consider s5(4). Consider appropriation debate. Consider problems with dishonesty. Consider alternative charges.

Suggested solution

When C enters the shop he decided to look around to see if there is anything worth stealing. In theory the prosecution could charge him with attempted theft of property unknown. The indictment does not have to specify the property C was attempting to steal; see *Scudder* v *Barret* (1979). Neither will it avail C to argue that there was nothing in the shop worth stealing. Impossibility is not a defence to a charge of attempted theft; see the Criminal Attempts Act 1981, as interpreted by the House of Lords in *R* v *Shivpuri* (1987). The major problem in actually securing such a conviction would be proof that he had taken steps more than merely preparatory to stealing, simply by looking around the shop; see *R* v *Gullefer* (1987).

C is more likely to be convicted of theft following his act of placing the teapot in his own bag. The teapot is property belonging to another as against C; see ss4(1), and

5(1) of the Theft Act 1968. In placing the teapot in his bag, C is assuming one of the rights of the owner; see the definition of appropriation provided by s3(1) of the 1968 Act. In *R* v *McPherson* (1973), the court had little hesitation in concluding that such behaviour could amount to an appropriation for the purposes of the 1968 Act, a view further endorsed by Lord Roskill in his speech in the later House of Lords' decision in *R* v *Morris* (1983). If any difficulty arises in relation to this theft charge it must be as regards the defendant's mens rea. Firstly he must be dishonest. C does not appear to come within any of the negative concepts of dishonesty as determined by s2 of the 1968 Act. It is submitted that, applying the common law definition of dishonesty provided by the Court of Appeal in *R* v *Ghosh* (1982), ordinary decent people would regard such behaviour as dishonest, and that C must surely have realised this. The remaining issue is that of C's intention to permanently deprive. C will undoubtedly contend that the fact that he replaced the teapot is evidence that he did not intend to keep it. Whilst his actions might be evidence of his remorse, and thus might be of relevance in considering the appropriate sentence, they are of little relevance to the substantive offence. The crucial issue is whether or not C intended to permanently deprive the owner of the teapot at the moment when he appropriated it by placing it in his bag. If he did, the theft is complete at that moment. Once the theft is complete it cannot be undone. It is submitted, however, that his action of replacing the teapot will create some evidential difficulties for the prosecution.

The question of whether or not C can be charged with burglary needs to be considered. That he has committed a theft seems likely for the reasons given above, but there may be difficulties with other elements of the offence.

Burglary requires proof that the defendant has entered a building as a trespasser. A shop is presumed to be open to the general public, and members of the public have a licence to enter. If a defendant enters a shop in order to steal an item within, it might be contended that he is entering for a purpose in excess of his implied permission, and thus enters as a trespasser; for further evidence in support of this approach see *R* v *Jones and Smith* (1976).

The difficulty for the prosecution in C's case is that he does not appear to have formed the intention to steal until he had already entered the shop. Once he had decided to steal he would have become a trespasser, but the wording of the two offences created by s9 of the 1968 Act requires proof that he either 'entered as a trespasser', or that he stole 'having entered as a trespasser'. There is no evidence to suggest that he enters any other part of the building occupied by the shop with an intent to steal, hence it is submitted that a charge of burglary would fail.

If one assumes that C picked the clock up and presented it at the counter, it is submitted that he cannot have committed any act of appropriation by selecting it. The item is correctly priced, hence the issues raised in the Divisional Court decision in *Dip Kaur* v *Chief Constable for Hampshire* (1981), do not arise.

Having purchased the clock, albeit at the wrong price, C will contend that the clock became his, and that a charge of theft could not be sustained because the clock was no longer property belonging to another. This argument will succeed unless the prosecution can establish that property in the clock did not pass to C. Section 5(4) of the 1968 Act states that where a defendant gets property by another's mistake and is under an obligation to make restoration of that property or its proceeds, then to the extent of that obligation the property or its proceeds shall be regarded (as against him) as belonging to the person entitled to restoration. Prima facie this section would seem to apply to C, thus effectively preventing property in the clock from passing to him, for the purposes of theft, because of the shopkeeper's mistake. The difficulty for the prosecution, however, is that s5(4) does not of itself create an obligation to restore goods obtained by another's mistake. Such an obligation must already exist in law. It is beyond doubt that such an obligation does exist where one obtains money as a result of another's mistake, but it is far less clear that any such obligation arises where the property so obtained takes some other form. It is instructive to note that s5(4) was specifically drafted to deal with the problem that arose from the decision in *Moynes* v *Cooper* (1956), ie a defendant receiving too much cash in his wage packet. It has been applied to similar situations since its enactment, eg *Attorney-General's Reference (No 1 of 1983)* (1984), but has not been applied to a situation where a defendant has received goods by mistake. On this basis it is suggested that a charge of theft would founder on the prosecution's inability to prove that the clock was property belonging to another when C left the shop.

If the above analysis is rejected by the court, either on the basis that s5(4) does prevent property from passing, or on the basis that the owner of the clock only intended ownership to pass if the proper price was paid, there would still be difficulties with appropriation. It should be remembered that Lord Roskill in *R* v *Morris* stated that any assumption of any of the owner's rights would suffice for the purposes of appropriation. In the same case, however, his Lordship does go on to state that '... the concept of appropriation in my view involves not an act expressly or impliedly authorised by the owner but an act by way of adverse interference with or usurpation of those rights.' The problem presented by this statement is that it suggests that appropriation has to be some sort of unauthorised act. C's action could arguably be regarded as authorised, since he is given the clock by the shopkeeper. A conflicting view of appropriation is offered, however, by the House of Lords' decision in *Lawrence* v *Metropolitan Police Commissioner* (1971), in which Viscount Dilhorne held that appropriation did not involve proof that the owner did not consent to the defendant's actions, and that furthermore, a defendant could appropriate property whilst becoming the owner of it. The argument that a defendant appropriates property where he has not paid the proper price for it, even though this is unknown to the victim at the time, has received further support in post- *Morris* cases such as *Dobson* v *General Accident (etc)* (1990). Even if the *Lawrence* view of appropriation is accepted, the difficult question remains of whether or not the defendant was dishonest. It is submitted that C might raise two arguments by way of defence on this point. First, that he honestly believed he had a right in law to take the item; see s2(1)(a) of the Theft Act 1968. In contract law terms he would surely have acquired voidable title. Secondly, C could argue that, following *R* v *Ghosh* (above), ordinary decent people would not regard his actions as dishonest, or at least that he did not realise that they would regard them as dishonest. Whether or not this latter argument succeeds would depend largely upon the amount by which the price of the clock was mis-stated by the shopkeeper. C's intention to permanently deprive the owner of the clock is evident.

If one assumes that the shopkeeper took the item from a shelf behind the counter and handed it to C, there is no question of C having appropriated it until he takes it from the store. It is submitted that the difficulties outlined above in relation appropriation would also arise in this case. C will not have assumed the rights of the owner until he takes possession of the clock, by which time he will have paid for it. C will contend that he had at least voidable title to the clock, and that until this is avoided by the shopkeeper he cannot commit an act of appropriation in relation to it. The law on this issue is currently rather confused. In *R* v *Morris* Lord Roskill rejected the introduction into the law of theft of such concepts as void and voidable contracts, but did not indicate how else such problems might be resolved. Arguably one could apply *Lawrence* and contend that C is appropriating the clock when it is handed to him, even though the owner consents to his actions, and even though he is becoming the owner of it. Such an analysis derives support from cases such as *Dobson*. Were this view to be accepted, there would still be the difficulty of establishing dishonesty on the part of the defendant for the reasons outlined above. Moreover, had C gone behind the counter he would have entered a 'part of the building' as a trespasser (there being no implied invitation to shoppers to go behind the counter) and therefore the above offences of burglary may have been committed.

There is the possibility that C could be guilty of obtaining the clock by deception, contrary to s15 of the 1968 Act, but the difficulty would lie in establishing a deception on his part. The prosecution may cite *DPP* v *Ray* (1974), and contend that by remaining silent C was representing that he honestly believed the price requested by the shopkeeper to be correct when this was not the case. The chief difficulty here is of course the fact that the price of the clock was determined by the shopkeeper, not C! Proving dishonesty would also be problematic, for reasons already given.

Question 15

D borrowed his father's car and took his girlfriend to a circus. D believed that his father would have given permission if asked although his girlfriend knew that no such permission would have been granted. D climbed over a barrier and entered the circus but D's girlfriend refused to join him and entered by paying for her admission. Inside, D bought ice creams for himself and his girlfriend and he received an excess of change which he did not notice till he returned home.

Advise the parties of their criminal liability.

University of London LLB Examination
(for External Students) Criminal Law June 1990 Q3

General comment

A fairly straight forward question. The most difficult point being D's liability for not paying his entrance fee. This must be considered even if the conclusion is that he incurs no liability. Similarly with burglary. Note that the s5(4) point arises for the second time in this paper. In the interests of clarity the liabilities of the parties should be considered separately.

Skeleton solution

D's liability for s12. Theft of the petrol. Deception offences. Making off without payment. Theft of excess change. Liability of D's girlfriend under s12 and for theft of the petrol.

Suggested solution

D may be charged with taking a conveyance without the consent of the owner contrary to s12(1) of the Theft Act 1968. To establish a taking of the car, the prosecution must prove that there has been some movement of it, which is evident here; see *R* v *Bogacki* (1973). Secondly, it must be shown that the taking of the vehicle was for the defendant's or another's own use. This essentially requires proof that the defendant used the car as a conveyance; see *R* v *Bow* (1976). Again it is evident that D has been carried in the car. It would appear from the facts given that the owner, D's father, has not granted permission for the car to be driven by D, hence the actus reus of the offence is made out. D has taken the conveyance without having the consent of the owner. D will rely, however, on s12(6) of the 1968 Act which provides that a person does not commit an offence under s12, if he takes a conveyance in the belief that he would have the owner's consent if the owner knew of his doing so and the circumstances of it. The test for this belief appears to be subjective; see *R* v *Clotworthy* (1981).

In driving the car D will be appropriating the petrol in the car's petrol tank, which is property belonging to his father. By driving the car he evidently intends to deprive his father of the petrol. D is unlikely to be convicted of theft of the petrol, however, as the prosecution will have great difficulty in establishing dishonesty. D would presumably rely on s2(1)(b) of the 1968 Act, in claiming that he honestly believed he had the owner's consent to taking the property.

By climbing over the barrier and entering the circus without paying, D enters the circus as a trespasser. On the assumption that the circus is housed in a tent of some description, the question arises as to whether or not this constitutes a building for the purposes of s9(1)(a) and (b) under the 1968 Act. It would appear that in order to qualify as a building for the purposes of burglary, the property entered must have some degree of permanence. The weight of academic opinion seems to suggest that a tent would not satisfy the definition of a building, even if it was being used as a home. Even if the court was willing to concede this point in the prosecution's favour, there would still be the difficulty of proving that D had any of the ulterior intents required under s9(1)(a), such as an intent to steal, rape, commit grievous bodily harm, or criminal damage, none of which is evident here.

When D climbs over the barrier to evade the entrance fee, he may have committed the offence of making off without payment, contrary to s3 of the Theft Act 1978. Payment for the service supplied by the circus is due at the point of entry, and by climbing in D could be described as making off from the spot where payment is due. A technical difficulty, however, is that s3 refers to a 'service done' and a 'service which has been provided'. There is, therefore some doubt as to whether the section extends to cover avoiding payment for service to be provided at some point in the future.

Prima facie it may appear that D, by avoiding payment of the entrance fee, has either obtained a service by deception, contrary to s1 of the 1978 Act, or has dishonestly, by deception, obtained exemption from liability to make a payment, contrary to s2(1)(c) of the 1978 Act. The difficulty in both cases would be in proving some deception on D's part either before obtaining the services, or before obtaining exemption from a liability. There is no evidence that he is trying to deceive anyone by his conduct. Arguably he is seen by members of staff once inside the circus, and is allowed to stay there because he is making the implied representation that he has paid the proper entry fee. On this basis there is the possibility of a s1 offence under the 1978 Act once he is allowed to remain by someone who believes he has paid; see *DPP* v *Ray* (1974). There is insufficient information in the question to be able to pursue this point in more depth.

Section 5(4) of the 1968 Act states that where a defendant gets property by another's mistake and is under an obligation to make restoration of that property or its proceeds, then to the extent of that obligation the property or its proceeds shall be regarded (as against him) as belonging to the person entitled to restoration. Prima facie this section would seem to apply to D, thus effectively preventing property in the change from passing to him. Section 5(4) does not, of itself, create an obligation to restore property obtained by another's mistake. Such an obligation must already exist in law. It is beyond doubt that such an obligation does exist, in quasi contract, where one obtains money as a result of another's mistake. Section 5(4) was specifically drafted to deal with the problem that arose from the decision in *Moynes* v *Cooper* (1956), ie a defendant receiving too much cash in his wage packet. It has been applied to similar situations since its enactment, eg *Attorney-General's Reference (No 1 of 1983)* (1985) (policewoman receiving too much in wages via a bank giro credit). Thus D appropriates property belonging to another when he leaves with the excess change, but at the time he is unaware of the overpayment, and thus would be able to claim that he was not dishonest. He may be guilty of theft if he later realises that he has been given too much change but fails to return it. Retaining the money could be a dishonest appropriation, subject to two caveats. Firstly, D may wrongly, although honestly believe that he has the right in law to keep the money; see s2(1)(a) Theft Act 1968. Secondly, if the sum involved is small, he may not be regarded as dishonest under the test laid down in *R* v *Ghosh* (1982).

D's girlfriend may have committed an offence contrary to s12 of the 1968 Act in allowing herself to be carried on a conveyance she knows to have been taken without the consent of the owner.

In theory D's girlfriend could be regarded as having stolen the petrol, as unlike D, she does not honestly believe that the owner would consent to its being taken, and she may be regarded as dishonest under the test in *R* v *Ghosh*.

7 OTHER THEFT ACT AND RELATED OFFENCES

7.1   Introduction

7.2   Key points

7.3   Recent cases and statutes

7.4   Analysis of questions

7.5   Questions

7.1   Introduction

In addition to the offences of theft and deception there are several related offences that must be known in order to have a complete understanding of the offences against property. These offences will invariably be examined within questions that relate mainly to the areas covered in the proceeding chapter and they provide an opportunity to gain extra marks for the well-prepared student.

7.2   Key points

a) *Robbery*

This is essentially a theft with the aggravating circumstances of the use of force or the fear of its use. The definition under s8 must be known. Most important is the time at which any force is used and if the force is used after the stealing is complete there is no robbery: *Corcoran* v *Anderton* (1980) 71 Cr App R 104. However students must be familiar with the Court of Appeal's ruling in *R* v *Hale* (1978) 68 Cr App R 415 concerning continuing appropriation.

b) *Blackmail - s21 Theft Act 1968*

The elements of the offence ie a view to gain or intent to cause loss/unwarranted demand menaces/believes reasonable grounds for making demand/use of menaces proper.

Note the different ways in which 'demands' may be made (*Treacey* v *DPP* [1971] AC 537) and what will constitute a 'menace': *R* v *Harry* [1974] Crim LR 32; *R* v *Garwood* [1987] Crim LR 476.

Note also the occasions where an accused believed that he was entitled to get his property back from another by these methods - *R* v *Harvey* (1980) 72 Cr App R 139.

c) *Taking a conveyance - s12 Theft Act 1968*

Again the definition must be known and the component parts understood.

'Taking' - *R* v *Bogacki* [1973] QB 832; *R* v *Bow* (1977) 64 Cr App R 54; *R* v *Marchant* (1985) 80 Cr App R 361; 'owner's consent' or 'lawful authority' - *R* v *McGill* [1970] RTR 4; *Whittaker* v *Campbell* [1984] QB 318; *R* v *Peart* [1970] 2 QB 672.

'Conveyance' - *Neal* v *Gribble* (1977) 64 Cr App R 54. Note also that it is an offence to allow oneself to be carried in or on a conveyance knowing it has been so taken, and the offence of unauthorised taking of a pedal cycle.

d) *Removal of articles*

Students should be aware of the specific offence under s11 of the 1968 Act dealing with removal of articles displayed to the public and how it differs from theft and burglary. Most importantly, the lack of a requirement for intention permanently to deprive must be appreciated (as with taking a conveyance).

e) *Going equipped*

The offence of 'going equipped' ie having with one any article for use in connection with any burglary, theft or cheat - s25 Theft Act 1968 is one which is often overlooked in answering questions: *R* v *Rashid* [1977] 2 All ER 237; *R* v *Bundy* [1977] 2 All ER 382; *R* v *Minor* (1987) 52 JP 30.

f) *Handling*

    i)   This is an important and relatively complex offence and its elements ought to be known in some depth.

        The concept of 'handling stolen goods' must be appreciated - the feeling among legislators is that, without 'fences' - ie receivers and handlers - there would be little theft. Therefore handling is viewed more seriously, and punished more harshly than theft. It follows that the thief cannot be the handler.

    ii) The offence can be committed in many different ways (18 to be precise).

        The handler must be dishonest. He must also 'know or believe' the goods to be stolen and these words are to be given their ordinary meaning: *R* v *Harris* (1987) 84 Cr App R 75. In *R* v *Hall* (1985) 81 Cr App R 260 the Court of Appeal laid down guidelines for directing juries on this matter and it was held that where the accused 'cannot say for certain that goods are stolen but there can be no other reasonable conclusion in the light of all the circumstances', such knowledge would suffice. Mere suspicion is not enough.

    iii) The various ways in which the offence may be committed must be known:

        • receiving (or arranging to do so);

- undertaking the retention, removal, realisation or disposal by or for the benefit of another (or arranging to do so);

- assisting in the retention, removal, realisation or disposal by or for the benefit of another (or arranging to do so).

iv) 'Stolen goods' must be understood - ie goods obtained by theft, blackmail, deception, or similar offences abroad which would have constituted theft, blackmail or deception had they been committed in England.

Note should be taken of when goods cease to be 'stolen' and the arguments arising in *Haughton* v *Smith* [1975] AC 476 and *R* v *King* [1938] 2 All ER 662.

g) *Forgery and counterfeiting*

Very briefly, it is useful to remember that there exist separate offences of forgery and counterfeiting. Forgery is basically making or using a document, stamp, tape etc which 'tells a lie about itself'. Counterfeiting involves making or using counterfeit currency or coins.

7.3 Recent cases and statutes

Blackmail:

R v *Bevans* [1988] Crim LR 236 - demanding painkiller at gun point - view to gain?

Taking a conveyance

R v *Gannon* [1988] RTR 49 - burden of proof of mistaken belief in lawful authority.

Going equipped

R v *Minor* (1987) 52 JP 30 - articles acquired at scene of crime - amounted to offence.

Handling:

R v *Park* [1988] Crim LR 238 - solicitor arranged to 'launder' stolen money which hadn't yet been stolen. Not handling - conspiracy more appropriate.

R v *Shelton* (1986) 83 Cr App R 379 - cannot convict of handling and theft on same facts.

Forgery:

R v *Gold and Shifreen* [1988] 2 WLR 984 - computer 'hacking' not forgery. No appropriate alternative in these circumstances.

7.4 Analysis of questions

There will usually be several of these theft-related offences hidden within the facts of questions and it is easy to remain pre-occupied with the obvious crimes revealed at first glance.

Occasionally a question will be largely concerned with one of these related offences usually taking a conveyance or blackmail.

7.5   Questions

Question   1(a)

Xeres and Yella decided that they would try to borrow a car to go for a drink. Xeres asked his brother for a loan of a car to go to town. In fact he wanted to borrow it and take Yella for a drink in a nearby village and he knew that if he told his brother the truth he would not lend it.

What crimes have Xeres and Yella committed?

Adapted from University of London LLB Examination
(for External Students) Criminal Law June 1983 Q6

General comment

A straightforward question on s12 of the Theft Act 1968 with consideration of a possible deception.

Skeleton solution

Taking a conveyance or being carried thereon - s12 TA 1968. Obtaining property/service s15 TA 1968 and s1 TA 1978.

Suggested solution

When Xeres and Yella borrowed Xeres' brother's car to go for a drink at a nearby village they may both have committed offences contrary to s12 of the Theft Act 1968. Section 12 provides that a person shall be guilty of an offence if without having the consent of the owner or other lawful authority he takes any conveyance for his own or another's use, or knowing that any conveyance is to be taken without such authority, drives it or allows himself to be carried in it or on it.

There is not a 'taking' of a conveyance until there is movement, *R* v *Bogacki* (1973) and furthermore the taking of the conveyance must be for use as a conveyance: *R* v *Bow* (1976). These elements of the offence would be satisfied on the facts in question. However, what may not be satisfied is whether the taking is 'without the consent of the owner'.

On the facts in question the consent is obtained by fraud. In this respect two particular cases must be considered. In *R* v *Peart* (1970) D persuaded P to lend him a van in order to go to A. In fact he wanted the van to go to B where he was found by police some time after the expiry of the period within which he should have returned the van. The conviction under s12 was quashed by the Court of Appeal because the consent which P had obtained was not vitiated by the deception. In that case the deception did not relate to a fundamental matter and therefore still operated. However, the court left open the question of whether a deception relating to a fundamental aspect would nullify consent.

In *R* v *McGill* (1970) it was held that D may be convicted of an offence if he has obtained consent to use a conveyance for a particular purpose and for a given time but uses it beyond that time for a different purpose. At the moment when he has completed the purpose for which the consent was originally given and he goes on to

141

use the vehicle for a different purpose there will be a fresh 'taking' of the conveyance under s12.

It is difficult to reconcile these two cases and it is submitted that the facts in question are more akin to those of *R* v *Peart* (1970) than *R* v *McGill* (1970). On that basis the deception is not fundamental and therefore the consent would still operate. However if this were not the case and the court found that there was a taking of the conveyance without consent, Xeres could be charged with taking and driving the conveyance contrary to s12 and Yella could be charged with allowing himself to be driven contrary to s12, but only if he knew that the taking was without consent. There would be no possibility of charging either party under s1 of the Theft Act 1968 (theft) or s15 of the Theft Act 1968 (obtaining property by deception) because although they have satisfied the actus reus and it is possible that they would be viewed as dishonest, they did not possess the necessary 'intention to permanently deprive'.

Similarly, a charge of obtaining a service from the brother under s1 of the 1978 Theft Act would be inappropriate as, although there is a 'benefit' conferred upon X and Y, it was not made on the understanding that it has been or will be paid for.

Question 1(b)

N and O, aged 17 years and 13 years, decided to borrow their father's car without asking. They suspected, though they did not know, that he would have refused. N drove them to a nearby cafe.

Advise N and O.

Adapted from University of London LLB Examination
(for External Students) Criminal Law June 1984 Q5

General comment

Again, a fairly simple examination of s12 with particular regard to 'consent' and the aggravating factor of the age of the accused.

Skeleton solution

Conspiracy - CLA 1977; mischievous discretion; taking a conveyance and being carried thereon - s12 TA 1968.

Suggested solution

When N and O decide to borrow their father's car without his approval, they may commit a conspiracy contrary to s1 of the Criminal Law Act 1977 in that they have agreed on a course of conduct which if carried out in accordance with their intention will necessarily amount to the offence contained in s12 of the Theft Act 1968. N is 17 years old and therefore for the purpose of criminal law is treated as an adult. However, O is 13 years old and because of this will only be a party to the conspiracy if it can be shown that he has 'mischievous discretion': *R* v *Gorrie* (1918) and *McC* v *Runneckles* (1984). The fact that they suspected, although they did not know, their father would have refused would not give them a defence to any change contrary to s12. Under s12(6) a person would not commit the offence of taking a conveyance if:

a) he believed he had lawful authority to take the conveyance; or

b) he believed that he would have the owner's consent if the owner knew of the circumstances.

Neither of those requirements are satisfied on the facts in question.

When N drives the car and O is carried in the car they commit offences under s12 of the Theft Act 1968. N would be liable for taking and driving a conveyance without the consent of the owner and O would be liable, presuming that he has mischievous discretion, for allowing himself to be driven in a conveyance, knowing that it has been taken without the consent of the owner. The 'taking' of the conveyance occurs at the moment of some movement: *R* v *Bogacki* (1973). Furthermore, the taking and driving was in this case for use as a conveyance in that both N and O were transported in the vehicle: *R* v *Bow* (1976) and *R* v *Stokes* (1982).

Question 2

G and I were students at the same college. G wrote to H, I's millionaire father, demanding payment to rag funds in return for I's release. I agreed to write to H saying that he had been held against his will. This was not true. On receipt of these letters H was very alarmed and told his wife what had transpired. She had a nervous condition and suffered a heart attack.

H paid the money to the rag fund. Earlier, G and friends had blocked the roads near the college demanding payment before permitting vehicles to pass.

Advise G, I and H on their criminal liability.

Adapted from University of London LLB Examination
(for External Students) Criminal Law June 1985 Q3

General comment

A fairly straightforward examination of making 'demands with menaces' and the possible overlap with deception.

Skeleton solution

Blackmail - s21 TA 1968; attempted deception s15 TA 1968; deception s15 TA 1968; robbery - s8 TA 1968.

Suggested solution

When G writes to I's father demanding payment to rag funds in return for I's release he may commit the offence of blackmail contrary to s21 Theft Act 1968. A person is guilty of blackmail if he makes an unwarranted demand with menaces with a view to gain for himself or another or to cause loss to another in money or other property.

A 'demand' can be made in any number of ways and on the facts in question it would be complete when the letter is posted. It is immaterial whether or not it is received by the victim: *Treacy* v *DPP* (1971). The term 'menaces' is not defined in the Act.

In *R v Clear* (1968) it was held that the demand was only menacing if it was accompanied by threats of such nature and extent that an ordinary person of normal stability would be influenced so as to accede to the demand. In *R v Harry* (1974) the organisers of a student rag wrote letters to local shopkeepers offering them immunity from rag activities if they contributed to rag funds. While some shopkeepers complained this was held not to be menacing because an average person would not have been affected. Possibly if G and I had appreciated the wife's nervous condition that would have been taken into account.

A demand with menaces is unwarranted unless:

a) the accused believes that he has reasonable grounds for making the demand; and

b) the accused believes that the use of menaces is a proper means of reinforcing the demand.

When I writes to his father saying falsely that he is being held against his will he may be liable for an attempt to obtain money by deception contrary to s15 Theft Act 1968. Section 15 of the Theft Act 1968 provides that a person who by any deception dishonestly obtains property belonging to another with intention to permanently deprive shall commit an offence. The deception must satisfy s15(4) and therefore must be either intentional or reckless and can be by words or conduct, as to fact or as to law, including a deception as to the present intentions of the person using the deception, or any other person.

The deception must be shown to be the operative reason for the obtaining of the property (in this case the money).

Undoubtedly, there is an intention to permanently deprive although it may not be so easy to satisfy the requirement for dishonesty. The question of dishonesty must be left to the jury to decide. In *R v Ghosh* (1982) the Court of Appeal adopted an essentially subjective approach. When deciding whether or not a person was acting dishonestly the jury had to decide whether according to the ordinary standard of reasonable and honest people the accused's conduct was dishonest. If it was not then the accused should be acquitted. If it was the jury should then consider when the accused viewed his conduct as dishonest by ordinary standards. If he realised that his conduct was dishonest by these standards he would still be dishonest even if he believed that he was morally justified in acting in the way he did act.

When H pays the money to the rag fund a full offence contrary to s15 of the Theft Act 1968 may have been committed. While the House of Lords was of the opinion in *Lawrence v MPC* (1971) that there was a certain overlap between s15 of the Theft Act 1968 and s1 of the Act it did not make clear when that overlap would occur. No further clarification was given to this point in *R v Morris* (1983). If ownership of the money has passed from H it seems most likely that s15 alone is satisfied as the overlap between s15 and s1 would more obviously occur if ownership of the money remained in H while possession and control passed to the rag fund.

When G and friends blocked the road demanding payment before allowing vehicles to pass, a further offence under s21 may be shown although it seems much less likely that their demands would be found to be menacing. As we are not told of any force or threatened force used towards the drivers it is unlikely that a charge of robbery under s8 of the Theft Act 1968 would be made out.

Question 3

Whilst waiting in a bank, T saw V make a large withdrawal which he decided to steal. T threatened to hit V and snatched the money. He then ran out of the bank pushing two customers out of the way. T stopped a passing motorist, X, telling him a lie that he urgently needed to visit his wife who had been taken into a local hospital after an accident. X drove T to the hospital where he was apprehended.

Advise T.

Adapted from University of London LLB Examination
(for External Students) Criminal Law June 1985 Q8

General comment

A fairly detailed question made simpler by the fact that there is only one accused. A well-prepared student would be able to get very good marks here.

Skeleton solution

Robbery - s8 TA 1968; assault and battery; obtaining service by deception - s1 TA 1978; taking a conveyance - s12 TA 1968.

Suggested solution

When T removes the money from V's bag he commits the offence of theft contrary to s1 Theft Act 1968. Under s1 there is theft when there is an appropriation of property belonging to another with a dishonest intention to permanently deprive the other of the property. Section 3 provides that an assumption by a person of the right of an owner will amount to an appropriation. In *R* v *Morris* (1983) the House of Lords held that it was not necessary for the prosecution to prove that an accused assumed all the rights. It was sufficient to prove that he assumed any of the rights. Furthermore, the concept of an appropriation involved an act by way of 'adverse interference with or usurpation of those rights'. The question of dishonesty must be left to the jury who should apply the test as stated in *R* v *Ghosh* (1982).

However, the theft here is aggravated by T's use of threats toward V.

Section 8 of the Theft Act 1968 makes it an offence of robbery where a person steals and immediately before or at the time of doing so, and in order to do so, he uses force on any person, or puts or seeks to put any person in fear of being then or there subjected to force.

In threatening V, T commits a common law assault and also, as he puts V in fear of being subjected to force in order to facilitate his theft, T commits robbery.

His use of force on the customers appears to come after the theft is complete in which case he would only commit an assault and battery at common law against them.

However, in *R* v *Hale* (1978) the Court of Appeal held that an appropriation could be regarded as a continuing act and when considering the time at which force was used, and the purpose therefor, it may be open to a jury so to conclude.

It is submitted that in this case the appropriation by T is complete before he pushes the customers.

When T stops a passing motorist and tells him a lie to persuade him to give him a lift, he may commit an offence contrary to s1 Theft Act 1978. Under s1(1) a person who by any deception dishonestly obtains services from another shall be guilty of an offence. The phrase 'deception' is defined in 15(4) Theft Act 1968 as any deception (whether deliberate or reckless) by words or conduct as to fact or as to law, including a deception as to the present intentions of the person using the deception or any other person.

The deception must be the operative reason for the obtaining of the services: *R* v *Clucas* (1949).

The term 'service' is defined in s1(2) of the Theft Act 1978 which provides that it is an obtaining of services where the other is induced to confer a benefit by doing some act, or causing or permitting some act to be done on the understanding that the benefit has been or will be paid for.

It is this last element of payment that does not on the facts appear to be satisfied.

T may also commit the offence of taking a conveyance without the owner's consent or other lawful authority contrary to s12 of the Theft Act 1968.

The question to be determined here would be whether T had 'taken' the conveyance. He has certainly used it as such, satisfying the requirements in *R* v *Bow* (1977).

Another requirement for the offence is that the taking is without the owner's consent. X here consents to the use of the vehicle but that consent is obtained by T's false representations. Does that vitiate the consent.

In *Whittaker* v *Campbell* (1984) it was held that in such circumstances it could not be said that the owner had not consented.

In *R* v *Peart* (1970) D made a false representation of an urgent need to make one journey, knowing that the owner would not have consented to the taking had he known of D's real intended journey. It was held that such a deception did not vitiate the owner's consent.

Therefore it appears that, even if a 'taking' could be established, T does not do so without the owner's consent.

Question 4

a) T took £450 from her boss's till despite having been expressly instructed not to do so. T intended to replace the money. T used the money to buy groceries from T's friend U having explained to U how she had come by the cash.

b) T believed that V had agreed to lend T his car to visit T's mother. In fact V had agreed to lend the car but only if T's husband drove it. T did in fact drive the car. Later, T went to a multi-storey car park to look for a car to take for a joyride. T took a set of duplicate ignition keys with him in the hope that one of them might fit one of the parked cars.

Advise T and U of their criminal liability if any.

Adapted from University of London LLB Examination
(for External Students) Criminal Law June 1986 Q8

General comment

A fairly straightforward question. Part (a) in particular covers an area of the syllabus that has frequently been examined. Part (b) deals with an area not quite so commonly examined. However an averagely well prepared student should be able to pick up good marks on this question.

Skeleton solution

a) Section 1 Theft Act 1968 - s2 Theft Act 1968: cases on dishonesty - s22 Theft Act: definition of stolen goods.

b) Section 12(1) Theft Act 1968 - s12(b) Theft Act 1968 - going equipped - s25 TA 1968.

Suggested solution

a) When T took £450 from her employer's till having been expressly instructed not to do so she may commit the offence of theft contrary to s1 Theft Act 1968. Under s1 a person is guilty of theft if he dishonestly appropriates property belonging to another with the intention of permanently depriving the other of it.

Undoubtedly on the facts there is the actus reus of theft. Furthermore she has an intention to permanently deprive because although she intends to return an equivalent sum of money she has the intention to use the money she removed for her own purposes. This would be an example of an intention to permanently deprive. The borrowing of the money is equivalent to an outright taking within s6(1) because T treats it as her own to dispose of regardless of the other's rights. (*R* v *Velumyl* (1989)).

The only question remaining is whether T is dishonest.

Section 2 Theft Act 1968 lists three instances when a person is not to be regarded as dishonest. These are:

a) if he believed he had the right in law to take the property;

b) where the accused believes the owner would consent if he knew of the circumstances; or

c) if he believed the owner cannot be found by taking reasonable steps.

147

None of these is available on the facts as given. It is therefore for the jury to decide whether T is dishonest: *R* v *Feely* (1973). The test to be applied is as stated in *R* v *Ghosh* (1982) and, if T claims that her behaviour was honest even though the majority of people would think it dishonest, a *Ghosh* direction is appropriate: *R* v *Price* (1990):

i) was T dishonest according to the standards of reasonable honest people. If no, T will not be guilty. If yes;

ii) did T realise that reasonable and honest people would regard what she did as dishonest. If yes, she is guilty. If no, she is not guilty.

U may commit an offence within s22 Theft Act 1968 when she accepts the money in payment for groceries knowing how T came by the cash. However before this offence is shown a number of points would have to be satisfied. Under s22 Theft Act 1968 U would be liable for handling stolen goods if (otherwise than in the course of the stealing) knowing and believing them to be stolen goods she dishonestly receives the goods, or dishonestly undertakes in their retention, removal, disposal or realisation by or for the benefit of another, or arranges to do so.

The first question to consider is whether the money can be regarded as 'stolen goods'. For the purposes of s22, 'stolen goods' includes goods taken contrary to s1 Theft Act 1968. Therefore only if T was dishonest in her appropriation - so that T is liable for theft, can the money be regarded as stolen and U be regarded as receiving stolen goods. However it must still be shown that U acted dishonestly (*R* v *Feely* and *R* v *Ghosh*) and that she had knowledge or a belief that the money was stolen. It should be noted that if the money is stolen the groceries purchased with the money may themselves be 'tainted'. Within s24(2) Theft Act 1968 'stolen goods' shall include any other goods which are directly or indirectly stolen goods in the hands of the thief.

Technically U may also commit the offence of theft as defined above at the same time as any s22 offence: *R* v *Sainthouse* (1980). However, U cannot on the same circumstances and facts, be convicted of both offences: *R* v *Shelton* (1986).

If U committed an offence under s22 T would be liable as an aider and abettor to the offence in that she was present assisting and encouraging at the scene of the crime *R* v *Coney* (1882) with full knowledge of the facts that constitute the offence: *Johnson* v *Youden* (1950).

b) It is necessary to consider the offence of taking a conveyance under s12 Theft Act 1968. Section 12 Theft Act 1968 provides that a person shall be guilty of an offence if, without having the consent of the owner or other lawful authority, he takes or drives any conveyance for his own or another's use. T had undoubtedly committed the actus reus of the offence. The car is a 'conveyance' within s12(3) and T takes it for use as a conveyance: *R* v *Bow* (1977). However, s12(6) provides that a person does not commit the offence of taking a conveyance if he believes that he had lawful authority to take the conveyance. Such belief need not be reasonable provided it is honestly held.

When T goes to the car park armed with the keys he may commit the offence under s25 of the Theft Act 1968, of going equipped as he, when not at his place of abode, has with him articles for use in the course of or in connection with a theft. Although taking a car for a joyride would not amount to 'theft' per s1 of the Act, it is sufficient for the purposes of s25 that his intention is to take a conveyance without consent.

Question 5

Wally decides to get himself some money to pay off gambling debts. He goes to a nearby shopping precinct, taking a child's halloween mask with him from his house.

Seeing Lindsey pushing a pram containing her three month old baby, Wally puts on the mask. He stops Lindsey and shouts 'Give me your purse or the baby gets it!'

Lindsey is terrified for her baby's safety and hands over the purse.

What offences, if any, has Wally committed?

Written by Editor

General comment

This question is a straightforward test of a student's knowledge of robbery and blackmail and the distinction between the two.

Skeleton solution

Robbery - s8 TA 1968; blackmail - s21 TA 1968; theft - ss1-7 TA 1968; going equipped - s25 TA 1968.

Suggested solution

When Wally leaves his house with the mask in his possession, he commits an offence under s25 of the Theft Act 1968 which states that:

'a person shall be guilty of an offence if, when not at his place of abode, he has with him any article for use in the course of or in connection with any burglary, theft or cheat.'

The term 'article' is very wide: *R* v *Rashid* (1977) and would cover the halloween mask under these circumstances.

Wally intends to use the mask in a future theft and therefore he has sufficient mens rea for this offence: *R* v *Ellames* (1974).

When Wally puts on the mask and threatens the baby, getting Lindsey to hand over her purse, he may be guilty of robbery under s8 of the Theft Act 1968.

A person is guilty of robbery if he steals, and immediately before or at the time of doing so, and in order to do so, he uses force on any person or puts, or seeks to put any person in fear of being then and there subjected to force.

149

In appropriating the purse, Wally 'steals' ie he dishonestly appropriates property belonging to another with the intention of permanently depriving the other of it (s1 Theft Act 1968). The question here is whether he has used force or sought to put a person in fear of being subjected to force.

It can be argued that he uses no force on Lindsey, neither does he seek to put her in fear of its use on her. Moreover, Wally cannot realistically be said to put the baby in fear of being subjected to force as, it is submitted, the baby is too young to appreciate the situation.

Therefore it is arguable that the fear instilled in Lindsey by Wally is insufficient to support a charge of robbery. Had he used force on the baby, that may have sufficed.

More appropriate would be a charge of blackmail contrary to s21 of the Theft Act 1968 which makes it an offence for a person, with a view to gain for himself or another, or with intent to cause loss to another, to make any unwarranted demand with menaces.

Here the demand is quite clear and it is made with a view to gain.

'Menaces' is to be given its ordinary meaning: *R* v *Lawrence and Pomroy* (1971) and in *Thorne* v *Motor Trade Association* (1937). Lord Wright held a menace to be a threat of 'any action detrimental to or unpleasant to the person addressed'.

This is clearly the case here and Wally's threat would be 'of such a nature and extent that the mind of an ordinary person of normal stability and courage would accede to the demand: *R* v *Clear* (1968).

Wally would not be able to avail himself of the provisions of s21 by claiming a belief that he has reasonable grounds for making the demand and that the use of the menaces is a proper means of reinforcing it.

If Wally knows that what he is threatening is a crime he cannot maintain that such a threat is proper: *R* v *Harvey, Ulyett and Plummer* (1980).

Question 6

'There is no overlap between theft and handling.'

Discuss.

University of London LLB Examination
(for External Students) Criminal Law June 1990 Q7

General comment

A straightforward question requiring a comparison of the elements of theft and handling. Some explanation of *Pitham and Hehl* is clearly needed, as well as a more general explanation of why the two offences need to co-exist.

Skeleton solution

Explain elements of both offences. Provide examples of cases where there may be an overlap. Look at the judicial response. Consider wider issues.

Suggested solution

Theft, as defined by s1(1) of the Theft Act 1968 involves the dishonest appropriation of property belonging to another with intention to permanently deprive that other of it. A central concept within this definition is that of appropriation. Section 3(1) of the 1968 further defines appropriation as an assumption of the owner's rights. Lord Roskill, in *R* v *Morris* (1983), explained that this could be any assumption of any of the owner's rights. Appropriation can take place, therefore, where a defendant sells another's property, pledges it, gives it away, uses it up, or merely takes it into his own possession.

Section 22(1) of the 1968 Act defines handling as occurring where a defendant who knows or believes goods to have been stolen, dishonestly receives them, or dishonestly undertakes or assists in their retention, removal, realisation, or disposal, for another's benefit, or by another person. Crucially, the section adds, in parenthesis, that all of this must occur otherwise than in the course of stealing.

It was clearly the intention of the legislators, therefore, that there should be a distinction between handling and theft. Prima facie they were to be mutually exclusive. If a defendant was stealing goods he could not at the same time be handling them. In reality the law has cause confusion. A number of scenarios need to be considered.

Where a defendant steals another man's wallet, he commits an offence contrary to s1(1) of the 1968 Act, but not s22(1). Although he has received stolen property he has done so in the course of stealing it, and thus is excluded from the ambit of s22(1). In a simple case such as this there is no problem. In any event the prosecution would be content to charge the defendant with theft.

Complications emerge where the defendant is accompanied by a friend. Let us supposed that D1 takes P's wallet whilst D2 keeps watch. Once he has taken the wallet, D1 passes it immediately to D2. Is D2 guilty of theft, handling, or both ? The correct answer would perhaps be either. D2 could be charged with theft as an accomplice to D1. He is clearly aiding in the commission of the offence, and has the necessary mens rea. Alternatively he could be charged with receiving stolen goods contrary to s22(1). In *R* v *Pitham and Hehl* (1976), D1 invited D2 and D3 to the house of X who was in prison at the time. D1 invited D2 and D3 to purchase some of the contents of the house, which they agreed to do. It was held that D1 was guilty of theft because he had offered to sell property belonging to another. D2 and D3 were held to be guilty of stealing the property. The theft, in the view of the court, was complete once the act of appropriation had been committed, ie once the offer to sell had been made. D2 and D3 could thus be charged with arranging to receive stolen property otherwise than in the course of stealing since the theft had ceased. It has been argued that the effect of this ruling has been to render the words 'otherwise than in the course of stealing' redundant. What it certainly illustrates is that the statement suggesting that theft and handling cannot overlap is somewhat dubious.

A further difficulty arises where stolen property passes from one defendant to another. Suppose that D1 steals a camera, and sells it to D2 at a considerable undervalue. D2 knows that the camera is stolen. That D1 is guilty of theft but not handling is evident from what has already been explained above. What of the liability of D2? By taking the stolen property into his possession, knowing it to have been stolen, D2 is clearly receiving stolen property contrary to s22(1). But is he not also committing theft? He cannot claim to have acquired good title to the camera, since he was not a bona fide purchaser for value without notice, hence the camera remains property belonging to another as against D2. By taking it into his possession he assumes the rights of the owner, and one can assume from the facts that he has the necessary mens rea. Prima facie it would appear that he cannot be convicted of handling the stolen camera, since he is at the same time stealing it, and the statute, as explained above, endeavour to keep the two offences apart. The same problem arises in relation to other forms of handling under s22(1). Disposal, retention, realisation, and removal of another's property could all be acts amounting to appropriation for the purposes of theft. Taken to its logical conclusion this argument would limit the scope of handling stolen goods to such an extent that the offence could become redundant. The courts have supplied at least a partial solution by way of decisions such as *R v Sainthouse* (1980), where it was held that the term 'otherwise than in the course of stealing' was meant to prevent the original thief from being charged with handling stolen goods whilst 'on the job'. The expression was not to be taken as preventing charges under s22(1) from being brought against a subsequent handler of those goods, even though technically he might be appropriating them.

On a more general level there are two good arguments for maintaining a separate offence of handling stolen goods, even though the offence may overlap with theft. Firstly, there may be some cases where it is debatable whether or not a handler is necessarily appropriating stolen goods, eg cases where D arranges to receive stolen property. Secondly, there may be cases where the original thief has obtained voidable title to the goods, for example where he has obtained them by deception, and as a result, the goods might not represent property belonging to another, as against the handler.

8   CRIMINAL DAMAGE

8.1	Introduction
8.2	Key points
8.3	Recent cases and statutes
8.4	Analysis of questions
8.5	Questions

8.1   Introduction

Criminal damage is an area of criminal law that is relatively straightforward and which usually forms the basis of at least one examination question. As with the Theft Acts offences, definitions should be learnt together with statutory defences.

8.2   Key points

a) The three broad categories of criminal damage must be known ie:

  i)   without lawful excuse, destroying or damaging property belonging to another, intentionally or recklessly (s1(1) Criminal Damage Act 1971);

  ii) destroying or damaging property belonging to self or another intentionally or recklessly, intending to endanger the life of another or being reckless as to whether the life of another is endangered (s1(2) CDA 1971);

  iii) arson - destroying or damaging property by fire (s1(3) CDA 1971).

b) Elements and their meanings must be known.

'Destroy or damage' - *Samuel* v *Stubbs* [1972] 4 SASR 200; *Hardman* v *Chief Constable of Avon and Somerset* [1986] Crim LR 330.

'Property' - note the overlap with theft. Also *Cox* v *Riley* (1986) 83 Cr App R 54 - erasure of programme from circuit card.

'Belonging to another' and the overlap with theft.

'Intentionally or recklessly' - the mens rea of criminal damage is probably the most difficult aspect of it. Cases such as *R* v *Smith* [1974] QB 354 and *R* v *Appleyard* (1985) 81 Cr App R 319 should be known.

Most importantly, *MPC* v *Caldwell* [1981] 1 All ER 961 must be known and contrasted with other forms of recklessness (see Chapter 2). Later cases such as *Elliott* v *C* [1983] 2 All ER 1005 should be learnt and the recent case of *Chief Constable of Avon and Somerset* v *Shimmen* (1986) 84 Cr App R 7.

'Lawful excuse' and s5 of the 1971 Act must be learnt, and occasions on which an accused may destroy or damage another's property without attracting criminal liability.

Where a charge under s1(2) is considered, the causal connection between the damage and the danger to life must be shown: *R* v *Steer* [1987] 2 All ER 833.

Note also that s1(2) will cover damaging one's own property if the attendant intention or recklessness is shown.

c) Finally, the offences of threatening to destroy or damage property, and having custody or control of anything intending to cause criminal damage should not be overlooked.

8.3 Recent cases and statutes

R v *Ashford and Smith* [1988] Crim LR 682 - CND member in possession of wire-cutters. Argued defence of protecting property from nuclear attack. Such a defence to be judged objectively.

R v *Hill*; *R* v *Hall* [1989] Crim LR 136 - again, CND member, with hacksaw. Held belief in nuclear attack too remote in law. No evidence of need for protection from immediate danger.

R v *Dudley* [1989] Crim LR 57 - arson - damage caused was only trivial - s1(2) referred to intended damage not actual damage.

Morphitis v *Salmon* (1990) 154 JPN 186 - person removed scaffolding clip and bar from barrier - no damage to either - although barrier itself was dismantled, and therefore was arguably 'damaged' on current authorities, no damage to component parts as charged.

Lloyd v *DPP* [1991] Crim LR 904 - wheelclamping 'trespassing' vehicle not criminal damage - removing such a device by damaging it does not attract defence of 'lawful excuse'.

R v *Whiteley* [1991] Crim LR 436 - deletion of computer program may be 'damage'.

Computer Misuse Act 1990 - creates offences of securing unauthorised access to computer programs with or without an ulterior intent, and causing unauthorised modification to the contents of a computer with the intention of preventing/hindering access.

8.4 Analysis of questions

Criminal damage questions rarely appear alone and the offences are usually included among other crimes eg burglary and theft. In many cases the destruction of property may also amount to a theft and the overlap between the offences must be appreciated.

8.5   Questions

Question 1

C and E were out poaching on D's land. C fell and injured himself and lay in the undergrowth for several hours. Eventually another poacher found C and alerted E who came onto the land deliberately damaging a fence, to take C to hospital.

Advise E of his criminal liability.

Adapted from University of London LLB Examination
(for External Students) Criminal Law June 1988 Q2

General comment

The issue of criminal damage needs to be considered carefully, step by step, especially whether E has any lawful excuse for what he did. Note that there is no defence of necessity in English law.

Skeleton solution

Fence damaged - Criminal Damage Act 1971 - 'damage' - 'property' - 'belonging to another' - mens rea - intention - recklessness - defences.

Suggested solution

When E deliberately damaged a fence in entering D's land in order to take C to hospital, he may have committed criminal damage contrary to s1(1) Criminal Damage Act 1971.

The actus reus of the offence consists of 'destroying' or 'damaging' 'property' 'belonging to another'.

The terms 'destroy' and 'damage' contemplate actual destruction or damage, ie some physical harm, impairment or deterioration which can be perceived by the senses. The actual damage need only be slight but there must be actual damage: *Eley* v *Lytle* (1885); *Gayford* v *Chouler* (1898); *Laws* v *Eltringham* (1881). How the defendant regards his conduct will be irrelevant if, in fact, damage was caused: *R* v *Fancy* (1980).

On the facts of the question, 'damage' appears to have been committed.

By s10(1) Criminal Damage Act 1971, property is widely defined so as to include all 'property of a tangible nature, whether real or personal'.

Clearly, a fence constitutes 'property' for the purposes of the Criminal Damage Act 1971.

An offence under the Criminal Damage Act can only be committed against property 'belonging to another'. By s10(2) Criminal Damage Act 1971, property will belong to another if that other has some proprietary interest in the property. There is no need for that other to own it.

From the facts, the fence appears to 'belong to another' within the meaning of the Criminal Damage Act 1971.

The mens rea of the offence of criminal damage consists of intention or recklessness, and an absence of lawful excuse. A person intends to cause a result if he acts with the purpose of doing so: *R v Moloney* (1985); *R v Hancock and Shankland* (1986); *R v Nedrick* (1986). The defendant must not only intend to do the act which caused the damage but also must have intended to cause the damage.

From the facts, it appears that E had the required mens rea.

By s5(2) Criminal Damage Act 1971, two grounds of justification are given for damage deliberately done, namely a belief in the consent of the person entitled to consent to the destruction or damage of the property and action taken in defence of property.

On the facts, E knew that D, the person who was entitled to consent had refused his consent.

As E damaged the fence in order to help C, he clearly cannot argue that he was acting in defence of property.

Therefore, these two limbs of the defence of lawful excuse are not available to E.

However, by s5(2) Criminal Damage Act 1971, the law recognises that there may be other circumstances, apart from a belief in consent or acting in defence of property, which could constitute a lawful excuse for it provides that 'this section shall not be construed as casting any doubt on any defence recognised by law as a defence to criminal charges'.

On the facts, it does not appear that E could avail himself of any defence recognised by law, eg infancy, insanity, duress. Therefore, E appears to have committed criminal damage.

Question 2(a)

N, aged 13 years, was pedalling his bicycle along a busy pavement, crashed the cycle through a shop window. N caused an electrical cable to short and a fire started in the shop window, spreading quickly to the interior.

Assess N's criminal liability.

> Adapted from University of London LLB Examination
> (for External Students) Criminal Law June 1985 Q5

General comment

This question, although complicated slightly by causation and mischievous discretion, is really a test of knowledge of the elements of criminal damage.

Skeleton solution

Criminal damage to shop - and causing fire - s1(1), 1(2) and 1(3) of the Criminal Damage Act 1971.

Suggested solution

When N crashes his bicycle into a shop window thus causing a cable to short and a fire to start he may commit a number of offences under the Criminal Damage Act 1971.

Section 1(1) of the Act provides that a person who without lawful excuse destroys or damages property belonging to another intending to destroy or damage any such property or being reckless as to whether any such property would be destroyed or damaged commits an offence.

Section 1(2) of the Act provides that a person who without lawful excuse destroys or damages property, whether belonging to himself or another with intent to endanger life or being reckless as to whether life is endangered shall commit an offence.

Section 1(3) of the Act provides that an offence under s1(1) or (2) committed by the use of fire is to be charged as 'arson'.

The test for recklessness was given by the House of Lords in *MPC* v *Caldwell* (1981). A person charged with an offence under the Criminal Damage Act 1971 is reckless if: ·

1) he does an act which in fact creates an obvious risk (of property being destroyed or damaged); and

2) when he did the act he either has not given any thought to the possibility of there being any such risk or he had recognised that there was some risk involved and has nonetheless gone on to take it.

In *Elliott* v *C (a minor)* (1983) it was held that the phrase 'creates an obvious risk' requires only that the risk would be obvious to a reasonably prudent man, not necessarily that the accused would have seen the risk had he given thought to it. Thus the fact that an accused was, for example, of subnormal intelligence or a child would not be taken into account.

Here, N's cycling down a busy pavement may amount to such an obvious risk.

It is submitted that, even if N were reckless under these circumstances, he would not be guilty of arson. Arson is a distinct and separate offence which, according to Smith and Hogan (6th Ed p687) requires intention or recklessness not merely that property would be damaged but that it would be damaged *'by fire'* and this is clearly not the case here.

It could not be said that N's conduct created an obvious risk of the shop being destroyed or damaged by fire although N, having started the fire, may have a duty to take some action to extinguish it: *R* v *Miller* (1983).

A defence may be available to N because he is only 13 years old. The defence of infancy is available to a child aged between 10-14 if it can be shown that he lacked 'mischievous discretion' ie a comprehension of the difference between right and wrong: *R* v *Gorrie* (1918); *McC* v *Runneckles* (1984), although the objective test in *Elliott* v *C* would apply to N's 'recklessness'.

CRIMINAL LAW

Question 2(b)

P, an anti-bloodsports demonstrator, spread chemicals on fields to make the hounds sneeze and to impair their sense of smell.

Advise P of his criminal liability if any.

Adapted from University of London LLB Examination
(for External Students) Criminal Law June 1985 Q6

General comment

A straightforward examination of simple damage and its component parts.

Skeleton solution

Criminal damage under s1(1) Criminal Damage Act 1971 to land - attempted criminal damage to hounds - s1(2) of the Criminal Damage Act 1971 - possessing articles - s3 CDA 1971.

Suggested solution

When P spreads chemicals on the land in order to divert the hounds from their trail he may commit an offence contrary to s1(1) of the Criminal Damage Act 1971

Section 1(1)provides that a person who without lawful excuse destroys or damages any property belonging to another intending to destroy or damage any such property or being reckless as to whether any such property would be destroyed or damaged shall commit an offence.

The expression 'destroy or damage' speaks for itself to a great extent although it should be noted that an article or object may be damaged even though it is not actually broken in any way and can serve to carry out its normal purpose: *Hardman* v *Chief Constable of Avon and Somerset* (1986).

Section 10(1) of the Criminal Damage Act contains the definition of property for the purposes of criminal damage. 'Property' means property of a tangible nature whether real property or personal property.

Applying these principles to the facts in question when P spread chemicals onto the land he was damaging property belonging to another in that the chemicals were to a degree spoiling the property. Undoubtedly P would wish to claim that he was acting with lawful excuse and therefore not liable for any offence.

A partial definition of 'lawful excuse' may be found in s5 of the Act. P's conduct would not fall within any of the specific situations mentioned in s5 ie belief that the owner would consent or defence of property. It would therefore be up to the jury to decide whether they thought he had a lawful excuse for his conduct. The mens rea of s1(1) is satisfied where in addition to acting without lawful excuse the destruction or damage of the property is shown to be either intentional or reckless in the *MPC* v *Caldwell* (1982) sense.

While D may not intentionally damage the land he would be 'reckless' within the *MPC* v *Caldwell* definition in that he created an obvious risk that the property would

158

be damaged and either he had given no thought to the possibility of the risk or he had seen the risk but had nevertheless gone on to take it.

P may commit a further offence under the Criminal Damage Act by attempting to damage property belonging to another. When he spreads the chemicals he does so in order to make the hounds sneeze and impair their sense of smell. The hounds would be 'property belonging to another' and what he intended would be sufficient to amount to 'damage'. In order to establish an attempt it must be shown that his act is more than merely preparatory: s1 Criminal Attempts Act 1981. This is for the jury to decide. Furthermore the mens rea for any attempt is generally the same as for the full offence except that as this is a result crime it must be shown that P intended the damage. Recklessness is not sufficient.

Additionally, by having the chemicals in his custody or under his control intending, without lawful excuse to use it to destroy or damage property belonging to some other person, P commits an offence under s3 of the Act.

Question 3

X and Y were members of a peaceful sect who were strongly opposed to war and violence of any description. Intending to cut holes in a perimeter fence of a military establishment, X and Y set off across nearby moorland armed with pliers.

They were apprehended before reaching the fence.

Advise X and Y of their criminal liability, if any, under the Criminal Damage Act 1971.

X and Y tell you that they intend to use the defence that they were acting in defence of their nearby property which would be endangered by the presence of the establishment in the event of war.

How far are they likely to succeed in this defence and would it make any difference if X and Y had carried out their damage?

Written by Editor

General comment

A fairly detailed question covering recent cases on criminal damage and in particular the statutory defence.

Skeleton solution

Possessing articles - s3 CDA 1971; lawful excuse - s15(2) and (3) CDA 1971.

Suggested solution

Where X and Y take up the pliers intending to cut the fence they commit the offence under s3 of the Criminal Damage Act 1971.

Under s3 a person who has anything in his custody or under his control intending without lawful excuse to use it or to cause or permit another to use it, to destroy or damage property belonging to some other person shall be guilty of an offence.

It is not necessary that they leave their house with the pliers or even that they have them with them, and the offence is complete as soon as they have custody or control of the implements with the relevant intention.

X and Y may argue that, although they did intend to cause damage to the fence, it was with a view to causing the military base to close, thereby removing the likelihood of a hostile attack on the area in the event of war. That being the case, X and Y may argue that they fall under the protection of s5(2)(b) which states that a person shall have a lawful excuse if he intended to cause damage in order to protect property belonging to himself or another and at the time he believed that the property was in immediate need of protection. Moreover, s5(3) states that such a belief, if honestly held, need not be justified.

However, it was held by the Court of Appeal in *R v Ashford and Smith* (1988) that such circumstances did not give rise to 'lawful excuse' and that the question of whether an act was done to protect property must be an objective one.

In *R v Hill*; *R v Hall* (1989) the Court of Appeal decided that the tests were twofold:

i)   what was in the accused's mind - a subjective test; and

i)   whether it could be said, as a matter of law, that on the facts as believed by the accused, the action would amount to something done to protect his/her home or that of others.

In similar circumstance to those encountered here it was held that the proposed act was too remote from the eventual aim and also that there was no evidence that there was a belief that the property was in need of immediate protection.

Therefore the defence would fail.

Section 5(2) and (3) also applies to actually damaging or destroying property and therefore the same test would be applied in determining whether or not X and Y had acted without lawful excuse.

9 INCHOATE OFFENCES

9.1   Introduction

9.2   Key points

9.3   Recent cases and statutes

9.4   Questions

9.1   Introduction

In addition to the substantive offences looked at in the preceding chapters, it remains to consider those offences which are committed on the way to the commission of a full offence.

Traditionally crimes of incitement and conspiracy are recorded under this heading.

However in this book those offences have been examined under the chapter dealing with participation (Chapter 3) and therefore we are concerned here with criminal attempts.

9.2   Key points

a) The reason behind offences covering attempts, both under individual statutes (eg s5 Road Traffic Act 1988) and under s1 of the Criminal Attempts Act 1981 must be appreciated.

There is a need for laws which will punish offenders and potential offenders who fully intend to commit crimes and take purposeful steps, beyond mere preparation, towards doing so.

b) Criminal Attempts Act 1981:

   i) The provisions of the Criminal Attempts Act 1981, especially s1 must be known.

   In particular students should be aware of the exclusion of acts which are merely preparatory to the commission of an offence from s1. A jury shall not be concerned with the law which obtained before the 1981 Act. They must decide whether the acts done by D were more than merely preparatory: *R* v *Campbell* [1991] Crim LR 268. Defining such acts is not straightforward and the courts have referred to common law tests in deciding questions of 'what is preparatory?': *R* v *Boyle* (1987) 84 Cr App R 270.

   However, some common law rules such as that laid down in *DPP* v *Stonehouse* [1978] AC 55 requiring the accused to go beyond the point of no return have gone: *R* v *Gullefer* [1987] Crim LR 195.

There must be sufficient proximity between the accused's acts and the commission of an offence: *R v Button* [1900] 2 QB 597.

ii) The pre-1981 problems with concepts such as the equivocality of an accused's conduct should be noted and, most importantly, that of impossibility.

The considerations raised in *Haughton v Smith* [1975] AC 476, regarding physical impossibility, and incompetence should be known and the content of s1(2) of the 1981 Act must be known and understood.

Students must be aware of the interpretation in *R v Shivpuri* [1987] AC 1 and the earlier decision in *Anderton v Ryan* [1985] AC 560.

Moreover, a candidate should be able to argue for or against such an interpretation and contrast the moral culpability of an accused who believes that he is committing an offence and does all in his power to commit it, but no such offence exists: see *R v Taaffe* [1984] AC 539.

iii) The mens rea of attempts generally should be learnt and the non-applicability of recklessness: *R v Millard* [1987] Crim LR 393. However, note *R v Khan and Others* [1990] Crim LR 519 where the mens rea for attempted rape was held, by the Court of Appeal, to be the same as that for the full offence namely that D knows, or could not care less, about the woman's absence of consent. D's intent is the same in each case in that he intends to have sexual intercourse and has knowledge of, or is reckless as to, the woman's absence of consent. The only difference between the attempted and the substantive offence is that in one intercourse takes place whereas in the other it does not. Such reasoning cannot, however, apply to all attempts (eg causing death by reckless driving).

Note the meaning of 'intent' in s1: *R v Pearman* (1984) 80 Cr App R 259 and also the difficulties involved in conditional intent: *R v Husseyn* (1977) 67 Cr App R 131 and the residual problems in framing indictments for such.

c) It may be worthy of note that, since the Criminal Justice Act 1988, the offence of taking a conveyance (see Chapter 7) is triable summarily only and therefore can no longer be 'attempted' under the 1981 Act.

9.3   Recent cases and statutes

R v Khan; *R v Dhokia*; *R v Banga*; *R v Faiz* (1990) The Guardian 1 February - mens rea for attempted rape same as for substantive offence - no question of attempting to achieve reckless state of mind - the attempt relates solely to physical activity.

Somchai Liangsiriprasert v Government of USA and Another (1990) The Times 3 July - Privy Council - common law conspiracy committed abroad - no overt acts took place within jurisdiction of court - held, as conspiracy had as its object the commission of a criminal offence (importing drugs) into the country - the conspiracy was triable there notwithstanding lack of overt criminal acts in that country.

R v *Sansom and Others* (1990) The Times 27 September - Court of Appeal approved *Somchai* case (above) as stating the law of England and as applying to statutory conspiracies under the Criminal Law Act 1977 as well as common law - facts of case were similar to *Somchai*, ie persons abroad conspiring to import controlled drugs.

R v *Siracusa and Others* (1990) 90 Cr App R 341 - conspiracy to import one class of drug could not be proved by showing conspiracy to import another class.

R v *Campbell* [1991] Crim LR 268 - jury to decide whether or not D's acts were more than merely preparatory.

9.4   Questions

Question 1

'Impossibility is no longer a defence.'

Discuss.

Adapted from University of London LLB Examination
(for External Students) Criminal Law June 1982 Q3

General comment

This question appeared in the June 1982 paper and, although students would be lucky to get such a straightforward essay in the future it is a useful title to expound the law concerning criminal attempts.

Skeleton solution

Section 1(1) and (2) Criminal Attempts Act 1981; recent cases.

Suggested solution

The Criminal Attempts Act 1981 has made substantial alternations in relation to the defence of impossibility in conspiracy and attempt. However, in order to see the full effects of these alterations the position pre-1981 must be considered.

There are three types of inchoate offence, incitement, conspiracy and attempt. Impossibility in relation to incitement can quickly be dealt with by saying that impossibility never was a defence. In *R* v *McDonough* (1962) the accused was convicted of incitement to receive certain stolen lamb carcasses even though there was no evidence that the carcasses existed at the relevant time. However, in order to be incitement the rule at common law is the act incited must be one which when done would be a crime by the person incited. Therefore, if the offence would never amount to a crime were it to be performed by the person incited, then it can be no crime of incitement. This common law rule has been altered by s54 of the Criminal Law Act 1977 in relation to certain sexual offences, however, the general rule is not affected.

The position in relation to attempt and conspiracy prior to the 1981 Act was governed by *Haughton* v *Smith* (1975). In *Haughton* v *Smith* a van loaded with stolen corned beef was captured by the police. It was allowed on its way with the addition of two officers and rendezvoused with the defendant who unloaded the beef in the belief that he was dealing with stolen property. D was not charged with handling stolen goods as the prosecution conceded that the goods were in police possession and by virtue of s24(3) of the Theft Act 1968 were not stolen goods. He was found liable for attempt. However, since the goods were no longer stolen goods it was legally impossible for him to attempt the offence and the House of Lords quashed the conviction.

Although *Haughton* v *Smith* was a case concerning legal impossibility the House of Lords expressed obiter opinions on other types of impossibility. Lord Hailsham drew distinctions between three particular types of impossibility:

i)   Physical impossibility due to ineptitude or insufficiency of means. Providing that the accused had done an act which was proximate to the full offence then the fact that the means could not possibly succeed was immaterial. (The proximity test has now been replaced by a new requirement contained in the Criminal Attempts Act 1981 that in order to amount to an attempt an act must go 'beyond preparation'.)

ii) Physical impossibility because the object of the crime is not there. This type of impossibility would be a complete defence to any charge of attempt because the act was not one which if completed could ever amount to a crime. Thus if a defendant took steps towards stealing a picture which was not in fact there, he could not be liable for attempted theft because the crime was physically impossible to commit.

iii) Legal impossibility, where unknown to the accused the facts which the accused believed to exist are not shown. An example of legal impossibility is shown in *Haughton* v *Smith* where although the defendant believed the goods to be stolen goods, they were not since the police had regained custody. Legal impossibility was a defence under the principles stated in *Haughton* v *Smith*.

Haughton v *Smith* had in effect overruled an earlier decision in *R* v *Ring* (1892) where one of the defendants was found liable for attempted theft when he put his hand into a man's pocket with intention to steal but in fact found there was nothing in the pocket.

Haughton v *Smith* was criticised for the very obvious reason that it allowed those with criminal intentions who took steps towards performing an offence to be acquitted because of the existence of facts unknown to them. The Law Commission examined the question of impossibility and recommended that impossibility no longer be a defence to a charge of attempt.

Haughton v *Smith* was concerned solely with attempt, however, the principles that it laid down in relation to attempt were applied to conspiracy in the House of Lords case in *DPP* v *Nock* (1978). The Law Commission sought to bring a uniform approach to impossibility for both attempt and conspiracy and recommended similarly that in relation to conspiracy, impossibility should no longer be a defence. Thus the Law Commission recommended that conspiracy and attempt be brought into line with the third inchoate offence of incitement.

The Criminal Attempts Act 1981 contains the provisions relating to impossibility for both conspiracy and attempt. Section 1(1) of the Act provides that a person is guilty of attempt where he does an act which is more than merely preparatory to the commission of the offence.

Section 1(2) goes on to deal with impossibility: 'a person may be guilty of attempting to commit an offence even though the facts are such that the commission of the offence is impossible.'

Similar provisions relate to conspiracy so that s1(1) of the Criminal Law Act 1977 is amended by s5(1) of the Criminal Attempts Act 1981 so that an offence of statutory conspiracy is committed:

i) 'if a person agrees with any other person or persons that a course of conduct shall be pursued which, if the agreement is carried out in accordance with their intentions either:

   a) will necessarily amount to the commission of any offence or offences by one or more of the parties to the agreement; or

   b) would do so but for the existence of facts which render the commission of the offence or any of the offences impossible.'

The effect of these provisions is that the three inchoate offences are now similarly treated where the question of impossibility arises.

Following the passing of the 1981 Act, however, the House of Lords decided that attempting to do what was in fact legal but what would have been unlawful had the facts been as the accused believed them to be, - Lord Hailsham's 'legal impossibility' - did not become a criminal attempt by virtue of s1(2): *Anderton* v *Ryan* (1985).

Nevertheless, in 1987 their Lordships reversed their opinion on this matter, holding that where an accused attempted to bring what he believed to be controlled drugs into Britain but they turned out to be innocuous powder, he was guilty of a criminal attempt: *R* v *Shivpuri* (1987).

The argument that had swayed their Lordships in *Anderton* v *Ryan*, namely that in cases of 'legal impossibility' there was no actus reus but only mens rea, did not so persuade them on this occasion. Therefore, generally, it is true to say that impossibility is no longer a defence. However, it should be remembered that in all instances whether it be in relation to incitement, conspiracy or attempt, a defendant can never be convicted where he has made a mistake as to what amounts to a crime and where he imagines certain conduct to constitute an offence when this does not. For example, if B believes adultery to be an offence, he cannot be convicted of attempting to commit such an offence if the crime itself is imaginary.

This was the case in *R* v *Taaffe* (1984) where the accused imported foreign currency believing that, by so doing, he was committing an offence. In fact there was no such offence at the time and the accused was acquitted.

From a moral standpoint it is difficult to distinguish the two cases but such a jurisprudential quandary will not avail a defendant!

Question 2

John believes that he can produce 'crack', a controlled drug by mixing bicarbonate of soda with weedkiller. In order to make a large quantity, John buys 2lbs of each powder and several plastic containers and puts them in a laboratory which he has set up to make the drug in this way.

John is told that Royal Jelly - a health food obtained from bees, is now a controlled drug having been found to contain morphine. This is untrue. However, John believes it to be true and puts small quantities of Royal Jelly in packets and sells them to people in his local nightclub.

Advise John of his criminal liability if any.

Written by Editor

General comment

The question examines a student's understanding of the Criminal Attempts Act 1981 particularly in relation to impossibility.

Skeleton solution

Criminal Attempts Act 1981 ss1(1) and 1(2) 'impossibility' - interpretation in recent cases.

Suggested solution

John commits no substantive criminal offence when he buys the powder and containers but he may be guilty of an attempt under s1 of the Criminal Attempts Act 1981 which states:

If, with intent to commit an offence to which this section applies - ie triable an indictment - a person does an act which is more than merely preparatory to the commission of the offence he is guilty of attempting to commit the offence.

John has 'done an act' in buying the items and setting up a laboratory and he has done with an intention of committing an offence under the Misuse of Drugs Act 1971.

However, his actions appear to fall within the proviso of the section, being 'merely preparatory'.

Whether they are merely preparatory is a question of fact for a jury: *R* v *Campbell* (1991).

The former test requiring an accused to have 'crossed the Rubicon and burnt his boats': *DPP* v *Stonehouse* (1978) has been disapproved and it is no longer necessary to prove that the accused has gone beyond the point of no return: *R* v *Gullefer* (1987).

Having regard to cases determined before the 1981 Act but dealing with the same question eg *Comer* v *Bloomfield* (1970) where the accused hid his van and wrote to the insurers asking whether he could claim on the policy - it would seem that John's acts were only preparatory and therefore without more, he is not guilty of attempting to produce a controlled drug.

John's liability in relation to the Royal Jelly is not so straightforward.

John sells packets of the substance believing it to contain morphine. This is not the case and therefore John does not commit an offence of unlawfully supplying a possessing of controlled drug.

However, s1(2) of the 1981 Act states that a person may be guilty of attempting to commit an offence even though the facts are such that the commission of the offence is impossible. Further, s1(3) provides that, in any case where:

a) apart from this subsection a person's intention would not be regarded as having amounted to an intent to commit an offence; but

b) if the facts had been as he believed them to be, his intention would be so regarded, then he shall be regarded as having an intent to commit that offence.

These subsections removed the 'defence' of impossibility which had existed at common law: *Haughton* v *Smith* (1975); *DPP* v *Nock* (1978).

Under subs (2) and (3), the fact that supplying Royal Jelly is not an offence will not save John who carried out the act of selling the substance believing it to contain a controlled drug. That belief is sufficient to attract liability for 'attempting' the offence: *R* v *Shivpuri* (1987).

Had John believed that selling Royal Jelly *per se* was an offence and had gone on to do so, he would not be liable for 'attempting' an offence. This is because his belief would relate to the existence of an imagined offence and therefore there would be no actus reus: *R* v *Taaffe* (1984).

In the instant case the offence of supplying morphine unlawfully does exist and as John believes - albeit erroneously - that that is what he is doing, he is guilty of an attempt notwithstanding the fact that the commission of the completed offence is impossible.

Question 3

H wrote to his friend, J, in France suggesting that they should rob a bank in London. The letter never arrived. H sent a similar letter to K in England who wrote to H agreeing to his proposal. K's letter never arrived at H's address. H contacted L and together they went to rob a bank but, on the way, H's car which was being driven by L was involved in a motoring accident and L was blinded. The accident resulted from a defect in the brakes which H knew about.

Advise the parties of their criminal liability.

University of London LLB Examination
(for External Students) Criminal Law June 1990 Q6

General comment

A complex question in which careful planning of the answer is of great importance. Deal with the liabilities of the parties separately. The question requires specific knowledge of the relationship between inchoate offences. It is not necessary to detail the statutory duty to maintain a motor vehicle as this offence is not on the syllabus.

Skeleton solution

Liability of H for attempted incitement and the completed crime. Conspiracy with K and L. Attempted robbery. Attempted murder of L, injury to L, based upon failure to act. Liability of K for conspiracy. Liability of L for conspiracy and attempted robbery.

Suggested solution

The incitement of another to commit an offence is itself an offence at common law. Normally the incitement must reach the mind of the incitee, but where this does not happen the defendant can still incur liability for attempted incitement. In *R* v *Banks* (1873), the defendant was convicted of attempted incitement where his letter was intercepted and never reached the incitee. See also *R* v *Ransford* (1874). There seems no doubt that H had the necessary mens rea for incitement to rob. He intended the suggestion to be acted upon by K. It should be noted that the charge would have to be one of attempted incitement to rob, rather than attempted incitement to conspire to rob, since incitement to conspire was abolished as an offence by s5(7) of the Criminal Law Act 1977. Provided the letter containing the incitement was posted in England, the English courts would have jurisdiction over the offence. As regards the letter sent to K, the incitement obviously reaches the mind of the incitee, who realises that what is being suggested is a criminal offence; see *R* v *Curr* (1968). It appears to have been the intention of H that the suggestion should be acted upon. There are no jurisdictional problems in this case. It is submitted, therefore, that H could be convicted of inciting K to commit robbery.

As noted below, H commits the offence of statutory conspiracy when he agrees to rob the bank with L. It is questionable whether or not their action constitutes an attempt to commit the offence; see below.

The prosecution may consider a charge of attempted murder in light of the fact that H allowed L to drive the car knowing it had defective brakes. A major stumbling block to liability would be that there is no evidence of a positive act, on the part of H, that causes death. He has not, for example, tampered with the brakes. If liability for failing to service the brakes is to be imposed, there must be a positive legal duty to act. In the present case the prosecution may wish to rely on the statutory duty resting upon a car owner to maintain the vehicle in a roadworthy condition. If one assumes for the sake of argument that the actus reus of the offence is made out (as to which see *R* v *Gullefer* (1987)), the problem would lie in establishing intent. Some older authorities, such as *R* v *Whybrow* (1951), suggest that the defendant must have the death of the victim as his purpose. It is submitted that there would at least have to be evidence that H foresaw the death of L as virtually certain before the jury could infer such intent. Note that intent to commit grievous bodily harm would not be sufficient on a charge of attempted murder. It is submitted that since he was also a passenger in the car, it may difficult to establish this intent.

It is worth noting that when the Road Traffic Act 1991 comes into force there will be a new offence of causing death by dangerous driving and that, in assessing whether driving is 'dangerous', regard will be had to the condition of the vehicle concerned. This new offence has been enacted specifically to deal with the type of situation above.

The blinding of L constitutes grievous bodily harm; see *R* v *Saunders* (1985). To begin to establish liability it would again be necessary to show that H had culpably failed to maintain his vehicle. The prosecution would then have to show that this failure to act caused the harm.

For the purposes of both s18 and s20 of the Offences Against the Persons Act 1861, this would involve proof that the injury was reasonably foreseeable. The fact that the injury was indirectly caused by H is no bar to liability; see *R* v *Martin* (1881). Under s18, H will have to be shown to have intended the grievous bodily harm; see *R* v *Belfon* (1976). If this cannot be established, a charge under s20 would require proof that he at least foresaw the possibility of some physical harm occurring to L, albeit slight; see *R* v *Cunningham* (1957), and *R* v *Mowatt* (1967). it is submitted that a charge under s20 is likely to succeed.

K agrees to carry out the robbery with H but his letter signifying this is never delivered. K could be charged with statutory conspiracy contrary to s1(1)(a) of the Criminal Law Act 1977. The act of posting the letter is evidence of his agreement. The fact that the letter is never delivered to H does not provide K with any form of defence based upon impossibility; see Criminal Attempts Act 1981. The prosecution have no choice but to proceed against K with a full charge of conspiracy, since the offence of attempted conspiracy was abolished by s5(7) of the 1977 Act.

In agreeing to rob the bank with H, L commits the offence of statutory conspiracy contrary to s1(1) of the 1977 Act. The parties clearly agree upon a course of conduct which if carried out in accordance with their intentions will necessarily result in the commission of a criminal offence. It is submitted that H and L could not be charged with attempted robbery on the basis that although they are on their way to rob the bank, they may not have committed any acts more than merely preparatory to the offence; see s1(1) of the Criminal Attempts Act 1981, as interpreted in *R* v *Gullefer*. In the final analysis the question of whether or not they have gone beyond mere preparation will be a question of fact for the jury.

10 DEFENCES

10.1   Introduction

10.2   Key points

10.3   Recent cases and statutes

10.4   Analysis of questions

10.5   Questions

10.1 Introduction

In answering any question concerning a person's criminal liability it must be remembered that, although a prima facie case may appear to be made out, that person may well have a general or specific defence.

Certain specific defences have been reviewed in the appropriate preceding chapters:

Consent, lawful correction, self-defence and lawful force - Chapter 4 - non-fatal offences against the person, provocation, diminished responsibility and suicide pacts - Chapter 5 - homicide.

Lawful excuse - Chapter 8 - criminal damage.

Such defences are usually only applicable to a particular crime - eg provocation in murder cases. There are however, general defences which may appropriately be raised in a number of circumstances and it is these defences which are examined here.

10.2 Key points

a) *Infancy or minority*

It is an irrefutable presumption that a child under ten years of age cannot commit a criminal offence.

For children between ten and 14 years there is a rebuttable presumption that a child is similarly incapable of committing an offence. This presumption may be rebutted by proof of mischievous discretion ie proof of knowledge that what was done was morally or legally wrong: *R* v *Gorrie* (1918) 83 JP 136; *McC* v *Runneckles* [1984] Crim LR 499.

b) *Mistake*

A mistaken belief may negate an accused's mens rea and may therefore amount to a defence. What students must note is that there is a distinction between a mistaken belief which is *reasonably* held and one which is not.

i) In the latter case a mistake, if honestly held, may negate mens rea where intention or recklessness is required: *DPP* v *Morgan* [1976] AC 182; *R* v *Williams (Gladstone)* (1984) 78 Cr App R 276; *R* v *Kimber* [1983] 3 All ER 316.

ii) Mistakes involving a belief which is not only honestly held but also reasonably held are the only type of mistakes that will avail an accused in cases of negligence. Moreover, if an accused claims 'justification' based upon a mistake, this too must be reasonable: *R* v *Gould* [1968] 2 QB 65.

iii) If a mistake precludes neither mens rea (intention or recklessness) nor negligence it cannot provide a defence.

c) *Intoxication*

Principally, intoxication is associated with alcohol, although the effects of drugs should also be considered.

Students should note that where drugs are known to produce aggressive or unpredictable behaviour, such drugs will be classed with alcohol for 'intoxication' purposes: *R* v *Hardie* [1985] 1 WLR 64.

i) Note that intoxication generally is not a defence. It may, however, negate the required mens rea.

Where a specific or ulterior intent is required, self-induced intoxication may preclude that intent: *R* v *Bailey* [1983] 2 All ER 503. Drunkenness may, for instance, prevent D from forming the intent required for murder - *R* v *O'Connor* [1991] Crim LR 135.

However note the decision in *Attorney-General for Northern Ireland* v *Gallagher* [1963] AC 349 in relation to drinking for 'dutch courage', having already formed the relevant intention.

ii) Voluntary intoxication will not be a defence for crimes of basic intent: *DPP* v *Majewski* [1977] AC 443.

Such offences are capable of being committed recklessly, a criterion which is itself met by the accused's becoming voluntarily intoxicated.

Where D because of self-induced intoxication forms a mistaken belief that he is using force to defend himself that plea of self-defence will fail - *R* v *O'Grady* (1987) 85 Cr App R 315.

However, an accused may form an honest belief whilst so intoxicated and thereby find a statutory defence such as 'lawful excuse' to damage another's property: *Jaggard* v *Dickinson* [1981] QB 527.

iii) Where intoxication is through a drug such as a sedative: *R* v *Hardie* - or failure to take a drug such as insulin: *R* v *Bailey* - that intoxication may provide a defence even for crimes of basic intent.

d) *Insanity*

Note the elements of *M'Naghten's Case* (1843) 10 Cl & F 200 and the requirements of 'disease of the mind' resulting in 'labouring under a defect of reason' and so the accused did not appreciate the 'quality or nature of his actions' or, if he did, then he did not know that they were wrong.

Students should know the leading cases concerning the elements in *M'Naghten*, ie 'disease of the mind': *R v Kemp* [1957] 1 QB 399; *R v Sullivan* [1984] AC 156; *R v Quick* [1973] QB 910; *R v Rabey* (1977) 37 CCC and in particular the 'internal/external' causes of insanity: *Bratty v Attorney-General for Northern Ireland* [1963] AC 386.

e) *Automatism*

This is really a lack of actus reus as opposed to a defence and proof of automatism would mean that an accused had not voluntarily carried out the proscribed act: *Hill v Baxter* [1958] 1 QB 277; *R v Boshears* (1961) The Times 8 February; *R v Kemp* (1986) The Times 3 May.

Care should be taken to distinguish automatism generally from acts done 'involuntarily' following self-induced intoxication (see (c) above).

Note should also be made of cases where the accused has voluntarily set in train a series of actions leading up to one which is then brought about inadvertently eg going armed with a loaded shotgun, robbing another person and pointing the gun at them. If the gun then 'goes off' without the accused intending it to, he may still be liable for any resultant injury or damage: *Ryan v R* (1967) 40 ALJR 577; *Gray v Barr* [1971] 2 QB 554.

f) *Necessity and duress*

i) The defence of necessity is very contentious and, despite numerous cases which appear to point to its existence eg *Mouse's Case* (1608) 12 Co Rep 63; *R v Bourne* [1939] 1 KB 687; *Johnson v Phillips* [1975] 3 All ER 682 - others deny its existence - *Southwark London Borough v Williams* [1971] 2 All ER 175; *R v Dudley and Stephens* (1884) 14 QBD 273.

ii) Closely related to necessity, if not in fact a part of it, is duress of circumstances: *R v Willer* (1986) 83 Cr App R 225; *R v Conway* [1988] 3 All ER 1025.

In these cases duress was seen as being separate from necessity but in *R v Martin* [1989] 1 All ER 652 it was recognised as being a party of necessity.

It should be noted that necessity or duress of circumstances will not provide a defence in cases of strict liability or murder: *R v Howe* [1987] AC 417.

g) *Duress*

This defence applies to all offences except murder (*R v Howe* (above)) and attempted murder (*R v Gotts* [1991] Crim LR 366) and arises where the accused commits a crime but he is forced to do so by the threats of violence by another.

Such violence must amount to death or serious bodily harm: *DPP for Northern Ireland* v *Lynch* [1975] AC 653; *R* v *Hudson and Taylor* [1971] 2 QB 202

In order to avail himself of the defence, an accused must display the steadfastness of an ordinary citizen in attempting to resist threat: *R* v *Graham* [1982] 1 All ER 801, and must take any reasonable opportunity to pursue an 'avenue of escape': *R* v *Shepherd* (1988) 86 Cr App R 47.

The threat must operate at the time of the commission of the crime, although it need not be capable of immediate execution.

The defence is not open to an accused who commits the offence under threats from members of a criminal organization of which he himself is a voluntary member: *R* v *Sharp* (1987) 85 Cr App R 207.

h) Note the specific defence of coercion under s47 of the Criminal Justice Act 1925 which applies **only** to a wife who commits the offence in the presence of her husband. The threats made need not only amount to death or serious injury and the defence is only available in a very limited number of crimes, including murder.

Like the *M'Naghten* (1843) rules it is of very limited practical significance.

i) Students should note the areas of self-defence and 'public defence' particularly in relation to 'reasonable force' and s3 of the Criminal Law Act 1967.

The recent cases of *R* v *Williams (Gladstone)* (1984) 78 Cr App R 276 and *Beckford* v *R* [1987] 3 All ER 425 must be known as should the tenor of the *Attorney-General's Reference (No 1 of 1975)* [1975] QB 773 per Lord Diplock.

The leading cases governing self-defence generally should be learnt, in particular *R* v *Browne* [1973] NI 96; *R* v *Bird* [1985] 2 All ER 513; *R* v *Field* [1972] Crim LR 435 (see also Chapter 4: *Non-fatal offences against the person*).

j) *Provocation*

It is interesting to note the 'defence' of provocation that was put forward in *R* v *Cocker* [1989] Crim LR 740 where the appellant was driven to killing his wife who was terminally ill, by her insistence on ending her life.

The wife deliberately wore down the appellant's self-control until he finally smothered her with a pillow and, although the appeal failed, the argument that such loss of self-restraint would in some cases fall within Lord Devlin's definition of provocation - *R* v *Duffy* [1949] 1 All ER 932 is supportable.

10.3 Recent cases and statutes

T v *DPP* [1989] Crim LR 498 - D's replies after caution, together with circumstances of theft enough to rebut presumption of *doli incapax*.

R v *Martin* [1989] 1 All ER 652 - duress of circumstances - requirements.

R v *Shepherd* (1988) 86 Cr App R 47 - accused must take 'reasonable opportunity' to pursue avenue of escape.

R v *Ball* (*Simon Leonard*) [1989] Crim LR 579 - assault on police officer while arresting another - D claimed honest belief that arrest was unlawful and excessive - held no defence to assault.

R v *Cocker* [1989] Crim LR 740 - provocation - husband of terminally ill wife driven to kill her - husband held to have been in full control.

R v *Roberts* [1990] Crim LR 122 - provocation - jury aware of D's relevant disabilities - no need to admit medical evidence of psychiatrist.

R v *T* [1990] Crim LR 256 - post-traumatic stress disorder following rape - held to be non-insane automatism caused by external force.

R v *O'Connor* [1991] Crim LR 135 - jury should have been warned that self-induced intoxication could have prevented D from forming intent to cause gbh.

R v *Burgess* [1991] Crim LR 548 - sleepwalking may amount to 'disease of the mind' (cf *Bratty* where *obiter dicta* said sleepwalking was non-insane automatism).

R v *Bingham* [1991] Crim LR 433 - need to distinguish between hyperglycaemia (too much sugar in the blood) and hypoglycaemia (too little). Hypoglycaemia was not caused by diabetes but by too much insulin/not enough food. In such cases 'insanity' defence inappropriate. Question in such cases was presence or absence of mens rea.

R v *Gotts* [1991] Crim LR 366 - defence of duress not available as defence to attempted murder.

R v *Clarke* [1991] Crim LR 383 - provocation - when considering whether reasonable man would do as D did jury must consider the whole course of D's conduct, not just the one act which probably caused death.

10.4 Analysis of questions

Questions on general defences will appear either in essay form or among the facts of a problem question and when answering the latter, students should always consider circumstances or facts which may provide a defendant with such a defence. However, that is not to say that a defence will be available in every case.

Occasionally questions will be split into an essay part and a problem part (see Question 3). This can help a student clarify the relevant law before applying it to specific situations and it is suggested that the essay part of such questions is tackled first.

10.5 Questions

Question 1

'The law regarding the defences of self-induced and insane automatism and voluntary intoxication is hopelessly confused.'

Discuss and illustrate your answer by reference to the relevant case law.

Adapted from University of London LLB Examination
(for External Students) Criminal Law June 1982 Q8(b)

General comment

Students could almost spend the entire examination answering this question in depth. Whereas it is difficult to keep an answer such as this concise as well as dealing with all the major issues, it is a good revision aid on a complex subject.

Skeleton solution

Self-induced automatism; insane automatism; voluntary intoxication; overlap *inter se* and cases illustrating difficulties.

Suggested solution

Insane automatism may provide an accused with a defence to a crime providing the accused can show that he falls within the *M'Naghten* (1843) rules. The law on insanity is still governed by these rules of 1843 which provide that it is a defence for the accused to prove 'that at the time of committing the act, the party accused was labouring under such a defect of reason, from disease of the mind, so as not to know the nature and quality of the act he was doing or if he did know it, that he did not know that what he was doing was wrong'.

In *R* v *Sullivan* (1984) the House of Lords accepted that the rules have been a comprehensive definition of insanity since 1843.

The term 'defect of reason' connotes that the accused must be deprived of reasoning. Simply a failure to use the reasoning powers that the accused possesses due to confusion or absent mindedness is not sufficient: *R* v *Clarke* (1972).

The question of whether or not the accused is suffering from a 'disease of the mind', is a legal question and not a medical question, although medical evidence is obviously relevant. In *R* v *Quick and Paddison* (1973), the Court of Appeal held that 'disease of the mind' meant a 'malfunctioning of the mind caused by disease'. It was not simply limited to a disease of the brain, but the term does not cover the transitory effect of such external matters as violence, drugs, alcohol and hypnosis. The term however does cover physical diseases which affect the mind. Thus in *R* v *Kemp* (1956) arterio sclerosis caused congestion of the blood in the defendant's brain and consequent lack of consciousness. It was claimed on the defendant's behalf that there was no insanity until degeneration of the brain cells occurred and in the absence of this, the defendant was merely suffering from automatism. The court rejected this argument. 'The law is not concerned with the brain but with the mind, in the sense that "mind" is ordinarily used. The mental facilities of reason, memory and understanding. If one reads for "disease of the mind", "disease of the brain", it would follow that in many cases, pleas of insanity would not be established because it could not be proved that the brain had been affected in any way.' The defendant was found to be insane.

'Nature and quality' refers to the physical quality of the act not to its moral or legal quality: *R* v *Codere* (1916).

'Wrong' means 'legally' wrong. If the accused knew that his act was contrary to the law or that it was wrong according to the ordinary standard of a reasonable man, he cannot be heard to say that he did not know the act to be wrong, even if he believes his action to be morally right: *R* v *Windle* (1952).

The effect of a successful plea of insanity is the verdict of 'not guilty by reason of insanity' Criminal Procedure (Insanity) Act 1964 s1. The defendant will then be sentenced to an indefinite period in a criminal mental hospital.

There has, for many years, been some problem in distinguishing circumstances where the defence of insanity should be available. Automatism has generally been regarded as a defence where the accused shows that his conduct was not 'willed'. An example given in *Hill* v *Baxter* (1958) would be where the defendant, while driving, was attacked by a swarm of bees and was disabled from controlling the vehicle. In these circumstances, it would be held that he would no longer be 'driving' because the movement of the defendant's limbs was involuntary. In *R* v *Boshears* (1961), the accused was acquitted of murder where he contended that he had killed a girl in his sleep. Similarly, in *R* v *Scott* (1967) the accused was held not liable for acts done while he was unconscious through concussion.

The effect of a successful plea of automatism is a complete acquittal. Obviously, this is preferable to a finding of 'not guilty by reason of insanity', which although a type of acquittal, results in the accused being incarcerated for an indefinite period in a criminal mental hospital. Therefore where possible, an accused would always wish to rely on the general defence of automatism rather than that of insanity. In *Bratty* v *Attorney-General for Northern Ireland* (1961), the appellant was charged with murder of a girl. There was evidence that he suffered from a form of epilepsy which could result in no recollection of acts done. The defence raised two possible defences, automatism which would result in acquittal or insanity. The trial judge refused to leave the defence of automatism to the jury and the appellant was found guilty of murder after the jury rejected the plea of insanity. He appealed unsuccessfully to the Court of Appeal for Northern Ireland and, thereafter to the House of Lords.

Viscount Kilmuir accepted that if a defence of insanity was raised unsuccessfully, there could, in certain circumstances be room for an alternative defence based on automatism, for example, a jury might reject evidence of a defect of reason from disease of the mind, but accept evidence that the accused did not know what he was doing, in which case the jury should find him not guilty. However, such a defence could only succeed where there had been positive evidence of something other than a defect of reason.

'Where the only cause alleged for the unconsciousness is a defect of reason from disease of the mind, and that cause is rejected by the jury, there can be no room for the alternative defence of automatism.' On the facts before the House, there was nothing to suggest any other pathological causes for automatism and the accused's appeal was dismissed.

This case outlined the link and also the difference between insane automatism and non-insane automatism. However, it did not cover every situation and it was accepted by the courts that there would be borderline situations. Nevertheless, it did outline the considerations which a court should bear in mind in considering whether both defences should be available to an accused or merely one of them.

Until 1973, there was never any suggestion in a case that the defence of automatism would not be available to an accused if it was shown that the automatism arose from the defendant's fault. However, in the case of *R* v *Quick and Paddison* (1973), the Court of Appeal proposed a new rule which did require the court to consider whether or not the accused was to blame for his automation state (obiter).

The general rule that the Court of Appeal laid down provides:

'A self-induced incapacity will not excuse, see *R* v *Lipman* (1969), nor will one which could have been reasonably foreseen as a result of either doing or omitting to do something, as, or for example, taking alcohol against medical advice after using certain prescribed drugs, or failing to have regular meals while taking insulin.'

However, in *R* v *Bailey* (1983) the Court of Appeal held that the defence of automatism may be open to an accused who fails to take the required amount of food after insulin. In such cases, the court must decide whether the accused has been proved to have been reckless in not taking sufficient food and, if he knows that by failing to do so he will become aggressive, unpredictable or uncontrolled, with the result that he may cause injury to others, he may be found to be reckless.

It is not clear whether a case such as *R* v *Bailey* is one of 'self-induced' automatism, although it is arguable that his omission to take food, combined with his knowledge of the attendant consequences, could make any ensuing automation state 'voluntary' or 'self-induced'. If an accused does not know that his failing to take the food will have those consequences then, according to the decision in *R* v *Bailey* the defence of automatism will be open to him.

A more clear-cut area of self-induced automatism is that of voluntary drunkenness and 'dangerous' drugs. The distinction between sedatives and the drugs with a merely soporific effect, and those drugs which induce aggressive or unpredictable behaviour appears to have been introduced by the Court of Appeal in *R* v *Bailey* and *R* v *Hardie* (1984).

In the latter case the accused took Valium pills and then, whilst under their influence, went on to damage property. The judge directed that such 'intoxication' was no defence, equating it with alcohol and the *DPP* v *Majewski* (1976) rule (below). However, the Court of Appeal made a distinction between drugs such as Valium and 'dangerous drugs' or alcohol.

In such cases as *R* v *Bailey* and *R* v *Hardie* the question will be one of recklessness and the *DPP* v *Majewski* restrictions will not be imposed upon the accused's raising the defence of intoxication.

Generally, voluntary drunkenness is not a defence to a criminal charge. The term 'drunkenness' includes a state of mind induced by voluntary drug taking: *R* v *Lipman* (1969).

There are difficulties surrounding 'voluntariness' here. In *R* v *Tandy* (1988) it was argued that a woman who was an alcoholic did not drink 'voluntarily' prior to committing a murder but had been driven to it by her alcoholism. Her argument failed to impress the Court of Appeal who held that at least her first drink of the day was taken voluntarily.

Similarly, in *R* v *Allen* (1988), where the accused argued that he did not know the strength of the drink he had consumed and that therefore his consumption of it was involuntary, the court held this to be voluntary intoxication.

However, in certain circumstances, drunkenness may be a defence:

1) If it causes a disease of the mind, eg delirium tremens. In these circumstances the accused will be entitled to an acquittal providing he can satisfy the requirements of the *M'Naghten* (1843) rules.

2) It may enable the defendant to establish a mistake of fact incompatible with criminal responsibility, eg *R* v *Letenock* (1917) (provocation).

3) Drunkenness may provide a defence to a crime, where the drunkenness totally negatives the specific intent necessary for the crime. In *DPP* v *Majewski* (1976), the accused who was drunk assaulted a police officer, who arrested him. The defendant's appeal against conviction for assault occasioning actual bodily harm was dismissed by the House of Lords, because the defence did not involve specific intent and his drunkenness was consequently immaterial.

This rule laid down in *DPP* v *Majewski* is plainly one of policy and is not one that has its roots in logic. Plainly, a sufficient degree of intoxication can negative mens rea totally but this will only be a defence where it negatives the mens rea in a crime of specific intent, not a crime of basic intent. The situation is further complicated, because a crime of 'specific intent' for the purposes of drink and drugs, will not necessarily be classified for other criminal law purposes as a crime of specific intent. Furthermore, a crime which might generally be classified as a crime of specific or ulterior intent for the purposes of criminal law generally may not be classified as a crime of specific intent for the purposes of the defence of drink and drugs. It is necessary to look to case law to discover what are crimes of specific intent for the purposes of drink and drugs and what are crimes of basic intent. This rather arbitrary classification by the courts is obviously subject to review and re-classification of offences which were previously held to be crimes of specific intent to crimes of basic intent have occurred. In the case of *MPC* v *Caldwell* (1981), the House of Lords considered the effect of *DPP* v *Majewski* on a charge under s1(2) of the Criminal Damage Act 1971, where the accused was charged with causing criminal damage, being reckless as to whether life was endangered. The court considered that the effect of *DPP* v *Majewski* was that if an accused was charged with causing criminal damage under s1(2) of the Criminal Damage Act with intent to endanger life, he would have a defence where he could show that voluntary intoxication made him unable to form the necessary mens rea. However, he would not have a defence where he was charged under s1(2), with being reckless as to whether life was endangered. *DPP* v *Majewski* provides that all crimes of recklessness must be crimes of basic intent and therefore, this anomalous situation arises.

The effect of this decision is to overturn a previously accepted rule that where an accused was voluntarily intoxicated to the extent that he was unable to form mens rea, he would have a defence under s1(2) of the Criminal Damage Act 1971, because this is a crime of specific intent, but he would not have a defence under s1(1) of the Criminal Damage Act 1971 as this is a crime of basic intent.

The rules laid out in *DPP* v *Majewski* have been severely critizised on the basis of their arbitrary and illogical nature. *MPC* v *Caldwell* serves to emphasise this as criticism and it is to be hoped that there will shortly be some clarification in this area.

A final area of self-induced intoxication is where the accused deliberately gets drunk in order to give himself 'dutch courage' to carry out a crime that he has formed the intention to commit. It was held in *Attorney-General for Northern Ireland* v *Gallagher* (1963) that 'he cannot rely on this self-induced drunkenness as a defence to a charge of murder, nor even as reducing it to manslaughter ... the wickedness of his mind before he got drunk is enough to condemn him' (per Lord Denning).

As with *DPP* v *Majewski* there is a strong element of policy evident in this decision which appears to contradict the general requirement that mens rea must coincide with actus reus and that an intention to commit some future act is not mens rea: *R* v *Jakeman* (1983).

Question 2

Una, a terrorist, forced Vernon into her car at gun point. Una said, 'We have your wife and children. Carry out your instructions and they will be safe.' Vernon was given a pistol, a photograph and detailed instructions which involved killing the person in the photograph when he came out of the nearby cathedral, 45 minutes later Una placed an electronic 'bug' under Vernon's watch and told Vernon 'If you take this off or contact the police, your children will die.' Vernon was dropped off at the cathedral. He did not know what to do. He telephoned his home but received no answer. Finally, Vernon walked up the cathedral steps and shot the victim as he was leaving. The victim was not killed but was severely wounded.

Advise Una and Vernon of their criminal liability. Would it make any difference to your advice if the victim had died or if Una never had Vernon's wife and children in her custody?

University of London LLB Examination
(for External Students) Criminal Law June 1982 Q8

General comment

The core of this question concerns the offence of attempted murder and the general defences which may be available to it. It is also concerned with the rather difficult principle of innocent agency and liability for an offence where the principal is not present. The two defences which have to be considered in relation to murder are duress and mistake. These are difficult defences in their own right and become exceptionally difficult when they are intermingled.

Skeleton solution

Assault; threats to kill s16 CLA 1977; false imprisonment; incitement, procurement of murder; attempt murder s1 CAA 1981; gbh, s18 OAP 1861.

Defence - duress - applicability to murder/attempt murder; mistake.

Suggested solution

When Una forced Vernon into the car at gun point she commits a common law assault in that she puts a person in fear of being then and there subjected to force. By making threats to kill Vernon's children she commits an offence contrary to s16 of the Criminal Law Act 1977 which states that a person who without lawful excuse makes to another a threat intending that that other would fear that it would be carried out to kill the other or a third person shall be guilty of an offence.

By forcing Vernon into her car she may commit the offence of false-imprisonment where the victim is unlawfully and intentionally or recklessly restrained from moving freely from a particular place. There may, furthermore, be the offence of kidnapping which is a particular type of false imprisonment involving the removal or secreting of a victim against his will.

However, the most serious offence that she commits is that concerning the plan to kill. By requiring Vernon to carry out this plan to kill she is at least inciting a murder. It is an offence under the common law to incite another to commit an indictable or summary offence. However, the incitement must be more than the mere expression of desire. It must be shown that Una urged or spurred Vernon on by advice, encouragement, persuasion, threats or pressure: *Race Relations Board* v *Applin* (1973). To be liable for incitement it is not necessary that the offence is actually committed. The crime is complete at the time of the persuasion even if the full offence never occurs. However, if the person incited does commit the offence the inciter becomes a participant in that offence and is guilty of counselling the offence.

It may be that Una is more than just an inciter or counsellor to the offence. It is possible that under the doctrine of innocent agency Vernon could be relieved of liability and Una would be deemed to be the principal offender in the offence. However, this doctrine will be considered at greater length when Vernon's liability and possible defences have been discussed.

When Vernon shoots at the victim severely wounding him, he performs the actus reus of attempted murder. For there to be an attempt it must be shown that there is an act beyond preparation towards the commission of the offence. Section 1 Criminal Attempts Act 1981. The mens rea for an attempt is generally the same as for the full offence. However, in a charge of attempted murder it must be shown that Vernon had intention to kill. Any lesser mens rea is insufficient for the charge although had Vernon actually killed he could have been liable for murder with a lesser mens rea. If Vernon did not intend to kill but merely intended grievous bodily harm he will have committed an offence contrary to s18 of the Offences Against the Person Act 1861 in that he caused grievous bodily harm with intent to cause grievous bodily harm.

It may be possible for Vernon to claim that he was acting under duress. For the defence to be operative it must be shown that Vernon committed the offence only because of an overriding threat of death or serious personal injury: *DPP for Northern Ireland* v *Lynch* (1975).

The threat must be 'immediate' in the sense that the accused had no reasonable opportunity to render it ineffective by seeking police protection. On the facts in question it should be noted that there was opportunity for Vernon to contact the police although he had been told that this would bring about his children's death. The jury would therefore have to decide whether or not the opportunity should have been taken by Vernon to contact the police. It should be noted that in *R* v *Hudson and Taylor* (1971) the accused was still able to claim the defence of duress even though they had not thought to contact the police because the police protection offered to them would have been ineffective.

It is not necessary that the threat be directed towards the accused. In *R* v *Hurley and Murray* (1967) the Supreme Court of Victoria (Australia) held that the threats to kill or seriously injure the defendant's common law wife were sufficient for duress, and this principle would clearly extend to an accused's family, and it was opined in *R* v *Shepherd* (1988) that there was nothing in principle to exclude threats made against an accused's relatives.

The test to be applied by the jury in deciding whether the defence is shown was outlined in the case of *R* v *Graham* (1982), the Court of Appeal stated that the jury should be directed to ask themselves 'whether the defendant was, or might have been, impelled to act as he did because of the result of what he reasonably believed the partner had said or done, the defendant had good cause to fear that, if he did not so act the partner would kill him'. If that was so, the jury must further be satisfied that a sober person of reasonable firmness sharing the defendant's characteristics would have responded to the situation by taking part in the killing. The test therefore is two limbed. The first limb is subjective - was the accused responding to a reasonably perceived threat to kill himself? The second limb is objective - would the ordinary man have responded to that threat by taking part in the killing?

However, the fact that Vernon has committed an attempted murder complicates the matter.

The House of Lords in *R* v *Howe* (1987) held the defence of duress not to be available in murder cases.

Addressing the question of attempted murder Lord Hailsham said that in such a case the defence would need to be reconsidered. Lord Griffiths felt that the defence would not be available and Smith and Hogan argue that if it were otherwise, the situation would be absurd (6th ed p233), with the law providing a defence for an act when it was done and then removing it after a year and a day if the victim died within that period.

Had the victim died, Vernon would not have the defence of duress open to him following *R* v *Howe* as Vernon would be either the principal offender or a secondary party.

It is unlikely then that Vernon will be able to bring himself within the ambit of 'innocent agency' thereby imputing liability as principal offender to Una.

Una would appear to be guilty of procuring the murder (s8 Accessories and Abettors Act 1861) and therefore would also be liable to be tried as a principal offender.

Had Una never had Vernon's family in custody, that fact alone should not deprive Vernon of any defence of duress which might otherwise be available to him. It will be a consideration in deciding whether or not his belief of the threat was reasonable and whether his reaction to the threat was one which might be expected of a sober person of reasonable firmness (per *R* v *Graham*) so, for instance, if it would have been almost impossible for Una to have had the family in custody eg they were abroad at the time - then Vernon's submitting to Una's threat would not meet the Graham requirements.

However, we are told that Vernon tried to contact his family without success.

If he could have expected them to be there, and had taken all reasonable steps open to him to ascertain the truth of Una's claim then it is submitted that he would be able to argue that he was acting under duress even though there was no threat to his family.

It is also submitted that, following *R* v *Williams (Gladstone)* (1987) (private defence) that Vernon should be judged on the facts as he believed them to be, whether reasonably or not (see Smith and Hogan 6th Ed p236).

Question 3(a)

Mistake operates by considering the position the accused thought he was in and on that assumption examines the legal significance of his acts.

Discuss.

University of London LLB Examination
(for External Students) Criminal Law June 1984 Q3(a)

General comment

Bearing in mind the recent case law and the academic discussion surrounding the defence of mistake and the problems that arise from it this question should be one that a well-prepared student would have been able to answer well and possibly would even have been pleased to see. The fact that it is half essay/half problem in its format may also assist a student because the essay aspect of the question will often help a student to recall clearly and accurately the necessary cases and principles that are to be applied in relation to the problem part of the question.

Skeleton solution

Mistake - negation of mens rea; 'honest and reasonable'; recent cases - removal of 'reasonableness' requirement except in certain cases.

Suggested solution

a) A mistaken belief held by an accused may be as to fact or as to law (either civil or criminal). It is necessary always to distinguish what particular type of mistake an accused may be labouring under as a mistake of law is usually to be regarded as no defence. In *R* v *Bailey* (1800) the mistaken belief that conduct was not criminal when in fact it was, was held to be no defence, although it went to mitigation. A mistake of fact may be a defence providing it negates the particular mens rea necessary to prove the crime charged.

A mistake which does not preclude the mens rea cannot provide a defence as it is irrelevant.

The difficulty for many years has been in settling what particular type of mistake of fact should enable an accused to be judged according to the position he thought he was in. Some early case law, for example *R* v *Rose* (1884), suggested that the mistake had to be both honest and reasonable. However, in *DPP* v *Morgan* (1975) a purely subjective approach was adopted. In that case D had invited three friends to have sexual intercourse with his wife. He told them that she would put up a struggle as this would increase her sexual pleasure. The men had intercourse with the wife and were convicted of rape. The men appealed against conviction to the House of Lords on a question of whether an honest though unreasonable belief in consent to intercourse was a defence. The House of Lords held that since rape required intercourse without consent, if an accused honestly (though unreasonably) believed that his victim was consenting the prosecution had failed to prove the necessary mens rea for the crime.

More recently there have been a number of cases which have suggested that in certain cases a mistake has got to be both honest and reasonable before it enables the accused to be judged on the basis of what he thought. For example in *Albert* v *Lavin* (1980) the Divisional Court considered the question of mistake in relation to a charge arising under s51 of the Police Act 1964. It was held that it was necessary to distinguish between mens rea required for the basic elements of the offence and the mental element required for a defence. In the former case an honest, albeit unreasonable, mistaken belief may negative mens rea; in the latter, only an honest and reasonable mistake would suffice. For example in the case of an assault charge under s51 a mistaken belief by the defendant that the victim had no right to detain him related to the nature of a defence and applying *Albert* v *Lavin* would have needed to have been reasonable as well as honest. However, more recently there has been a move away from this approach. In *R* v *Kimber* (1983) it was stated that, on a charge of indecent assault, if an accused honestly believed a victim was consenting then he would be entitled to be acquitted. The question of whether his belief was reasonable or unreasonable was irrelevant save in so far that it might have assisted the jury to decide whether an accused did believe what he said he did. Furthermore in *R* v *Williams (Gladstone)* (1984) it was held to be a material misdirection when it was not made clear to the jury that it was for the prosecution to eliminate the possibility that the appellant was acting under a genuine mistake of fact. Once again the Court of Appeal stated that the question of reasonableness of the appellant's mistaken belief was material only to the question of whether or not the belief was in fact held.

In *Beckford* v *R* (1987), where the Privy Council described Morgan as 'a landmark decision in the development of the Common law', the court approved the decision in *R* v *Williams (Gladstone)* (1984). That decision was that, in relation to assaults, 'the mental element necessary ... is the intent to apply unlawful force' and that if the accused believed, reasonably or otherwise, in the existence of facts which would justify his using that force in self-defence, then he did not have the required mens rea.

Since *Beckford* v *R* then, the distinction made in *Albert* v *Lavin* (1981) between elements of the offence and these of a defence has been removed.

It is therefore true to say that mistake generally operates by considering the position the accused thought he was in and on that assumption examines the legal significance of his acts. There do appear to be exceptions to this rule, for example in *DPP* v *Morgan* (1976) the House of Lords refused to overrule *R* v *Tolson* (1889). In that case the accused had been deserted by her husband for five years and believed him to be dead. She remarried whereupon her first husband reappeared. Her conviction for bigamy was quashed because her belief was not only an honest one but also based upon reasonable grounds. Lord Hailsham stated in *DPP* v *Morgan* that he viewed *R* v *Tolson* as a narrow decision based on the construction of a statute which prima facie seemed to make an absolute statutory offence with a proviso of the statutory defence. In Lord Hailsham's view there was a distinction between *R* v *Tolson* and other cases based on statute and the more general situation in *DPP* v *Morgan*.

This view is supported by *Westminster City Council* v *Croyalgrange* (1986).

However, in *R* v *O'Grady* (1987) it was held that where D, because of self-induced intoxication, formed a mistaken belief that he was using force to defend himself his plea (of self-defence) failed.

Finally, where a crime is one capable of commission by negligence, the requirement of reasonableness in mistake persists as an unreasonably held mistaken belief is itself negligent.

Question 3(b)

I was a plain clothes policeman arresting a violent criminal dressed as an old lady. J saw the incident and honestly believed that I was attacking an old lady. J hit I over the head with his bag.

Advise J.

Adapted from University of London LLB Examination (for External Students) Criminal Law June 1984 Q3(b)

General comment

A simple test of the application of the principles relating to mistake and justified use of force.

Skeleton solution

Assault - s51 Police Act 1964; prevention of crime s3 CLA 1967; mistake.

Suggested solution

I should be advised that J may have committed a number of serious offences against him. In particular, s51 of the Police Act 1964. However, it may be open to J to claim the benefit of s3 of the Criminal Law Act 1967 in conjunction with his genuine mistake of fact.

Under s51 of the Police Act 1964 a person who assaults a constable in the execution of his duty shall be guilty of an offence. It is not necessary that an accused knows that it is a constable he is assaulting provided that the constable is acting 'in execution of his duty'. In order for J to be convicted of an offence contrary to s51 it must be shown that the initial arrest being effected by I was lawful: *Riley* v *DPP* (1989). I would seem to be acting in the execution of his duty as his conduct falls within the general scope of preventing crime and catching offenders: *R* v *Waterfield* (1964). J could not be liable under s51(2) for wilfully obstructing a constable in the execution of his duty because on the facts in question he was not acting wilfully as he did not know I was a policeman.

J will wish to claim the defence contained in s3 of the Criminal Law Act 1967 in conjunction with the defence of mistake. The facts in question are very similar to those contained in *R* v *Williams (Gladstone)* (1984). In that case the accused saw M knock a youth to the ground. M said that he was arresting the youth for mugging a woman. The accused did not believe his story and the struggle ensued during which the accused punched M who sustained injuries to his face. The accused was charged under s47 of the Offences Against the Person Act 1861 and put forward the defence that he had honestly believed M was unlawfully assaulting the youth. The trial judge directed that the accused could only rely on his mistake if it was both honest and reasonable. The accused was found guilty and appealed to the Court of Appeal where it was held that there had been a material misdirection in that it had not been made clear to the jury that it was for the prosecution to eliminate the possibility that the appellant was acting under a genuine mistake of fact. The question of whether or not that mistake was reasonable was relevant only in deciding whether the belief was honestly held.

Furthermore, following the Privy Council decision in *Beckford* v *R* (1987) the question to be asked will be did the accused believe, reasonably or not, in the existence of facts which would justify his use of force under the circumstances?

Applying that principle to the facts in question, providing J honestly believed that I was attacking an old lady his criminal liability must be judged on the basis of what he perceived the facts to be.

185

He would therefore be able to claim the defence contained in s3 of the Criminal Law Act 1967 which provides that a person may use such force as is reasonable in the circumstances in the prevention of crime. This defence will not be available to him if he used excessive force in the light of all the circumstances.

The test of what is 'reasonable' here will be an objective one: *Farrell* v *Secretary of State for Defence* (1980), however, account will be taken of the 'heat' of the situation and allowances made therefor.

J will be judged, in respect of his use of force, by the standards of a reasonable man under those particular circumstances and not by those of a reasonable man who is able to exercise detached reflection in the cold light of day: *R* v *Whyte* (1987).

Question 4

R was climbing with his friends S and T. They were roped together and were climbing a particularly dangerous Welsh mountain. T, who was on the bottom of the rope, fell away from the face and dragged S off. R was supporting S and T but they were heavy. R was not able to hold their weight for long so he shouted to S to cut the rope below him. S said, 'But this would be murder.' R said, 'Unless you do so I will cut you both free and you will both be killed.' Reluctantly, S cut the rope and T, who was unconscious, plunged to his death several thousand metres below.

Advise the parties of their criminal liability.

University of London LLB Examination
(for External Students) Criminal Law June 1987 Q6

General comment

This question appeared in the June examination of 1987 and, in view of the recent appeal cases in this area, such a question was to be expected.

This question was relatively straightforward, although the aspect of causation was not easy. The link between necessity and duress required careful consideration.

Skeleton solution

S Murder - causation, necessity, duress - availability to murder.

R Aid/abet murder - necessity.

Suggested solution

The question requires consideration of a number of difficult aspects of the law of homicide. The type of extreme situation described has never come before the courts in practice and much of the law to be considered in this situation may at first glance appear incongruous in its application as the case law involved is more obviously 'criminal' than the facts in question.

The core of the question concerns whether or not R and S can be liable under the criminal law for the death of T. There is nothing in the question to indicate that R and S have acted recklessly in relation to the mountaineering itself. Nor is there anything to indicate that they did anything that would amount to a crime in itself separate from possible liability for the death. Therefore killing by reckless conduct and constructive manslaughter do not appear to be in any way appropriate on the facts.

The most obvious charge that could apply is that of murder. Murder is established when a person unlawfully kills another with 'malice aforethought'. The technical term 'malice aforethought' encompasses two particular types of mens rea - intention to kill and intention to do grievous bodily harm. Either one of these states of mind will be sufficient mens rea for murder: *R* v *Moloney* (1985); *R* v *Hancock and Shankland* (1986); *R* v *Nedrick* (1986).

The term intention includes direct intent (desiring a particular result) and oblique intent (knowledge that a particular result is certain or virtually certain to occur). On the facts in question the prosecution would allege that S had oblique intention to kill, ie he knew that it was certain to occur as a result of what he did even though he did not desire it.

However S could only be liable if he was regarded as the legal cause of T's death. Causation is a mixed question of fact and law. Undoubtedly it must be shown that S's act is a sine qua non of the event. This is a question of fact and in the facts in the question it would seem indisputably satisfied. Even so in law S's act may not be regarded as the cause of the death. Sometimes it is stated that the act must be 'substantial' before it can be regarded as the legal cause of a result. However this is now regarded as being too favourable to the accused. Generally all that need be established is that the accused is a cause of the death and that his contribution is not so trivial that it should be ignored.

Killing a person is merely accelerating an inevitable event. A very trivial acceleration should be ignored and will not be regarded as a legal cause of death. It could therefore be argued that by cutting the rope thus allowing T to fall to his death, S has merely hastened T's death by a matter of seconds and such a slight speeding up of death could not be regarded as the legal cause of the death.

There is therefore a strong argument for suggesting that S is not the legal cause of T's death and therefore is not liable for murder. However in order to examine all aspects of the question it will be assumed that S is the legal cause of T's death and could be liable for murder because he kills intending to kill. In this event it is necessary to consider whether S would be able to claim a defence.

The most obvious defence to consider on these facts is that of necessity. In essence this is a plea that S's intentional conduct, which otherwise would be criminal, was not criminal because what he did was necessary to avoid some other greater evil. However English law does not recognise a general defence of necessity. Thus in *R* v *Dudley and Stevens* (1884) the necessity for self-preservation was no defence to a charge of murder, arising out of the killing and eating of a cabin-boy by shipwrecked sailors adrift on an open boat and without food.

Furthermore, Lord Denning in *Southwark London Borough* v *Williams* (1971) dismissed the notion of such a defence ever existing in English law in relation to certain crimes.

However there has emerged recently a trend in the courts toward a recognition of a defence of 'duress of circumstances' which is a type of necessity. The Court of Appeal accepted such a defence to a charge of reckless driving in *R* v *Willer* (1986) and similarly, the defence was accepted in *R* v *Conway* (1988) as a type of duress.

Whatever the nomenclature, in *R* v *Martin* (1989) the Court of Appeal held that necessity and duress overlapped and that:

i)   in extreme circumstances the law does recognise the defence of necessity;

ii) it is a defence which is only available if, objectively viewed, the accused can be said to be acting reasonably and proportionately in order to avoid a threat of death or serious injury; and

iii) if the defence is available to the accused, the issue should be left to the jury.

They must be directed to determine whether the accused was impelled - or may have been impelled - to act as he did because, as a result of what he reasonably believed, he had good cause to fear that death or serious injury would otherwise ensue.

If that were the case, the question will then be 'would a sober person of reasonable firmness, sharing the characteristics of the accused, have responded to that situation by acting as the accused did?

Here, it is submitted that the above criteria are met, at least by S and possibly by R, although, as the defence of duress is not available in cases of murder (see below), the overlapping concept of 'duress of circumstances' or necessity is unlikely to be open to S and R.

Duress is a further example of what might be regarded as a limited defence of necessity. Duress may be available where S has committed the offence only because of a threat of death or serious personal injury: *DPP for Northern Ireland* v *Lynch* (1975).

For many years it was unclear whether or not duress was available to a principal charged with murder. In *DPP for Northern Ireland* v *Lynch* the House of Lords had allowed a plea of duress where an aider and abettor had taken part in a murder under duress. In *Abbott* v *R* (1976) the Privy Council held by a majority that the defence was not available to a principal charged with murder. The minority view was that since there was no compelling authority or public policy to the contrary, the defence should be available to a principal offender.

The lack of clarity on this area of law was further emphasised in *R* v *Graham* (1982) where the prosecution conceded that the defence could raise a plea of duress even though the accused was charged as a principal to murder.

Recently the House of Lords had opportunity to review the law in this difficult area. In *R* v *Howe* (1987); *R* v *Bannister* (1962); *R* v *Burke* (1987) and *R* v *Clarkson* (1987) the House, after much deliberation, departed from its own decision in *DPP for*

Northern Ireland v *Lynch* and held that the defence of duress was no longer available to an accomplice to murder, including an aider and abettor. Indeed it was not available to a principal or accomplice charged with murder as there was no proper distinction that could be drawn between a principal and an accomplice. The inconsistency of approach in this area has therefore been corrected. Furthermore the House affirmed the approach as stated in *R* v *Graham* that in any event a defence of duress would fail if the prosecution proved that a person of reasonable firmness sharing the characteristics of the defendant would not have given way to the threats as did the defendant.

Thus it is clear that S could not plead duress. Had S been able to plead duress R would have become a principal offender via the doctrine of innocent agency. However his only possible liability now must be an an aider and abettor. An aider and abettor is one who is present at the scene of the offence assisting or encouraging: *R* v *Coney* (1882); *R* v *Clarkson* (1971). To be an aider and abettor an accused must have full knowledge of the facts that amount to the crime: *Johnson* v *Youden* (1950). Patently this is established on the facts in question. R would be unable to claim any defence in law. Self defence is only available where an accused is countering a threat from a person. Necessity is not available as a defence in English criminal law. R, like S, would appear to be liable for murder. However, it must be remembered that this application of the law would not be appropriate if S was not the legal cause of T's death.

Question 5

G had invited H to a party given at G's house. H was a well known total abstainer. G believed that H had walked to the party whereas in fact H had come by car. G laced H's drink to see how H would react. In fact H became ill and decided to drive home. H was aware that he was not himself but he did not know that his disability was the result of the laced drink. H drove home and on the way collided with a parked car damaging it and causing severe anger to its owner who was some distance away. When H arrived home he found an intruder in his house and chased him intending to catch him. The intruder fell down stairs whilst being chased and broke a leg.

Advise the parties of their criminal liability.

University of London LLB (Examination)
(for External Students) Criminal Law June 1990 Q5

General comment

A question requiring a good knowledge of automatism and intoxication. The question raises the interesting issue of non-reckless intoxication. Far more space should be devoted to H's liability than that of G.

Skeleton solution

Liability of H. Criminal damage. automatism and non-reckless intoxication. Injuries to intruder. Causation. Consider mens rea for ss18, 20, and 47. Defence under s3 1967 Act. Liability of G. Administering a noxious substance. Accessorial liability.

Suggested solution

H has obviously damaged property belonging to another, contrary to s1(1) Criminal Damage Act 1971. The difficulty surrounding his liability for this offences stems from the fact that he was unwell/intoxicated at the time and thus may have a defence based on the submission that he was not responsible for his actions at the time. The most attractive argument to rely on from H's point of view, is that because of the effect of the alcohol on his nervous system he was in a state of automatism at the time of the collision. If this argument were to succeed it would result in H being totally relieved of all criminal liability for the collision. Automatism has been defined, in cases such as *Bratty* v *Attorney-General for Northern Ireland* (1963), as 'something done by the muscles without the control of the mind'. It is generally accepted that it takes the form of some external factor operating upon the brain, such as hypnotism. In theory the effect of alcohol upon the brain could come within this category, although there are two difficulties with this line of argument.

The first difficulty is that there must be evidence that H was really in an automatic state. If there is evidence that he was actually conscious of his actions, for example that he knew he was driving, the defence will not be available to him; see *Broome* v *Perkins* (1987). Secondly, there is evidence to suggest that he knew he was feeling unwell. The court may take the view that he should not have attempted to drive at all in such a situation, and that there is a degree of fault to be found in his deciding to drive; see *R* v *Bailey* (1983). A possible distinction between 'Bailey' and the present case is that H did not know the cause of his illness, and thus may not have been expected to know its possible consequences.

If the defence of automatism is not available to H, the defence of intoxication will have to be considered. It is well established that the defence of intoxication is normally only available to defendants charged with crimes of specific intent. Criminal damage contrary to s1(1) of the 1971 Act is a crime of basic intent. Following the House of Lords' decision in *DPP* v *Majewski* (1976), the mens rea required for the crime of basic intent, i.e recklessness, is to be found in the defendant's recklessness, or fault, in becoming intoxicated in the first instance. At this point a possible distinction between most cases of intoxication and the case of H emerges. H may contend that he was not at fault in becoming intoxicated since there was nothing that would have alerted him, or even the reasonable person, to the fact that his drink had been laced with alcohol. The concept of so-called 'non-reckless intoxication' was considered by the Court of Appeal in *R* v *Hardie* (1984). There the court held that where there is evidence that a defendant charged with a basic intent crime may not have been reckless in becoming intoxicated, the issue ought to be left to the jury. On this basis it is submitted that H may succeed with the defence of intoxication.

It is submitted that there will be no criminal liability for causing the car owner to be enraged. Such a condition is unlikely to constitute actual bodily harm contrary to s47 of the Offences Against the Persons Act 1861, as defined in *R* v *Miller* (1954), neither is it a common assault as the owner did not apprehend immediate physical violence.

In suffering a broken leg, the intruder in H's house incurs grievous bodily harm, as defined in *R* v *Saunders* (1985). H will be regarded as having caused the injury on the basis that the intruder's reaction, ie that of running away in haste, was a reasonably foreseeable consequence of his being chased by H; see *R* v *Roberts* (1971). There is no evidence of the intruder doing anything 'daft' that would break the chain of causation.

For liability under s18 of the 1861 Act, H will have to be shown to have intended to cause the intruder some grievous bodily harm; see *R* v *Belfon* (1976). On the facts this may be difficult to prove, as H will claim that his intention was to catch the intruder. More likely perhaps is a charge of inflicting grievous bodily harm contrary to s20 of the 1861 Act. For this offence it would have to be shown that H was 'malicious', ie that he foresaw at least the possibility of some physical harm occurring to the intruder albeit slight; see *R* v *Cunningham* (1957), and *R* v *Mowatt* (1967). H could escape liability under s20 if he can show that he never foresaw the possibility of any physical harm occurring to the intruder. It is submitted that if this proves to be the case, H might still be guilty of an offence contrary to s47 of the 1861 Act. The mens rea for s47 is intention or recklessness; see *R* v *Venna* (1976). In *Venna* the court took recklessness to mean subjective recklessness, basing this decision on the earlier case of *R* v *Cunningham* (above). Subjective recklessness requires proof that the defendant was aware of the risk that the victim would apprehend immediate physical violence. It would appear that the application of this form of recklessness to assault remains unaffected by developments in cases such as *MPC* v *Caldwell* (1982). *R* v *Spratt* (1990), and *R* v *Parmenter* (1991) both confirm that, s47 requires proof of *Cunningham* type recklessness.

By way of defence H can contend that he was using reasonable force in effecting or assisting in the lawful arrest of a suspected offender; see s3 Criminal Law Act 1967. It is submitted that his intoxication is irrelevant here since there is no evidence of his having misjudged the use of force necessary in the circumstances.

By placing alcohol in H's drink G may have committed either the offence of maliciously administering a noxious substance so as thereby to endanger life, contrary to s23 of the 1861 Act, or the offence of maliciously administering a noxious substance, with intent to injure aggrieve or annoy, contrary to s24 of the 1861 Act. Alcohol can be a noxious substance in certain circumstances; see *R* v *Cato* (1976), and *R* v *Marcus* (1981). A charge under s23 would be appropriate if the collision is seen as placing H's life in danger. Under s23, G does not need to have foreseen the collision, merely that there was a risk that H would suffer some physical harm; see *R* v *Cunningham*. It is submitted that H probably did have the mens rea required by s24, namely the intent to injure annoy or aggrieve.

H cannot be regarded as the innocent agent of G, as he was aware of his actions at the time of the collision, and when chasing the intruder. By causing H to become intoxicated, however, G may incur liability as an accessory to the criminal damage; see *Attorney-General's Reference (No 1 of 1975)* (1975).

11 UNIVERSITY OF LONDON LLB (EXTERNAL) 1991 QUESTIONS AND SUGGESTED SOLUTIONS

UNIVERSITY OF LONDON
INTERMEDIATE EXAMINATION IN LAWS
for External Students

CRIMINAL LAW

Tuesday, 11 June 1991: 10.00am to 1.00pm

Answer *four* questions

1. A and his next door neighbour, B, had quarrelled because of loud noises emanating from B's house at night. A intended to frighten B and he rewired B's burglar alarm to go off in the middle of the night. The alarm went off causing B's grandmother, who was an unexpected overnight visitor, to have a stroke from which she died thirteen months later. Also, C, one of B's children, in her rush to leave the house, fell down the stairs and broke her leg. A fire engine which had been called by a neighbour was rushing to B's house at a speed in excess of that lawfully permitted, when it collided with a car driven by D, who died from the injuries. Advise A and B of their criminal liability.

2. E went into F's camera shop to steal a 'Flashman' camera. He could not find one there and left having been told by a sales assistant that they did not have one in stock. Next E went into Gutrum Cameras to see if there was a 'Flashman' on the premises to steal on a subsequent visit. He found the camera and while the sales assistant's attention was elsewhere E changed the price labels on the camera putting a lower price label on the 'Flashman' camera. He then realised that the shop was protected by closed circuit television. E left the camera and rushed out of the store, forgetting to pay for a roll of film which he had picked up. As he was leaving, E pushed aside a customer who was entering the shop. Advise E.

3. H was a world-famous darts player. He was demonstrating his skills at an outdoor fete in aid of a charity. H offered £50 to anyone who would place an apple on his head and permit H to throw a dart at it. H contemplated the risk of hitting such a person. I volunteered, placing the apple on his head. H threw the dart but a sudden gust of wind caused the dart to deviate from its trajectory, and hit I's ear. I's blood dripped onto I's coat. The dart continued on to hit an electric cable, setting fire to a fete tent. Advise H of his criminal liability.

4. L telephoned M suggesting that they should enter Z's house, 'to do it over.' Z was their teacher. M understood L to be suggesting that they should look over the house and hide one or two of Z's things and leave messages in shaving soap on Z's mirrors. L meant that they should take anything of value and damage the rest of Z's property with paint. M said, 'Alright I'll see you at 8 pm tonight.' In fact, M failed to turn up having thought the matter over. Later, L recruited O to his plan and together they went to Z's house. Unexpectedly, Z returned home and discovered L and O. L hit Z over the head with a poker. Advise the parties of their criminal liability. What difference, if any, would it make to your advice if M was 16 years old?

5. X drove onto Y's self-service garage and filled up his tank with petrol. On the petrol pump was a notice which read, 'This petrol is not yours until it is paid for.' Having filled his tank, X realised that because he had forgotten his wallet he did not have sufficient money to pay for the petrol. X went to tell the attendant and to ask what to do. The attendant told him to walk the eight miles home to collect the money. This X refused to do and, despite protestations from the attendant, drove home. There X realised that the attendant had failed to make a note of X's name, address or vehicle registration number. X decided that because of the attendant's unhelpful attitude he would not return to pay. Advise X.

6. P hid a bomb aboard a plane. He telephoned the airline while the plane was on a transatlantic flight. He demanded payment of £1 million to tell them where the bomb was hidden. The airline refused to pay the money despite advice to the contrary from a security firm. As a result the plane was blown up and all the passengers and crew were killed. Advise P of his criminal liability. What difference, if any, would it make to your advice if P believed that in demanding payment he was divinely inspired to raise the money to further his religious ends?

7. G telephoned H and told him to pick up a package from a given address and place it outside K's church. G threatened that if H failed to comply he would tell H's employer about H's affair with his secretary. H was frightened by this because he was afraid of losing his job and his reputation as he was a well-known lay preacher. H picked up a package at the address and placed it outside the church. However, by mistake he picked up a different package belonging to K and it was subsequently stolen from the church doorstep where H had left it. The other package which he was meant to pick up exploded injuring a passer-by. Advise the parties of their criminal liability. What difference, if any, would it make to your advice if G had threatened to injure H's son whom H believed to be in G's custody?

Question 1

A and his next door neighbour, B, had quarrelled because of loud noises emanating from B's house at night. A intended to frighten B and he rewired B's burglar alarm to go off in the middle of the night. The alarm went off causing B's grandmother, who was an unexpected overnight visitor, to have a stroke from which she died thirteen months later. Also, C, one of B's children, in her rush to leave the house, fell down the stairs and broke her leg. A fire engine which had been called by a neighbour was rushing to B's house at a speed in excess of that lawfully permitted, when it collided with a car driven by D, who died from the injuries. Advise A and B of their criminal liability.

University of London LLB Examination
(for External Students) Criminal Law June 1991 Q1

General comment

Concentrate on the liability of A as there is little if any evidence to suggest criminal liability on the part of B. Deal with each type of harm caused in turn, and in the order in which it occurs. With many of the incidents it is the absence of mens rea which prevents liability from arising. At the time the question was set the issue of the mens rea for s47 was unresolved; this doubt should be reflected in the answer given.

Skeleton solution

Criminal damage simple and aggravated. Death, year and a day rule. Assaults. Issues of causation, problems with mens rea. Broken leg, mens rea issue. Death of D, causation. No recklessness.

Suggested solution

a) *Criminal damage*

In rewiring B's burglar alarm, A may be guilty of criminal damage contrary to s1(1) Criminal Damage Act 1971. Under s1(1), a person who without lawful excuse destroys or damages any property belonging to another intending to destroy or damage any such property or being reckless as to whether any such property would be destroyed or damaged is guilty of the offence. The alarm is clearly property belonging to another. By rewiring it interferes with its effectiveness, and this is sufficient to constitute 'damage' as that term has been interpreted under the Act; see *Hardman* v *Chief Constable of Avon and Somerset Constabulary* (1986), *Roe* v *Kingerlee* (1986), and *Morphitis* v *Salmon* (1990). A clearly has the intent to commit this offence. A does not have any lawful excuse, as that term is understood under s5(2) of the 1971 Act, which would relieve him of liability. A charge of aggravated criminal damage contrary to s1(2) of the 1971 Act would seem more speculative. Under s1(2), the defendant must be shown to have destroyed or damaged property, intending by the destruction or damage to endanger the life of another or being reckless as to whether the life of another would be thereby endangered. The prosecution must show that the defendant was at least reckless as to whether or not the criminal damage itself would endanger life; see *R* v *Steer* (1987).

Following *MPC* v *Caldwell* (1982), the defendant must be shown to have been aware of the risk that life would be endangered, or to have failed to give any thought to an obvious risk that life would be so endangered. The test is objective, in that the risk must be one that would have been obvious to a reasonable prudent bystander; see *R* v *Sangha* (1988). A might still escape liability if he thought about the risk of his criminal damage endangering life but decided that there was no such risk; see *Chief Constable of Avon and Somerset Constabulary* v *Shimmen* (1986).

b) *Grandmother's death*

A is the cause in fact of the grandmother's death, but any charge of murder/manslaughter would be prevented by the rule in *R* v *Dyson* (1908), which requires that death should result within a year and a day of the act alleged to have caused the death.

c) *Grandmother's injuries*

A causes the grandmother to suffer a stroke. 'But for' his tampering with the alarm she would not have suffered from shock; see *R* v *White* (1910). The frailty of the victim will not be a factor amounting to a novus actus interveniens; see *R* v *Blaue* (1975). Suffering a stroke could be regarded as grievous bodily harm; see *R* v *Saunders* (1985). The problem for the prosecution will be in establishing any mens rea on the part of A. His stated intention was to frighten. The fact that he has B as his intended victim, but causes fright to other will not relieve him of liability, see the principles of transferred malice expounded in *R* v *Latimer* (1886). Grievous bodily harm, however, requires proof of intent if charged contrary to s18 of the Offences Against the Persons Act 1861, or recklessness if charged contrary to s20 of that Act. In *R* v *Cunningham* (1957), as interpreted by Diplock LJ in *R* v *Mowatt* (1968), the defendant charged under s20 must at least have been aware of the possibility that his actions might cause some physical harm to a victim, albeit slight. It is significant that A only intended to frighten. In *R* v *Sullivan* (1981) the defendant was acquitted under s20 precisely because he only intended to frighten his victim, and a conviction under s47 of the Offences Against the Persons Act 1861 was substituted.

Could A be charged under s47? Again the difficulty is establishing the mens rea. It is now clear that the recklessness involved in the offence is *Cunningham* subjective recklessness; *DPP* v *Khan* (1990), doubted in *R* v *Spratt* (1990). *Cunningham* preferred by the Court of Appeal in *R* v *Parmenter* (1991).

The remaining question is that of what risk the defendant must have been aware of: merely assaulting the victim, or the risk that the assault would occasion actual bodily harm? The matter is currently the subject of conflicting judicial dicta in *R* v *Spratt*, *R* v *Parmenter*, and *R* v *Savage* (1990). If the defendant merely has to be aware of the risk of assault (ie frightening his victim), then A might incur liability. If foresight of the risk of actual bodily harm is required, it is submitted that, on the given facts, the prosecution would be in some difficulty.

d) *C's broken leg*

The broken leg would constitute grievous bodily harm. The chain of causation might not have been broken by C's running downstairs, if it is regarded as a reasonably foreseeable consequence of the alarm going off. See further *R* v *Martin* (1881). It is submitted that there would be the same problems in relation to mens rea as already outlined above at (c).

e) *Death of D*

A has caused the death of D, in fact, and it could be argued that the actions of the fire brigade in responding to the call were reasonably foreseeable and thus do not break the chain of causation; see *R* v *Pagett* (1983). The prosecution are unlikely to be able to establish the requisite mens rea, however. The minimum would be *Caldwell* recklessness, outlined above in relation to criminal damage. The reasonable person may well ask why, if it is a burglar alarm that has gone off, is it the fire brigade that is responding?

f) *Liability of B*

In the absence of any evidence that B failed to act to prevent any of the harm that has occurred, it is submitted that there is no basis for imposing any criminal liability.

Question 2

E went into F's camera shop to steal a 'Flashman' camera. He could not find one there and left having been told by a sales assistant that they did not have one in stock. Next E went into Gutrum Cameras to see if there was a 'Flashman' on the premises to steal on a subsequent visit. He found the camera and while the sales assistant's attention was elsewhere E changed the price labels on the camera putting a lower price label on the 'Flashman' camera. He then realised that the shop was protected by closed circuit television. E left the camera and rushed out of the store, forgetting to pay for a roll of film which he had picked up. As he was leaving, E pushed aside a customer who was entering the shop. Advise E.

University of London LLB Examination
(for External Students) Criminal Law June 1991 Q2

General comment

There are a number of points to watch in attempting this question. E does not intend to steal the camera when he visits the second shop but is planning to return on another occasion. How does this affect his liability? What is his state of mind when he leaves the shop with the film? We are not given clear guidance on this. It is suggested that the examiner clearly wanted candidates to consider robbery, although on the facts it seems unlikely that such a charge could succeed.

Skeleton solution

Section 9(1)(a) burglary in both shops. Label switching as theft. Attempted s15. Effect on burglary. Not paying for the film. Theft. Problem with dishonesty. Making off. Battery. Robbery.

Suggested solution

a) *Section 9(1)(a) burglary*

E may have committed burglary contrary to s9(1)(a) of the Theft Act 1968, when he entered F's camera shop intending to steal the 'Flashman' camera. The shop is clearly a building. Byles J, in *Stevens* v *Gourley* (1859), stated that a building was 'a structure of considerable size and intended to be permanent or at least to endure for a considerable length of time'. E has clearly entered the shop; *R* v *Brown* (1985). Section 9(1)(a) requires proof that E entered the shop as a trespasser. Clearly an honest shopper has permission to enter a shop and thus does not commit trespass as that concept is understood at civil law. In *R* v *Smith and Jones* (1976), the defendants visited the house of Smith's father and stole his television set. They were convicted under s9(1)(b) and appealed on the basis that they had permission to go into the house and thus could not have been trespassing. The court held that the defendants were rightly convicted under the subsection, on the basis that a person enters a building as a trespasser where he realises he has exceeded his permission, or is reckless as to whether he has done so. The defendants might have had permission to enter the house for normal domestic purposes, but not to enter in the middle of the night to steal.

Similarly E will not have had intention to enter the shop in order to steal and will have been aware of this. The fact that the camera he sought was not available will not affect E's liability. The Court of Appeal's decision in *Attorney-General's References (Nos 1 and 2 of 1979)* (1979) establishes that the essence of the offence is the defendant's state of mind at the time of entry, the intent to steal can exist quite independently of any property that he can or wants to steal.

E may also incur liability under s9(1)(a) in respect of his visit to 'Gutrum' cameras, although he may contend that as he does not intend to steal the camera there and then he does not have the present intention to steal which is one of the ulterior intents required for liability under s9(1)(a).

b) *Label switching: theft and burglary*

In switching labels on the cameras E may have committed theft. The cameras are obviously property belonging to another. Section 3(1) of the Theft Act 1968 defines appropriation as '... any assumption by a person of the rights of an owner ...'. In *R* v *Morris* (1983) this was held to extend to label switching on the basis that the defendant was assuming the owner's right to determine the price to be paid for the goods. In acting in this way E is clearly dishonest; see s2(1) of the 1968 Act and *R* v *Ghosh* (1982). There remains the question of whether or not he has intention to permanently deprive the store of its property. If he intended to take the camera to the counter there and then the answer would be 'yes', but the difficulty here is the evidence that he intends to return on another occasion to steal it. In this situation it may be wiser to charge E with the alternative offence of attempting to obtain property by deception. If he had presented the camera to the assistant with the lower price label and been permitted to purchase it at this lower price he would have obtained the camera by deception, hence his actions in swapping labels are acts more than merely preparatory to the deception offence; see s1(1) Criminal Attempts Act 1981, and comments by Lord Roskill in *R* v *Morris* (above). The fact that E changes his mind once he realises he has been observed is irrelevant. he has already committed the attempt, and possibly the theft, if he swapped labels with the requisite mens rea.

c) *Not paying for the film*

The film is property belonging to the store. It is submitted that despite the views expressed by Viscount Dilhorne in *Lawrence* v *MPC* (1972), E does not appropriate then film until he commits an unauthorised act in relation to it, ie leaving the store without paying for it; see the most recent re-affirmation of this approach in *R* v *Gomez* (1991). If E does not realise that he has the film he may not have any intention to permanently deprive the store of its property, in which case a charge of theft will not be sustainable. If he realises he has the film, but mistakenly thinks he has paid for it, then he will not be dishonest, by virtue of s2(1)(a) and (b) Theft Act 1968, which provide that

'A person's appropriation of property belonging to another is not to be regarded as dishonest – (a) if he appropriates the property in the belief that he has in law the right to deprive the other of it ...; or (b) if he appropriates the property in the belief that he would have the other's consent if the other knew of the appropriation and the circumstances of it ...'

E will believe he has the right in law to take the film if he thinks he has paid for it. Similarly he will believe that the owner consents for this reason. If a charge of theft cannot be sustained, then no question of liability under s9(1)(b) arises (entering as a trespasser and stealing).

As an alternative the prosecution may contemplate a charge under s3(1) of the Theft Act 1978, which creates the offence of making off without payment. Under s3 a person who, knowing that payment on the spot for any goods supplied or service done is required or expected from him, dishonestly makes off without having paid as required or expected and with intent to avoid payment of the amount due is guilty of an offence. A number of difficulties are evident with such a charge. First does E make off dishonestly? The test here is that laid down in *R* v *Ghosh* (above). If he thinks he has paid would he realise that ordinary and decent people would regard his actions as wrong? Secondly, does he make off with intent to avoid payment? Again, if he thinks he has paid, or even if he has simply forgotten, the answer must be 'no'.

d) *Robbery?*

The fact that E pushes aside a customer as he is leaving the shop is unlikely to give rise to a criminal charge. Technically E could be charged with battery as he has inflicted unlawful force on another; see *Cole* v *Turner* (1705), but the police are unlikely to entertain such a complaint. A private prosecution would have to be brought to pursue the matter. If prosecution form the view that E is committing theft of the film in leaving the store without paying for it, the matter becomes more serious. E could then be charged with robbery. Under s8 of the 1968 Act, a person is guilty of robbery 'if he steals, and immediately before or at the time of doing so, and in order to do so, he uses force on any person or puts or seeks to put any person in fear of being then and there subjected to force.'

There is no doubt here that force has been used (on the customer) but the question would arise as to whether or not it coincided with the theft. E may contend that the theft had already occurred, but the prosecution will rely upon the Court of Appeal's decision in *R* v *Hale* (1978), to the effect that appropriation could be a continuing act, the point at which it ceased was being determined by the jury on the facts of each case. Where, therefore, D steals property belonging to P, is discovered by P, and threatens P that unless he is allowed to escape without the police being called he will assault P, D will be guilty of robbery. The threats to P are made whilst the theft (appropriation) is continuing, and are made in order to accomplish the theft. It is submitted that even if the prosecution does persist in a charge of theft, E will rely upon the decision in *R* v *Robinson* (1977), in which the Court of Appeal held that a defendant should be found not guilty of robbery where he honestly believed he had a right in law to take the property, ie where the defendant falls under s2(1)(a) of the 1968 Act.

Question 3

H was a world-famous darts player. He was demonstrating his skills at an outdoor fete in aid of a charity. H offered £50 to anyone who would place an apple on his head and permit H to throw a dart at it. H contemplated the risk of hitting such a person. I volunteered, placing the apple on his head. H threw the dart but a sudden gust of wind caused the dart to deviate from its trajectory, and hit I's ear. I's blood dripped onto I's coat. The dart continued on to hit an electric cable, setting fire to a fete tent. Advise H of his criminal liability.

University of London LLB Examination
(for External Students) Criminal Law June 1991 Q3

General comment

Essentially a recklessness question. The question first raises the issue in relation to malicious wounding, and then in relation to criminal damage. A clear explanation of the difference between *Cunningham* and *Caldwell* is therefore required. When considering the criminal damage charges the examiner expects candidates to explore the 'gap' alleged to exist between the two types of recklessness.

Skeleton solution

Liability for wounding. Recklessness involved in malice. Section 47 alternative. Consent. Simple criminal damage. Recklessness. Lawful excuse. Aggravated offence.

Suggested solution

a) *Injury to I's ear*

The injury to I's ear constitutes a wound within the context of ss18 and 20 of the Offences Against the Persons Act 1861. Following *JJC* v *Eisenhower* (1983) a wounding must involve a rupturing of both the dermis and the epidermis. Clearly if I suffers a loss of blood as a result of the injury this requirement has been satisfied. H can only contend that the gust of wind which blew the dart off course amounted to a novus actus interveniens if it was something so unexpected that ordinary reasonable persons would not have foreseen it. It is submitted that this is unlikely to be the case. If, therefore, H is regarded as having caused the injury, the question of his mens rea has to be considered. Liability under s18 would seem to be precluded by the need to prove that, in throwing the dart, he intended to cause grievous bodily to I. Under s20 of the Offences Against the Persons Act 1861 he must be shown to have acted 'maliciously'. The basis for the modern interpretation of this term is the decision of the Court of Appeal in *R* v *Cunningham* (1957), where it was held to involve either an actual intention to do the particular kind of harm that in fact was done or recklessness as to whether such harm should occur or not (ie the accused must have foreseen that the particular kind of harm might be done and yet has gone on to take the risk of it). A gloss was placed upon the definition in *Cunningham* by Diplock LJ in the later case of *R* v *Mowatt* (1967) where his Lordship explained the term as requiring proof that the defendant should have foreseen that some physical harm to some person, albeit of a minor character, might result. It is clear that the 'recklessness' involved in the offence is subjective. The defendant must be aware of the risk of some physical harm. An intention to frighten, or foresight that the victim will be frightened is insufficient; see *R* v *Sullivan* (1981). So-called *Caldwell* recklessness is of no application under s20; see *W* v *Dolbey* (1983), and *R* v *Grimshaw* (1984). As a professional darts player, H may have determined that in his case there was no risk, and therefore cannot be regarded as reckless. The prosecution may wish to pursue a lesser charge under s47 of the Offences Against the Persons Act 1861, but should be advised that here too they will need to establish subjective risk taking on the part of H, which for reasons just stated may not be easy; see *R* v *Spratt* (1990).

Although I consents to take part in the darts demonstration, his consent will not afford H any defence if he is charged. *R* v *Donovan* (1934), provides that, subject to certain well established exceptions such as sporting contests and cosmetic/medical treatment, a victim can only validly consent to harm if it amounts to less than actual bodily harm. The fact that I is involved in a charity event will not, it is submitted, have any bearing on this matter. One cannot consent to being stabbed in the ear. (It is assumed for these purposes that ear-piercing constitutes cosmetic/medical treatment.)

b) *Damage to the coat*

H may incur liability for criminal damage contrary to s1(1) of the Criminal Damage Act 1971 in respect of the blood that drips onto I's coat. Under s1(1) a person who, without lawful excuse destroys or damages any property belonging to another intending to destroy or damage any such property or being reckless as to whether any such property would be destroyed or damaged is guilty of an offence.

The coat is clearly property belonging to another. The fact that the blood could be removed by cleaning does not mean that it does not constitute damage for the purposes of the Act. In *Hardman* v *Chief Constable of Avon and Somerset Constabulary* (1986), and *Roe* v *Kingerlee* (1986), defendants were convicted of damage to property even though the harm done in both cases involved substances being applied to surfaces that could be removed simply by cleaning.

H does not appear to have any lawful excuse for his actions unless he can bring himself with s5(2) of the 1971 Act by showing that at the time of the act or acts alleged to constitute the offence he believed that I had consented to the damage. This seems unlikely on the facts, although H may argue that the £50 offered to volunteers compensated them for any damage to their clothing that might occur.

H clearly did not intend to damage the coat, but under s1(1) recklessness is sufficient. Following *MPC* v *Caldwell* (1982), it is enough that he was either aware of the risk or gave no thought to an obvious risk that such harm would occur. There are a number of difficulties for the prosecution here. Given that H was a professional darts player, would the reasonable prudent bystander have thought that there was an obvious risk of criminal damage? See *R* v *Sangha* (1988). If not, the test is not satisfied. Was H aware of any risk? He may have decided that, given his skill, there was no risk. That a defendant might escape liability for criminal damage in such circumstances was adverted to by the Divisional court in *Chief Constable of Avon and Somerset Constabulary* v *Shimmen* (1987).

c) *Damage to the tent*

Again H may incur liability for criminal damage in respect of the damage to the electric cable and the tent. They are both property belonging to another, and the damage and destruction in both cases is evident. The same issues in relation to recklessness already discussed above would arise here. The additional factor to consider is that of whether or not H could be charged with aggravated criminal damage contrary to s1(2) of the 1971 Act.

The aggravating factor is the defendant's intention that the criminal damage should endanger life, or his recklessness as to whether the life of another would be thereby be endangered. If H lacks the recklessness for the damage to the electricity cable (for reasons already set out) there will be no basis for a charge under s1(2). Even if he is shown to have been reckless as to the damage to the cable, following the House of Lords' decision in *R* v *Steer* (1987), the prosecution will have to show that he was reckless as to whether or not that damage would endanger life further.

Question 4

L telephoned M suggesting that they should enter Z's house, 'to do it over.' Z was their teacher. M understood L to be suggesting that they should look over the house and hide one or two of Z's things and leave messages in shaving soap on Z's mirrors. L meant that they should take anything of value and damage the rest of Z's property with paint. M said, 'Alright I'll see you at 8 pm tonight.' In fact, M failed to turn up having thought the matter over. Later, L recruited O to his plan and together they went to Z's house. Unexpectedly, Z returned home and discovered L and O. L hit Z over the head with a poker. Advise the parties of their criminal liability. What difference, if any, would it make to your advice if M was 16 years old?

University of London LLB Examination
(for External Students) Criminal Law June 1991 Q4

General comment

The question raises a wide range of issues. Particularly trick points to watch for are the possibility of attempted incitement, and the possible absence of any agreement with regard to the conspiracy. The attack upon Z clearly requires reference to the 'Wilson and Jenkins' point on burglary. The point relating to M's age is curious. It would have made more sense if the question had stated that he was under 14, and then asked how his liability would differ.

Skeleton solution

Incitement. Curr point. Possible attempt. Conspiracy. Whether any agreement. Conspiracy with O. Burglary. Section 9(1)(a). Assault on Z. Section 9(1)(b). *R* v *Jenkins*. Principal deliberately departs from the common design. The age of M.

Suggested solution

a) *Incitement and conspiracy*

L suggests the commission of a number of offences to M. He may incur liability for common law incitement. The actus reus of incitement is committed where a defendant suggests the commission of an offence to another person. It has to be shown that the suggestion from the incitor has reached the mind of the incitee, but there is no need to provide evidence that the incitee acted on the suggestion; see comments of Lord Denning MR in *Race Relations Board* v *Applin* (1973). Generally, the incitee must know of the facts that make the conduct incited criminal. Hence a defendant can only be guilty of incitement to handle stolen goods if the incitee knew or believed the good in question to be stolen; see *R* v *Curr* (1968). In that case the defendant ran a loan business whereby he would lend money to women with children in return for their handing over their signed Family Allowance books. He would then use other women to cash the family allowance vouchers. He was convicted of inciting the commission of offences under s9(b) of the Family Allowance Act 1945, which made it an offence for any person to receive any sum by way of Family Allowance knowing it was not properly payable, but appealed successfully to the Court of Appeal, where it was held that the trial judge had erred in not directing the jury to consider whether those women, who were being incited to use the signed allowance books to collect money on behalf of the defendant, had actually known that what they were being asked to do was unlawful. In the present case L may contend that as he and M were at cross purposes, M may not have realised that what was being incited was unlawful. If this were the case, L might be charged with attempted incitement; see *R* v *Ransford* (1874).

It would appear that L did have the mens rea for incitement. In *Invicta Plastics* v *Clare* (1976), the Divisional Court defined it as involving not only an intention to incite, but also an intention that the incitee should act upon the incitement.

L and M may be charged with statutory conspiracy given that they agree to enter Z's house for an unlawful purpose, but there are difficulties here. Section 1(1) of the Criminal Law Act 1977 (as amended) provides that if a person agrees with any other person that a course of conduct shall be pursued which, if the agreement is carried out in accordance with their intentions, either will necessarily amount to or involve the commission of any offence or offences by one or more of the parties to the agreement, he is guilty of conspiracy to commit the offence or offences in question. The problem is that there is no meeting of the minds. Arguably the parties have not even agreed that any offence will be committed. Note that L cannot be charged with attempted conspiracy as the offence was abolished by s5 of the 1977 Act.

From the evidence provided it appears that there is much clearer evidence of a conspiracy between L and O, and that both could be charged with conspiracy to commit burglary contrary to the 1977 Act.

b) *Burglary*

The evidence provided indicates that when M entered the property owned by Z he intended to steal and commit criminal damage. O appears to have been fully aware of this. Under s9(1)(a) of the Theft act 1968, a person is guilty of burglary if he enters any building or part of a building as a trespasser and with intent, inter alia, to commit the theft of anything in the building, or of with the intent of doing unlawful damage to the building or anything therein.

M and O clearly enter a building and have no permission to be there. Provided the prosecution can establish that the defendants knew they were trespassing, or were at least reckless as to whether they were trespassing, the basis of the offence is made out. The recklessness here is 'subjective' as in *R* v *Cunningham* (1957) , and not objective as in *MPC* v *Caldwell* (1982). It is submitted that the offence under s9(1)(a) will be made out.

c) *Assault on Z*

In striking Z on the head with the poker, L commits an assault, quite probably grievous bodily harm or wounding, depending upon the severity of the injuries. The harm appears to have been inflicted intentionally, thus L may incur liability under s18 or s20 of the Offences Against the Persons Act 1861. A further possibility is that L might be charged under s9(1)(b) of the 1968 Act which provides (inter alia) that a person is guilty of burglary if having entered any building as a trespasser and inflicts on any person therein any grievous bodily harm. Whether or not L entered as a trespasser has already been discussed. Note that L need not have had the intention to steal or inflict grievous bodily harm when he entered the building as a trespasser; such intent can be formed subsequent to entry. The infliction of grievous bodily harm under s9(1)(b) does not have to constitute an offence; it simply requires L to have inflicted grievous bodily harm upon Z. The Court of Appeal in *R* v *Jenkins* (1983) contemplated that a defendant would be guilty under s9(1)(b) where he entered a house as a trespasser and was observed by an occupant of whose presence he was unaware. Should the occupant suffer a stroke as a result of this shock, the defendant would have inflicted grievous bodily harm regardless of his lack of mens rea. The House of Lords, although allowing the defendant's appeal, in *R* v *Jenkins*, did not dissent from the above analysis of s9(1)(b).

O will contend that he is not guilty under s9(1)(b) since the attack upon Z was not part of the original agreement. The general rule is that an accomplice will be liable for all the accidental, or unforeseen consequences that flow from the common design being carried out, but where the principal deliberately departs from the common design, an accomplice ceases to be a party to his actions. Thus in *Davies* v *DPP* (1954), which concerned a gang fight in which the principal offender had killed an opponent with a knife, the defendant accomplice was acquitted of being an accomplice to either murder or manslaughter because the use of a knife during the attack was beyond the scope of what had been contemplated by him. Thus the attack upon Z is likely to be seen as something not contemplated by O when he agreed to accompany L.

d) *The age of M*

There is no evidence to suggest that M is not an adult and the suggestions above have been based upon that assumption. If M were below the age of ten he could not incur any criminal liability. Between the ages of 10 and 14, he can only be criminally liable if he is shown to have had 'mischievous discretion', or to have understood that what he was doing was seriously wrong. At the age of 16 he is to be treated as an adult for the purposes of establishing the mental element of criminal liability. The only relevance of his being 16 might relate to whether or not he realised that what was being suggested to him by L was wrong. This matter has already been considered.

Question 5

X drove onto Y's self-service garage and filled up his tank with petrol. On the petrol pump was a notice which read, 'This petrol is not yours until it is paid for.' Having filled his tank, X realised that because he had forgotten his wallet he did not have sufficient money to pay for the petrol. X went to tell the attendant and to ask what to do. The attendant told him to walk the eight miles home to collect the money. This X refused to do and, despite protestations from the attendant, drove home. There X realised that the attendant had failed to make a note of X's name, address or vehicle registration number. X decided that because of the attendant's unhelpful attitude he would not return to pay. Advise X.

University of London LLB Examination
(for External Students) Criminal Law June 1991 Q5

General comment

A question essentially about the interaction between theft and the offence of making off without payment. The point concerning the passing of property needs to be clearly spelt out. In relation to the making off offence it is the elements of mens rea that require detailed consideration.

Skeleton solution

Elements of theft. Nature of appropriation. When does it occur? Whose property was it at the time? The need for the s3 offence. Elements of making off. The existence of the debt.

Suggested solution

There is no evidence that X knew he was unable to pay for the petrol prior to his filling the petrol tank, thus no possibility of a charge under s15 of the Theft Act 1968 arises. His liability for theft of the petrol is dependent upon the prosecution making out the elements of the offence as laid down in s1(1) of the 1968 Act. The petrol is clearly property capable of being stolen; see s4(1). Not withstanding the decision of the House of Lords in *R* v *Lawrence* (1972), it is submitted that the offence requires an appropriation of another's property in the form of an act or series of acts that the owner has not authorised; see Lord Roskill in *R* v *Morris* (1983). The issue of whether or not appropriation requires an act to which the owner does not consent has been the subject of conflicting judicial dicta of late. In *R* v *Fritschy* (1985) the Court of Appeal supported the 'unauthorised act' view. But this was not followed in *R* v *Philipou* (1989), nor by the Court of Appeal (Civil Division) in *Dobson* v *General Accident plc* (1990). Most recently, however, the Court of Appeal in *R* v *Gomez* (1991), seems to have expressed preference for the unauthorised act concept of appropriation, and it is that interpretation which is, with respect, followed here.

On this basis, X cannot commit theft of the petrol until he commits some act which is not authorised by the garage owners. The appropriation of the petrol therefor occurs at the moment he begins to drive off without having paid for it.

At that moment is the petrol property belonging to another? If X's petrol tank had been empty when he started to fill it up, there might be distinct property to which the garage could point as being their own. Given that he drives onto the forecourt, the evidence suggests that the new petrol has been mixed with his own, thus making it impossible for the garage to identify which petrol is theirs and which is his. It may not be a simple matter of working out how much X had to begin with and subtracting that from the amount he now has. The two quantities may be different grades of petrol that have now become mixed. It is submitted that, on the facts, property in the petrol will be treated as having passed to X as no distinct property belonging to the garage can be identified. It is analogous to the situation where a diner in a restaurant consumes a meal and then decides not to pay. A sign to the effect that the food did not become his until he had paid for it would have little legal effect once the food had been eaten! It is to deal with situations such as that under consideration that s3(1) of the Theft Act 1978 was enacted. Section 3(1) provides that a person who, knowing that payment on the spot for any goods supplied or service done is required or expected from him, dishonestly makes off without having paid as required or expected and with intent to avoid payment of the amount due shall be guilty of an offence.

There is clearly evidence of X having 'made off'. The phrase suggests a departure at high speed, but obviously this is not necessary for conviction. The defendant must have made off without having paid as required and expected. Failing to make any payment at all would clearly satisfy this requirement. X must know that payment on the spot for any goods supplied or service done is required or expected from him, and must be dishonest at the time of his making off. The test in *R* v *Ghosh* (1982), despite the fact that it was a case concerned with obtaining property by deception, may provide the 'model direction' for cases under s3. The court held that the jury should be directed in the following terms:

'Was the defendant dishonest according to the standards of ordinary decent people? If yes, did the defendant realise that what he was doing was dishonest by these standards?'

There is a rider to this test, to the effect that the defendant is to be regarded as dishonest even where he believes his actions to be morally justified, if he nevertheless realises that ordinary decent people would regard them as wrong. A possible loophole in this test is that a defendant may not have thought about whether ordinary decent people would have regarded his actions as dishonest, or even if he had, he may not have been able to tell. Essentially, if X was intending to obtain the money to pay for the petrol at the time he made off, then a jury is unlikely to regard him as dishonest, especially if the alternative was an eight mile walk.

Section 3(1) further requires proof of an intention to avoid payment. The House of Lords in *R* v *Allen* (1985) held, however, that the section should be interpreted to as to require proof of an intention to permanently avoid payment. If X, at the time he made off, intended to return with the money for the petrol he will not have done so with intent to permanently avoid payment.

X's decision, once home, not to pay for the petrol, does not create any criminal liability. He owes the garage the price of the petrol and is thus in debt, but the creation of a debt is not a crime. The garage will have to pursue their civil remedies against X.

Question 6

P hid a bomb aboard a plane. He telephoned the airline while the plane was on a transatlantic flight. He demanded payment of £1 million to tell them where the bomb was hidden. The airline refused to pay the money despite advice to the contrary from a security firm. As a result the plane was blown up and all the passengers and crew were killed. Advise P of his criminal liability. What difference, if any, would it make to your advice if P believed that in demanding payment he was divinely inspired to raise the money to further his religious ends?

University of London LLB Examination
(for External Students) Criminal Law June 1991 Q6

General comment

A relatively straightforward question requiring an examination of blackmail and murder. Points to watch are the relationship between mental abnormality and the question of whether or not the defendant's demands are warranted, and also the issue of jurisdiction over the blackmail.

Skeleton solution

Blackmail. Menaces. Purpose of demand. Whether warranted. Homicide. Mens rea for murder. Diminished responsibility. Insanity.

Suggested solution

a) *Blackmail*

In demanding a payment of £1m in return for the information as to the whereabouts of the bomb on the plane, P may be guilty of blackmail, as defined by s21(1) of the Theft Act 1968. Section 21(1) provides that a person is guilty of blackmail if, with a view to gain for himself or another or with intent to cause loss to another, he makes any unwarranted demand with menaces; and for this purpose a demand with menaces is unwarranted unless the person making it does so in the belief:

'(a) that he has reasonable grounds for making the demand; and (b) that the use of the menaces is a proper means of reinforcing the demand.'

P has clearly made a demand. The fact that the bomb might have exploded in mid-Atlantic does not raise jurisdictional difficulties. On the basis of *Treacy* v *DPP* (1971), the critical factor is where the demand is made. The prosecution will allege that P's demand was made with menaces. It has been suggested, by Cairns LJ in *R* v *Lawrence and Pomroy* (1971), that menaces is an ordinary English word which would normally call for no elaboration on the part of a trial judge, unless there were exceptional circumstances where what would not normally be menacing to an ordinary person, was menacing to the victim. The prosecution must establish that P was acting with a view to gain or loss. Clearly the demanding of £1m is a demand with a view to gain.

Finally, there is the question of whether or not the demand is warranted. A demand will be unwarranted unless the defendant makes it in the belief that he has reasonable grounds for so doing, and in the belief that the use of the menaces is a proper means of reinforcing the demand. The test is prima facie subjective, in that the defendant's belief does not have to be reasonable, although the more unreasonable it is the less likely the jury are to believe him. Further, note that both states of mind have to be established.

The defendant may honestly believe that there are grounds for making the demand for any number of reasons. He does not have to establish any particular legal, moral or factual basis for his belief, he will nevertheless have to provide evidence upon which a jury can act, that he honestly believed such grounds to exist. In the present case there is little prospect of P persuading a jury that he honestly believed he had grounds for making the demand. On the alternative assumption that he believes himself to be divinely inspired to collect funds for religious purposes there clearly would be some basis for his claim to have held such a belief, although in such circumstances it is submitted that the prosecution would lead evidence of insanity; see below.

b) *Murder*

By placing the bomb on the plane P has caused the death of the passengers. On the basis of *R* v *Hancock* (1986), the mens rea that has to be established is an intention to kill or do grievous bodily harm. Intention here is used in the broad sense of what the defendant foresaw. A defendant cannot be assumed to foresee a consequence simply because it is a natural result of his actions. The jury must consider the evidence of what the defendant actually foresaw, and the more evidence there is that the defendant foresaw death or grievous bodily harm, then the stronger the inference that he intended either of those consequences. In *R* v *Nedrick* (1986), the Lord Chief Justice suggested that a jury would have to be satisfied that a defendant foresaw death or grievous bodily harm as a 'virtual certainty' before they would be entitled to infer that he had intended either consequence.

Assuming that P had the requisite mens rea for murder the question of defences arises.

c) *Diminished responsibility*

The defence of diminished responsibility was introduced by s2(1) of the Homicide Act 1957, which provides that where a person kills or is party to a killing of another, he shall not be convicted of murder if he was suffering from such abnormality of mind (whether arising from a condition of arrested or retarded development of mind or any inherent causes or induced by disease or injury) as substantially impaired his mental responsibility for his acts and omissions in doing or being a party to the killing. Given that the standard of proof that P has to satisfy (balance of probabilities), he will have to obtain cogent medical evidence as to his condition. The nature of abnormality of the mind, as that term is used in s2(1), was considered by the Court of Appeal in *R* v *Byrne* (1960), where Lord Parker CJ explained that it was a state of mind that the reasonable person would find abnormal, and that this was essentially a matter of fact for the jury to determine. It may well be that the medical evidence in P's case reveals that the effect of his religious delusions was to substantially impair his responsibility for his action. If P succeeds with the defence his liability will be reduced to manslaughter.

d) *Insanity*

Insanity is a general defence that can be pleaded in relation to any offence. It is thus of relevance to P's liability for murder and blackmail. The definition is based upon the so-called rules established in *M'Naghten's Case* (1843), which provide that the defendant must establish that he was suffering from a defect of reason arising from a disease of the mind, having one of two results, either that the defendant was unaware of the nature and quality of his act, or that he did not realise that his actions were wrong. For these purposes the expression 'disease of the mind', according to Lord

Denning in *Bratty* v *Attorney-General for Northern Ireland* (1963), is a disorder that manifests itself in violence and is likely to recur.

P's beliefs would seem to satisfy this requirement. The disease of the mind must have one of two consequences. Either P becomes unaware of his actions, or he is shown not to have known that his actions were wrong. 'Wrong' in this context has been interpreted to mean wrong in law, as opposed to simply immoral: see *R* v *Windle* (1952). It may be that because of his beliefs P thought his actions were justified in law. Such evidence would bring him within the scope of the defence.

Question 7

G telephoned H and told him to pick up a package from a given address and place it outside K's church. G threatened that if H failed to comply he would tell H's employer about H's affair with his secretary. H was frightened by this because he was afraid of losing his job and his reputation as he was a well-known lay preacher. H picked up a package at the address and placed it outside the church. However, by mistake he picked up a different package belonging to K and it was subsequently stolen from the church doorstep where H had left it. The other package which he was meant to pick up exploded injuring a passer-by. Advise the parties of their criminal liability. What difference, if any, would it make to your advice if G had threatened to injure H's son whom H believed to be in G's custody?

University of London LLB Examination
(for External Students) Criminal Law June 1991 Q7

General comment

A distinctly odd question. The examiner provides so little information on some key points that it is impossible to provide anything more than a generalised answer. Much time will be spent explaining why the parties involved do not incur liability, which is never entirely satisfactory. It is advisable to go into depth where sufficient evidence is provided.

Skeleton solution

Liability of H for injuries and theft. Issues of dishonesty. Availability of duress. Liability of G. Blackmail. Assault.

Suggested solution

a) *Liability of H*

Prima facie H incurs no criminal liability in respect of his action. He has picked up a box, being innocent of its contents and has left it outside a church from where it has been stolen.

The prosecution may want to charge H with theft of K's box as principal. It is property belonging to another, as against H, and he does assume the rights of the owner by taking possession of it and leaving it outside the church. There are likely to be problems with mens rea, however. Given the threats made by G to expose H's affair with his secretary, H may honestly believe that K would consent to his taking

209

the box; see s2(1)(a) Theft Act 1968. If this is established, H cannot be dishonest. More generally he may seek to rely on the common law definition in *R v Ghosh* (1982), on the basis that he did not believe that ordinary decent people would have regarded it as wrong to act as he did, given the nature of the threats. By leaving the box outside K's church, H may contend that he did not have any intention to permanently deprive K of his property. Much will depend on the view of the jury. Under s6(1) of the 1968 Act, a defendant can be deemed to have had intention to permanently deprive, where he treats the property as his own to dispose of, regardless of the owner's rights. It is a question for the jury to determine whether or not H has acted in this way.

He cannot be charged as a party to the theft of the box since, despite the fact that he facilitated its theft by leaving it where it could be stolen, he did not act with the intention of assisting in the offence. He was not party to any agreement that it should be stolen.

Similarly he cannot incur liability for the injuries caused to the passer-by. Theoretically, by not collecting the correct box he causes the injuries to the passer-by that might otherwise have been avoided, but no liability can be based upon his failure to act as he was under no legal duty to collect the box.

If G had threatened to injure H's son, H would have had a much stronger claim to the defence of duress in relation to any charges brought against him. The model direction to be given to a jury where the defendant has raised the defence of duress is that laid down by the Court of Appeal in *R v Graham* (1982). The jury should first consider whether or not the defendant was compelled to act as he did because, on the basis of the circumstances as he honestly believed them to be, he thought his life was in immediate danger. If the jury concludes that this was not the case, then the defence falls at this stage. If, however, they are of the opinion that the defendant has satisfied this first subjective test, they should then consider the second, more objective test; would a sober person of reasonable firmness sharing the defendant's characteristics have responded in the same way to the threats? A defendant wishing to succeed with the defence of duress must provide evidence that he had no reasonable opportunity to avoid having to comply with the demands made upon him. In this sense it is said that the threat that forms the basis of the alleged duress must be immediate. In the present case H may have difficulty in showing why he did not simply contact the police.

b) *Liability of G*

G could be charged in relation to the injuries suffered by the passer-by, but the facts reveal little evidence as to its contents or his state of mind. The injuries could have been accidental or deliberate. It is impossible to advise any more precisely without further and better particulars. He cannot be charged with theft of the box through the actions of an innocent agent as there is no evidence that he wanted H to take K's box.

In threatening to reveal H's affair with his secretary unless he delivers the box, G may appear to be committing blackmail contrary to s21(1) of the Theft Act 1968.

He makes a menacing demand which appears to be unwarranted. The difficulty with such a charge, however, would be in establishing that the demand was made with a view to loss or gain as defined in s34(2)(a) of the same Act. It is not at all clear what, if anything, G serves to gain from having the box delivered, or what loss may be caused. It should be remembered that it was not his intention that K should lose his box. Acting with a view to cause H to lose his job, and thus his income may be enough to bring it within the section.

G's threats to injure H's son would not constitute an offence of assault, as this requires the victim to be then and there put in fear of violence. Words alone cannot constitute an assault, a priori where they are conditional; see *R* v *Meade and Belt* (1823).

HLT GROUP PUBLICATIONS FOR THE LLB EXAMINATIONS

Our publications, written by specialists, are used widely by students at universities, polytechnics and colleges throughout the United Kingdom and overseas.

Textbooks
These are designed as working books to provide students with a valuable framework on which to base their studies. They are updated each year to reflect new developments and changing trends.

Casebooks
These are designed as companion volumes to the Textbooks and incorporate important cases, statutes as appropriate, and other material, together with detailed commentaries.

Revision Workbooks
For first degree law students, these provide questions and answers for all topics in each law subject. Every topic has sections on key points, recent cases and statutes, further reading etc.

Suggested Solutions
These are available to past London University LLB examination papers and provide the student with an invaluable revision aid and an insight into the techniques essential to examination success.

The books listed below can be ordered through your local bookshops or obtained direct from the publisher using this order form. Telephone, Fax or Telex orders will also be accepted. Quote your Access or Visa card numbers for priority orders. To order direct from the publisher please enter the cost of the titles you require, fill in the despatch details and send it with your remittance to The HLT Group Ltd.

ORDER FORM

LLB PUBLICATIONS	TEXTBOOKS Cost £	£	CASEBOOKS Cost £	£	REVISION WORKBOOKS Cost £	£	SUG. SOL 1986/91 Cost £	£	SUG. SOL 1992 Cost £	£
Administrative Law	£18.95		£19.95				£9.95		£3.00	
Commercial Law Vol I	£18.95		£19.95		£9.95		£9.95		£3.00	
Commercial Law Vol II	£17.95		£19.95							
Company Law	£19.95		£19.95		£9.95		£9.95		£3.00	
Conflict of Laws	£18.95		£17.95		£9.95					
Constitutional Law	£16.95		£17.95		£9.95		£9.95		£3.00	
Contract Law	£16.95		£17.95		£9.95		£9.95		£3.00	
Conveyancing	£19.95		£17.95							
Criminal Law	£16.95		£18.95		£9.95		£9.95		£3.00	
Criminology	£17.95						£4.95†		£3.00	
English Legal System	£16.95		£14.95		£9.95		£8.95*		£3.00	
European Community Law	£17.95		£19.95		£9.95		£4.95†		£3.00	
Equity and Trusts	£16.95		£17.95		£9.95					
Evidence	£19.95		£18.95		£9.95		£9.95		£3.00	
Family Law	£18.95		£19.95		£9.95		£9.95		£3.00	
Jurisprudence	£16.95				£9.95		£9.95		£3.00	
Land Law	£16.95		£17.95		£9.95		£9.95		£3.00	
Law of Trusts							£9.95		£3.00	
Public International Law	£18.95		£18.95		£9.95		£9.95		£3.00	
Revenue Law	£19.95		£19.95		£9.95		£9.95		£3.00	
Roman Law	£14.95									
Succession	£19.95		£18.95		£9.95		£9.95		£3.00	
Tort	£16.95		£17.95		£9.95		£9.95		£3.00	

* 1987–1991 papers only   †1990 and 1991 papers only

cut along dotted

DETAILS FOR DESPATCH OF PUBLICATIONS

Please insert your full name below

Please insert below the style in which you would like the correspondence from the Publisher addressed to you

TITLE Mr, Miss etc.   INITIALS   SURNAME/FAMILY NAME

Address to which study material is to be sent (please ensure someone will be present to accept delivery of your Publications).

POSTAGE & PACKING

You are welcome to purchase study material from the Publisher at 200 Greyhound Road, London W14 9RY, during normal working hours.

If you wish to order by post this may be done direct from the Publisher. Postal charges are as follows:

UK   - Orders over £30: no charge. Orders below £30: £2.60. Single paper (last exam only): 55p
OVERSEAS - See table below

The Publisher cannot accept responsibility in respect of postal delays or losses in the postal systems.

DESPATCH All cheques must be cleared before material is despatched.

SUMMARY OF ORDER

Date of order:

			£
Cost of publications ordered:			
UNITED KINGDOM:			

OVERSEAS:	TEXTS		Suggested Solutions (Last exam only)	
	One	Each Extra		
Eire	£5.00	£0.70	£1.00	
European Community	£10.50	£1.00	£1.00	
East Europe & North America	£12.50	£1.50	£1.50	
South East Asia	£12.00	£2.00	£1.50	
Australia/New Zealand	£14.00	£3.00	£1.70	
Other Countries (Africa, India etc)	£13.00	£3.00	£1.50	

Total cost of order: £

Please ensure that you enclose a cheque or draft payable to **THE HLT GROUP LTD** for the above amount, or charge to ☐ Access   ☐ Visa   ☐ American Express

Card Number

Expiry Date ....   Signature ....